Constitutional Law in Belarus

Constitutional Law in Belarus

Second Edition

Grigory A. Vasilevich

This book was originally published as a monograph in the International Encyclopaedia of Laws/Constitutional Law.

General Editors: Roger Blanpain, Frank Hendrickx
Volume Editors: André Alen, David Haljan

Wolters Kluwer

Published by:
Kluwer Law International B.V.
PO Box 316
2400 AH Alphen aan den Rijn
The Netherlands
Website: www.wklawbusiness.com

Sold and distributed in North, Central and South America by:
Wolters Kluwer Legal & Regulatory U.S.
7201 McKinney Circle
Frederick, MD 21704
United States of America
Email: customer.service@wolterskluwer.com

Sold and distributed in all other countries by:
Turpin Distribution Services Ltd.
Stratton Business Park
Pegasus Drive, Biggleswade
Bedfordshire SG18 8TQ
United Kingdom
Email: kluwerlaw@turpin-distribution.com

Printed on acid-free paper

ISBN 978-90-411-6680-7

This title is available on www.kluwerlawonline.com

Printed and Bound by CPI Group (UK) Ltd, Croydon, CR0 4YY.

The Author

Grigory A. Vasilevich was born on 13 February 1955 in the City of Minsk. He began his career as a workman before performing military service in the Soviet Army. In 1980 he graduated from the Law Faculty of Belarusian State University, and where he subsequently completed his post-graduate studies. He was a Professor at the Law Faculty of Belarusian State University from 1983 to 1986. In 1986 he was appointed Deputy Head of the Law Department at the Secretariat of the Supreme Soviet, then Head of the Law Department (1989–1994). He has been a Judge of the Constitutional Court of the Republic of Belarus since April 1994, and Chairman of this organisation since January 1997. He was a member of the Constitutional Committee from the moment of its creation in July 1990 until the conclusion of its deliberations in March 1994, during which time he served as Deputy Head of the Panel on the elaboration of a new Constitution.

He presented his doctoral thesis in the sphere of labour relations law in 1984 at Kharkov Law Institute and in 1994 at Belarusian State University. His thesis is entitled ‘Legislative barriers to the activities of the Supreme Soviet of the Republic of Belarus’.

His scientific interests include constitutional law, labour law, state and legal theory, the organization of state bodies, the legal status of the individual, and relations between the individual and the State.

He is the co-author of fifty books and penned more than twenty others on his own. He also co-wrote eight textbooks. He has written more than 500 scientific articles, and has been a regular contributor to Belarus’ many newspapers on legal and political subjects. His most significant works include: *The Parliament of the Republic of Belarus (Constitutional and legal aspect)*, Minsk: Law and economy, 1995; *The Constitution of the Republic of Belarus: Scientific and Legal Commentary* (co-authorship), Minsk: Belarus, 1996; *Bodies of state power of the Republic of Belarus: Constitutional and legal status*, Minsk: Law and economy, 1999; *The Constitution and Aspects of Protection of the Rights and Liberties of Citizens*, Minsk: Knowledge, 1999; *Enforceable enactments of state bodies of the Republic of Belarus*, Minsk: Law and economy, 1999; *Legal Bases of Mutual Relations Between the Individual, Society and The State*, Minsk: Law and economy, 1999; *Responsibility of parties of a labour contract for damage caused*, Minsk: Belarus, 1989;

The Author

Material responsibility of the employee for damage caused for the employer, Minsk: Amalthea, 1994; *Damage. Labour. Responsibility*, Minsk: Vedy, 1997; *Labour Law: a Textbook for Higher Educational Institutions* (co-authorship), Minsk: Amalthea, 1997; *Bases of law: a Textbook for Secondary Educational Institutions* (co-authorship), Minsk: Amalthea, 1998; *Constitution. Person. State*, Minsk: Law and Economy, 4 volumes (2000, 2001, 2002 & 2004), *The Constitution of the Republic of Belarus: Scientific and practical comments*, Minsk: Law and economy, 2001; *The Labour Code: Scientific and practical comments*, Minsk: Amalthea, 2000. (co-authorship); *Referenda in the Republic of Belarus and the Road Towards Independence at the End of the 20th Century*, Minsk: Young scientific society, 2001; *The Law on enforceable enactments of the Republic of Belarus: Comments*, Minsk: Inter press Service, 2003; *Constitutional Law of the Republic of Belarus*, Minsk: Inter Press Service, 2003; *Legal Guide to the Parliament*, Minsk, Dicta, 2004; *The Bases of the Belarusian State Ideology*, Minsk, 2004 (co-authorship); *Constitutional Law of the Republic of Belarus*, Minsk: Book House, 2005; *The Constitution of the Republic of Belarus: Scientific and Practical Comments*, Minsk: BSU, 2005; *Sources of Belarusian Law: Principles, Normative Acts, Customs, Precedents, Doctrine*, Minsk: Theseus, 2005; *The Belarusian government at the turn of the century*, Minsk: *Law and economics, 2007; The offense, the law of responsibility*, Minsk: Law and economics, 2011; *1991: Chronicle dive country*, Minsk: Law and economics, 2012; *The Constitution – the foundation of the national legal system*, Minsk: Law and economics, 2012; *Some aspects of the application of criminal and criminal procedural law (ideas, suggestions, critical eye)*, Minsk: Law and economics, 2013; *Constitutional Justice*, Minsk: BSU Publishing Center, 2014; *Draft Constitution of the Republic of Belarus: the search for the optimal model*, Minsk: Law and economics, 2014; *Anti-corruption*, Minsk: Law and Economics, 2015.

Publications in Russia, Ukraine, Lithuania, Armenia, Poland, Bulgaria, France, Turkey, Greece; Research director of fifteen doctoral theses of post-graduate university students on legal matters and two post-doctoral theses; Chairman of the Council of Experts on Legal Subjects of the Supreme Attestation Committee of the Republic of Belarus; Member of the Republican Council of Judges; Member of the International Academy of Organizational and Managerial Science; Arbitrator, Court of Conciliation and Arbitration within the OSCE on the part of the Republic of Belarus; International Biographical Centre (Cambridge, England) member of list of outstanding people of the twentieth and twenty-first centuries; Member of the General Assembly of the National Academy of Sciences of Belarus. Reporter on many international conferences, including the conference of the World Jurists' Association in Stuttgart (2002), dedicated to constitutional issues and the increased effects of mobility and transportation on the environment; on the European Court of Human Rights in Strasbourg (2002) and at many other conferences in Russia, Ukraine, France, Italy, Turkey and other countries.

Table of Contents

List of Abbreviations

BSSR	Belarusian Soviet Socialist Republic
BSU	Belarusian State University
CIS	Commonwealth of Independent States
CPSU	Communist Party of Soviet Union
MIM	Minsk Institute of Management
NPS (Chernobyl)	Chernobyl Nuclear Power Station
UNESCO	United Nations Educational, Scientific and Cultural Organization
USA	United States of America
USSR	Union of Soviet Socialists Republics

List of Abbreviations

General Introduction

Chapter 1. Concise History of Constitutional Law of the Republic of Belarus

§1. Introduction

1. The term 'Constitutional Law of the Republic of Belarus' may be used in three independent and, at the same time, interrelated meanings. First, it can be considered as a branch of law, a body of legal norms that comprise constitutional legal relations. Second, it is a branch of legal study, made up of an accumulation of knowledge and analyses on the subject of constitutional law. Finally, it is an academic subject taught and studied in institutions of higher education. This study uses the norms of the Constitution, other existing norms and even other academic disciplines which allow a broader view of the true meaning of the constitutional sphere. In future, unless otherwise mentioned, in this book I shall speak about the constitutional law as a branch of law.

2. Constitutional law (its norms), unlike other branches of the law, regulates public relations in all spheres of society: political, economic, social and spiritual. It creates a legal framework for the most important relations that exist between individuals and state organs. Other bodies of legal norms, such as labour law or contract law, are more in-depth, and practical spheres which deal with precise issues in people's everyday lives. This is the principal difference between constitutional law and other branches of law.

3. Because of this, the constitutional law in the Republic of Belarus is considered as basis of all other branches of law. Constitutional law contains the fundamental principles of the relations between the State and the individual. The norms of constitutional law determine the process of the formation of law itself. They fix the system by which the State wields its power: the status of public bodies, the form of the State, the form of State system and the way that the State is governed, and envisage forms of ownership, economic principles, types of legal acts and their elaboration.

4. Constitutional law is closely connected with other branches of law. Constitutional law is the starting point for forming national law. Sources of other branches of law are based in constitutional law. Constitutional norms shall find their further development in other branches of law, whether administrative, civil, financial, labour or criminal.

5. Constitutional law in the Republic of Belarus has passed through several stages and that have been marked in the renewal of the texts of the Constitution. In the whole history of the development of Belarus, there have been five adopted Constitutions (in 1919, 1927, 1937, 1978 and 1994).

6. The first four Constitutions of the Republic of Belarus had their specific characteristics, which we will emphasize *below*. However, they had in common, obviously, class struggle, the domination of one prevailing ideology over all others, the absence of a multi-party system, the denial of a variety of forms of ownership and the subordination of every human activity to the interests of the party and the system. As a rule, the most important international instruments of human rights and freedoms had no place in these texts. Many of the norms were of a declarative character and had no direct effect in practice and, at times, other texts prevailed over the Constitution.

7. During the first period of Soviet power, rights and freedoms existed only for industrial workers and farmers. 'The exploiters' were restricted in their rights. This class approach clearly became softer during the period of 'developed socialism'; however, everything was subordinated to the interests of strengthening socialist relations and the development of communism. In the field of rights and liberties, collectivistic principles were predominant. Everything was subordinated to the will of the 'majority'. The individual was considered to be a 'pawn' in the complex system of societal relations.

8. The first Constitution of Belarus was adopted on 3 February 1919 by the First All-Belarusian Congress of Soviets. Its content was inspired by the idea of the dictatorship of the proletariat that was enshrined directly in the Constitution. It proclaimed the absolute power of the Soviets and created a new system of state bodies for Belarus. It abolished private ownership of land and ordered transfer of the ownership of estates and agricultural enterprises to the State. There were also progressive norms that, in practice, unfortunately were not realized. The freedom of worship was proclaimed, although anti-religious propaganda was, in reality, given priority. Under the Constitution of 1919, the independence of the press was declared. However, in reality, only the official point of view was expressed. The rights of working people to public assembly and demonstration were also granted. Equality, irrespective of race or nationality, was guaranteed in the constitution. The Belarusian, Russian, Polish and Yiddish languages were declared state languages in the territory of the Belarusian Soviet Socialist Republic (BSSR). The basic inspiration of the first Constitution was 'those who do not work do not eat'.

9. The second Constitution was adopted on 11 April 1927 by the Eighth All-Belarusian Congress of Soviets of workers, peasants and red army deputies, subsequent to the formation of the USSR (30 December 1922). In 1924 the Constitution of the USSR was adopted by the Republics and, in the process, parts of its composition were incorporated in their own Basic Laws. The Constitution of 1927 once again brought the rights of 'workers' to the forefront. 'Non-workers' were deprived of a number of rights, for example, to hold public office. The honourable right to protect the revolution with weapons was bequeathed only to the workers and peasants.

10. In the middle of the 1930s, the USSR began building a socialist system. Socialist policies became predominant in the economic, political and welfare spheres, requiring new constitutional specifications. In 1936 a new Soviet Constitution was adopted. The third Constitution of Belarus was adopted on 19 February 1937. It reflected the victory of socialism, a socialist system of government and socialist property structures; the reaffirmation of the dictatorship of the proletariat into the Nation-State; the abolition of restrictions on the electoral rights of 'non-workers'; a stipulation of equality for all citizens, and a broad-spectrum extension of the circle of rights and freedom for citizens. Ensuring the inviolability of an individual, his or her dwelling and his or her personal correspondence was envisioned. Unfortunately, constitutional guarantees of these rights were not realized in practice.

11. The fourth Constitution of the BSSR was adopted by the Supreme Soviet of the BSSR on 13 April 1978. In 1977 the Constitution of the USSR was adopted, which proclaimed the building of a highly developed socialist state. In its real meaning, these provisions also found their reflection in the Republic's Constitution. Unfortunately, its drawback was in its excessively declarative nature and the absence of concrete mechanisms for its execution. The communist party was maintained as the main force in society and the State, which was directly fixed in the relevant Articles of the Constitution. In fact, public authorities were an appendage of the party. It is necessary to note that the Constitution of 1978, after ten years in existence, underwent some crucial changes in 1989 to 1990. In 1989 there were large-scale alterations concerning the organization and activities of the Councils of Deputies, including the Supreme Soviet and its Presidium and elections to these bodies. In 1990 alterations were made in certain Articles of the Constitution that led to the liquidation of the monopoly of power for the communist party and stipulations concerning private property.

12. On 22 June 1990 the Supreme Soviet of Republic of Belarus adopted its Decision on the formation of the Constitutional Commission. Its full composition was determined by 20 July 1990. It consisted of sixty-one deputies and thirteen experts in the field of law (scientists and practical workers). Within the framework of the Constitutional Commission two working groups were immediately set up for the preparation of alternative drafts. After their preparation, the joint session of working groups in the summer of 1991 decided to propose a uniform text of the draft to the Supreme Soviet. It should be noted, that, as a matter of fact, the draft Constitution was made available in the middle of 1991. For the first time, it was subject to consideration at the seventh session of the Supreme Soviet in November 1991.

13. On 11 November 1991, the Supreme Soviet adopted its Resolution on the draft Constitution of the Republic of Belarus. The basic provisions of the draft were approved. It was decided to publish the draft in the press for national discussion, and the executive and the administrative bodies of the local Councils of Deputies were instructed to ensure careful accounting and generalization of the proposals and the remarks made as regards the draft by workers' collectives, public associations, and citizens and to forward them on or before the first and the fifteenth of each month to the Supreme Soviet of the Republic of Belarus. The results of the discussion of the draft Basic Law had to be covered by the Republic's mass media. The Constitutional Commission was empowered by the Resolution to elaborate and finish the draft Constitution, taking into account the proposals and the remarks expressed by the deputies of the Supreme Soviet of the Republic of Belarus, as well as those obtained in the process of the national discussion.

14. A major part in bringing the adoption of the new Constitution closer to fruition was played by the Resolution of the Supreme Soviet of 29 October 1992 that adopted the Statement 'On the necessity of acceleration of constitutional transformations in the Republic of Belarus'. The object of its adoption was the proposal of a group of citizens to hold a national referendum with the following wording: 'Do you consider it necessary to hold elections in autumn 1992 to the supreme body of state power of the Republic of Belarus on the grounds of the Law on elections of people's deputies of the Republic of Belarus, the draft of which was made by the opposition BNF to the Supreme Soviet, and due to this, dissolve the present Supreme Soviet'. By declining the proposal on the holding of a referendum, the Supreme Soviet, taking the political situation into account, found it necessary to focus its attention on the acceleration of constitutional reforms in the Republic. Adoption of the new Constitution (Basic Law) of the Republic of Belarus by 1993 was fixed as the main task. Thus, there was a specific date to finish the work on the draft Constitution for its adoption. Very often, opponents in cases of emerging serious political disputes referred themselves to the aforementioned Statement as one of their arguments. In particular, when the issue of the election of the President was opened, some deputies made a proposal to hold elections for a new Parliament and then to adopt the Constitution and to elect the President. However, the majority did not support this.

15. It should be emphasized that at the end of 1991 and in 1992 there were many changes that affected the pace and essence of work for the draft of a new Basic Law of Belarus. On 25 August 1991 the Declaration on State Sovereignty of the Republic of Belarus was adopted by the Supreme Soviet of the Republic of Belarus of 27 July 1990 and was granted the status of a constitutional act with higher legal status than the Constitution of 1978. The Declaration, according to Article 12, is the foundation for the elaboration of a new Constitution. On 8 December 1991 it concluded the Agreement on the creation of the Commonwealth of Independent States as an alternative to the USSR (ratified on 10 December 1991 with reservations on 16 January 1992).

16. Until 23 October 1992 the draft was published twice for national discussion (in December 1991 after discussion at the seventh session and in August 1992 with the remarks in the course of the national discussion). Publication of the draft for its discussion had brought to life debates in society regarding the Basic Law of the country. The Constitutional Commission, before the ninth session, received more than 7,000 proposals and remarks by citizens expressed in the press, by radio, television, and at meetings and in letters. In spite of certain critical remarks, a majority of individuals and bodies made favourable references to the draft.

17. In comparison to the seventh session, the draft presented for the tenth session went through significant changes. More precise content was given to section I 'Principles of the Constitutional System' and, first of all, to provisions related to state sovereignty, certain other institutions of democracy and the status of the Belarusian language. Taking into account the International Covenant on Civil and Political rights, the International Covenant on Economic, Social and Cultural Rights, the Universal Declaration on Human Rights, and the country's own historical experience, there were elaborate wordings in section II on 'The Individual, Society and The State' concerning human rights, liberties and obligations. Special attention was given not only to individual political rights and freedoms, but also to social and economic rights, especially those which generated the greatest interest of the citizens during the process of the discussion of the draft. These specifically included the right to labour, housing, education and medical care. Other sections and chapters underwent essential changes, including two crucial aspects. The Constitutional Commission, by not refusing the proclaimed principle of separation of powers, had presented the draft for the tenth session which specified that Belarus should become a Parliamentary Republic (with the President as Head of State, but without the power to carry out the leadership of the Executive).

18. The draft Resolution of the Supreme Soviet, prepared by the Constitutional Commission, presupposed the approval of the draft in its second reading and then put it up for discussion in the third reading, which was not in line, as a whole, with the Provisional Rules of Procedure of the Supreme Soviet and, in particular, with Article 102. However, the deputies of the Supreme Soviet did not agree with that approach. There were serious debates regarding the major provisions of the draft Constitution. 'Rating voting', as well as adoption of the final Resolution of 5 February 1993 'On the draft Constitution of the Republic of Belarus' made things clear. The Constitutional Commission and its working group, as a result of the discussion of Resolution of the Supreme Soviet of 5 February 1993, were empowered to finish the draft Constitution, taking into consideration the proposal and the remarks expressed by the deputies, and to enshrine in it the following fundamental provisions: (a) the State shall be formed on the principle of the separation of powers; (b) the Supreme Soviet is the body of state power, part of whose deputies may work on regular basis and another part may combine the duties of a deputy with professional or service activities. Belarus is a Presidential Republic, where the President is the leader of the Executive; (c) there should be a five-year term of office for deputies of the Supreme Soviet of Republic of Belarus; (d) local self-government shall be exercised by the citizens through local representative bodies, local referenda, meetings of citizens and others forms of direct participation of the population in public affairs within the competence granted to them by the law; (e) the powers of bodies of local self-government in terms of their inner organization and in the creation of their executive bodies shall be specified by the law; (f) the State guarantees to all citizens equal rights in carrying out economic and other activities, except for those prohibited by the law, as well as the creation of equal conditions for the development of all forms of ownership; (g) the accessibility of free and medical service, and free education in state institutions.

19. The Constitutional Commission was empowered to study in detail the proposals related to state social protection of Belarusian citizens; in case of necessity to determine more principled issues of the draft Constitution of the Republic of Belarus which may be put to a referendum; the relevant proposals shall be submitted for consideration of the Supreme Soviet of the Republic of Belarus.

20. The same Resolution approved the 'Procedure of ending work on the new draft Constitution of the Republic of Belarus'. This important document made it possible to control work on the draft Basic Law and to keep it going in the right direction. In reality, after two and a half years of work, the special Rules of Procedure of the Constitutional Commission were adopted with norms higher than those of the Provisional Rules of Procedure of the Supreme Soviet. Subsequently, the deputies were guided strictly by a fixed procedure.

21. Remarks and proposals of persons and bodies entitled to legislative initiative, and those declined by the Constitutional Commission, were subject to submission for consideration at the session in summarized form and with explanatory notes.

22. During the work of the twentieth session, from 19 May 1993 to 7 July 1993, the constitutional majority partially adopted the Preamble, sixty-nine Articles in full and nineteen Articles in part, as well as the draft Law 'On the Procedure of Enforcement of the Constitution' in its first reading.

23. The thirteenth session of the Supreme Soviet, which started its work in November 1993, finished work with the draft Basic Law. Up to that point, most parts of the Articles were adopted by the necessary qualified majority, and the attitudes of the deputies towards the organization of state power, both on national and local levels, were brought to light. Certain issues in that part remained open. In the summer of 1993, S. Shushkevich, the Chairman of the Supreme Soviet of Republic of Belarus, offered to adopt it by June in the Constitutional Assembly, the body specially created for those purposes.

24. The historical decision to finally adopt the constitution was made by the deputies on 15 March 1994 after almost four years of consultation. The adoption required the formation of a constitutional practice that met the letter and the spirit of the Basic Law, to secure direct implementation of the Constitution, and its uniform application. The Law on enforcement of the Constitution was entrusted to the Chairperson of the Supreme Soviet of Republic of Belarus who signed the document at a solemn session of the Presidium of the Supreme Soviet on 28 March 1994. On 30 March 1994 the Constitution was published in the national newspapers. The day of its enforcement, 15 March, was the actual day of adoption of the Constitution and was proclaimed to be the red-letter day in Belarus.

25. At the same time, a conflict emerged at the end of 1994 between the President, who was elected in July of that year, and the Supreme Soviet. Both parties contributed to the political conflict. The Supreme Soviet had held a monopoly on power since 1990 and did not wish to reduce its claims due to the new democratic Constitution of 30 March 1994. Among its major principles were: the separation of powers and the interaction of authorities, a variety of forms of ownership and their equal protection, political pluralism, rule of law, and a mutual responsibility between the State and man. For a year after the adoption of the Constitution there were no parliamentary elections. Contrary to the requirements of the Constitution, the laws were enforced by acts of Parliament. The ratification of international treaties, meant to be subject to a signature of the Head of State, was carried out by resolutions of the Supreme Soviet with the signature of the speaker.

26. Certain contributions to the conflict were caused by the actions of the Constitutional Court. According to the Constitution, the Court had the right to institute proceedings regarding the conformity between the Constitution and the normative acts of any state body. Unfortunately, it did not even attempt to demonstrate its impartiality. During the first year and a half, the Constitutional Court had initiated only considerations of the acts of the President and only before the autumn of 1996 did it consider some acts of the Supreme Soviet. To a certain extent its influence was affected by the composition of the Constitutional Court, which was formed by former deputies of the Supreme Soviet. Moreover, it was only the Supreme Soviet that appointed the Constitutional Court. The Republic of Belarus appeared to be the only country in the CIS where the President was elected after the adoption of the new Constitution and who did not participate in its creation as the Head of State, and who had no right to participate in the formation of the Constitutional Court.

27. In March 1996 the President of the Republic of Belarus submitted to the Supreme Soviet a small draft of a law amending the Constitution of Republic of Belarus. However, it was not even included in the legislative agenda. The Parliament blocked it illegally. The President of the Republic of Belarus proposed the formation of the Constitutional Court on the principle of parity. Years later, even some deputies of the opposition in the Supreme Soviet found the non-consideration of the draft law proposed by the President of Republic of Belarus a mistake. Faced with no alternative, the President decided to address the revised wording of the Constitution to the people by way of a referendum held on 24 November 1996. The Supreme Soviet proposed its own draft. In many respects it was similar to the Constitution of 1978.

28. What was essentially new in the Constitution after the referendum of 24 November 1996? The Basic Law fixed the principle of the supremacy of the law (Article 7) (previously the supremacy of acts). This secured more entirely the actual realization of the concept of separation of powers and gave more freedom to the judicial bodies to administer justice, meaning a delivery of decisions grounded, first of all, not on the acts of one kind, but on the law. Such an approach allowed the relevant demands of bodies realizing norm-making activities to go to the courts, which were called to administer justice; constitutional justice was included in this. The most essential changes were in section IV which were devoted to the organization and activities of the supreme state bodies, such as the President, the Parliament, the Government and the courts. The rights of the citizens were also extended. There was a redistribution and specification of powers between the bodies in question. It is not true that only the President received additional rights and duties. The scope of powers of the Government was also increased considerably. The mechanism of interaction between the representative and executive powers was formed in more concrete ways. The legislative process was formulated so as to minimize and reduce the disputes between its participants. The Parliament of Belarus became bicameral. The Constitution contains no provision providing joint sessions of the chambers for the adoption of any decisions. Each chamber has its own competences. Only the adoption of the laws shall be the competence of both chambers, and any draft law, unless otherwise stipulated by the Constitution, shall be considered in the House of Representatives of the Republic and then in the Council of the Republic. The Constitution stipulates for the participation of two branches of power, the legislative and the executive, in the formation of other bodies: the Constitutional Court, the Central Commission on Elections and Holding of National Referenda, the Supreme Court and the Supreme Economic Court.

29. Draft laws allocating, decreasing or increasing expenditures, would be submitted to the Parliament only with the consent of the President or on his instruction and with the consent of the Government. Thereafter, this process would be more thought-out and contributory to the preparation of the drafts. There appeared to be a new norm granting the President (Government) the right to require voting for the submitted draft as a whole or to preserve only those amendments offered or accepted by the Head of State or by the Government. The Constitution, having maximum legal force, defines the hierarchy of sub-constitutional normative acts. Following the Basic Law, there are constitutional laws, including the acts of interpretation of the Constitution adopted by the Parliament, then ratified international treaties, laws, decrees, edicts, and acts of the Government. A special place among the laws is basic directions of internal and external policy of the Republic of Belarus, or on military doctrine, that are broad programmes rather than narrow dispositions. This means that all the other sub-constitutional acts should be based on these important laws.

30. Where there is a discrepancy between a law, a decree or an ordinance and the Constitution, the Constitution shall apply. Where there is a discrepancy between a decree or ordinance and a law, the law shall apply when the powers for the promulgation of the decree or ordinance were provided by the law (Article 137). This is the major aspect of the concept of separation of powers according to which the acts of the President and the Parliament should be based primarily on the Constitution. Certainly, there may be several readings of the Constitution. In such a case, it is the business of the Constitutional Court to settle the dispute and to define, which of the acts in question (decree, law or edict) are based on the Constitution, and which ones violate it. Only then, when the powers for issuing a decree or edict were granted by law, shall such a law have supremacy.

31. The President, as previously stated, has the right to veto an adopted law. However, what is new here is that the law is not considered to be signed and enforced if it cannot be returned to the Parliament due to the termination of a session. This is a so-called 'pocket' veto, like the one stipulated in the Constitution of the USA. The Constitution of Belarus envisages the right of the President to state objections concerning certain provisions of the law that are brought back for repeated voting. In this case, before the relevant decision of the House of Representatives and the Council of the Republic, the law shall be subject to signing by the President and becomes effective except for those provisions that have objections thereto. This should help avoid a situation where the law may not be enforced because of any particular remarks.

32. One of the most important principles of the law is the constitutional norm in the provision in Article 104 of the Constitution about not giving a retroactive effect to the law, unless it extenuates or revokes the responsibility of citizens. Unfortunately, in our history there were many cases when a retroactive effect was given to adopted acts. Only the Criminal Code and the Administrative Code contain Articles which make it impermissible to provide a retroactive effect to acts that find or strengthen responsibility. I believe that this constitutional norm should also be treated as the order for enforcement of all normative acts, and not only laws. A similar approach obliges all the law-making bodies to organize their activities in a manner that insures that their legal norms do not infringe upon the rights and freedom of citizens, and do not inflict upon them additional burdens, without informing them about this beforehand.

33. The principle of judicial protection of rights and freedoms of citizens finds its development in the Constitution. First, Article 60 of the Basic Law assures the right of everyone to the protection of rights and freedoms by a competent, independent and impartial court of law within the time periods specified by the law. Second, according to the new wording of Article 61, everyone has the right, in accordance with international legal instruments ratified by the Republic of Belarus, to appeal to international organizations to defend their rights and freedoms, provided all available interstate means of legal defence have been exhausted. This constitutional standard establishes additional guarantees of the rights and freedoms of citizens by allowing them to call on international law, if it is not possible for the State to defend their rights. Relevant international treaties provide the grounding for this. Third, since 30 March 1994, Article 112 of the Constitution enshrines the rule that if, during the hearing of a specific case, a court concludes that an enforceable enactment is contrary to the Constitution, it shall make a ruling in accordance with the Constitution and raise, under the established procedure, the issue of whether the enforceable enactment in question should be declared unconstitutional.

34. In other countries there are, traditionally, norms that secure the stability of the Constitution. For these purposes, the Basic Law defines what constitutional provisions can be changed only by way of popular vote. These are sections devoted to the bases of the constitutional system, the individual, society, state, organization and activity of the supreme state bodies, as well as to the effect of the Constitution and to the procedure of its amendment. Such an approach describes the circumstances by which decisions adopted by referendum can be cancelled or changed only by referendum, unless otherwise stipulated. On first sight the formula seems to be complex. However, its essence is that the people, by taking this or that decision, may delegate a part of their authorities to any state body, for example, the President or the Parliament. If the Parliament makes amendments to the Constitution, then the relevant law may be adopted, as in Italy, after two discussions and approvals by the Parliament, with an interval of not less than three months.

35. As a whole, by evaluating the Constitution, despite some drawbacks, it is possible to say that it creates conditions for the formation of strong state legal mechanism. Therefore, it is very important that the driving force behind the activities of the State bodies should be their aspiration towards democracy, as well as ensuring the rights and freedoms of citizens.

36. On 17 October 2004 a national referendum was held, in which more than 77% of citizens from the total number of those on the voting lists expressed their opinions for the new edition of part one of Article 81 of the Constitution, which removes the two-term limit previously imposed on the President.

Chapter 2. Profile of the Form of Government

37. The President of the Republic of Belarus takes a special place in the system of the State bodies. According to Article 79 of the Constitution, the President shall be the Head of State, the guarantor of the Constitution of the Republic of Belarus, and of human rights and liberties. The President shall personify the unity of the nation, the implementation of the main guidelines of domestic and foreign policy, and shall represent the Republic of Belarus in relations with other states and international organizations. The President shall provide for the protection of the sovereignty of the Republic of Belarus, its national security and territorial integrity, shall ensure its political and economic stability, the continuity and the interaction of the bodies of state power and shall play an intermediary role between the bodies of state power. Thus, the Constitution of the Republic of Belarus gives the Head of State responsibility for the most important functions and tasks.

38. The obligation of the President of the Republic of Belarus to be the guarantor of the Constitution, human rights and civil liberties is stipulated by the task to ensure stability of the constitutional order and to guarantee the rights and liberties of individuals and citizens. For these purposes, the President is given the function of arbitrator between the different authorities in place. Providing the interconnection of the State bodies and acting as intermediary between them, the President stands above all the other state bodies. From my point of view, the intermediary role of the President is more of a political than a legal one. It is the Constitutional Court of Belarus that judicially has more rights, including the settlement of conflicts by verifying the constitutionality of enforceable enactments.

39. A peculiarity of the status of the President of the Republic of Belarus is that, on the one hand he acts as an arbitrator, and on the other hand he may actively administer the Government and subordinated bodies. The President has exceptional individual authority. There is no need of countersigning or any other participation of a state body (e.g., to make proposals, coordination, etc.).

40. Traditionally, the science of constitutional law shall include three types of republic: parliamentary, presidential, and the combined state system often referred to as a semi-presidential republic. Each of them has their own features. The Republic of Belarus is a republic with a combined state system, where the main figure on the political scene is the President. What are the arguments for a combined state system in the Republic of Belarus and not a presidential one? There are peculiarities that testify to the borrowing of some elements of a parliamentary republic. However, this borrowing usually leads not to the decrease of the authority of the President, but to its strengthening. Here it is possible to talk about the combined state system only in a formal sense. Thus, as a result of the transformation from a presidential republic (according to the Constitution of 15 March 1994) to a combined state system (according to the Constitution of 24 November 1996), the authority of the President had increased. Although, there still is a system of checks and balances, there are added new elements that shall be applied by the President, for instance, the dissolving of the chambers of Parliament in the case of regular or gross violation of the Constitution.

41. The President of the Republic of Belarus is not only the Head of State, but legally and nominally the head of the executive branch. However, it is not stated directly in the Constitution that he is the head of the executive branch. This may, however, be assumed on the grounds of analysis. As the Head of State he represents the State domestically and internationally, conducts negotiations, concludes (signs) international treaties of the Republic of Belarus, appoints diplomatic representatives, receives the credentials of the accredited diplomatic representatives of foreign countries, grants citizenship, solves other issues related to citizenship, grants asylum, bestows state awards and grants pardons to convicted citizens. As the head of the executive he determines the structure of the Government, forms it, appoints the Prime Minister, with the consent of the Parliament, dismisses the ministers, chairs the meetings of the Government, and has the right to abolish acts of the Government incompatible with legislation or the structure of local executive power.

42. A peculiarity of the classical presidential republic is the President's inability to dissolve the Parliament and the absence of the right to a vote of no-confidence in the Government. The latter circumstance, by force of certain rules in the Constitution, is also an argument for the combined state system of governing, and therefore demonstrates that the Republic of Belarus cannot be considered a presidential republic in its classical form.

43. In its status the Government of the Republic of Belarus is accountable to the President and the Parliament. It is interesting that, in presidential republics, there is no combination of duties for a member of the Government and a parliamentarian. Under Article 92 of the Constitution, a deputy of the House of Representatives may simultaneously be a member of the Government.

44. It is possible for the Republic of Belarus, under a system of checks and balances, to grant the Parliament the right to dismiss the President (the so-called procedure of impeachment).

Chapter 3. State Territory and Trust or Other Non-self-governing Territories (Geographical Data)

45. The Republic of Belarus is situated in the central part of Europe at the watershed of the Baltic Sea and the Black Sea. It has a territory of 207,600 square kilometres that comprises about 2% of the area of Europe. The length of the territory from the North to the South is 560 kilometres and from the West to the East is 650 kilometres. Minsk is the capital of the Republic of Belarus and is situated at the centre of the country. Belarus borders on five countries: Poland in the west, Lithuania in the north-west, Latvia and Russia in the north, Russia in the northeast and in the east and the Ukraine in the south.

46. Belarus is primarily a flat country with flat, lowland landscapes dotted with bogs and lakes. Average altitude is 160 metres above sea level. The highest hill is 345 metres and the lowest locality is 80–90 metres above sea level.

47. The climate of Belarus is temperate continental with regular western winds. Winter is mild with long thaws and summer is moderately warm. Average annual temperature in January ranges between four and eight degrees below zero and in July between seventeen and nineteen degrees above zero. The average annual level of precipitation is between 550 and 700 millimetres.

48. The development of its own mineral resources provides the country with potash, common salt, limestone, raw materials for cement, ceramic and refractory clay, sands, construction and gravel materials, building stone and fresh underground mineral water. At the same time, due to the lack of certain mineral resources, the Republic imports many raw materials, in particular: oil, gas, coal, oil-shale, glass sands, etc.

49. The water resources of Belarus include rivers, lakes, storage ponds, ponds, and subsoil and underground waters. In the Republic of Belarus there are about 21,000 rivers and brooks with a total length of 90,600,000 kilometres. The largest rivers (with a length of 500 kilometres) are the Neman, the Viliya, the Pripyat, the Zapadnaya Dvina, the Dnepr, the Zapadny Byg, the Sozh and the Berezina. There are 11,000 lakes with the total surface area of about 2,000 square kilometres. There are a great number of lakes in the North and in the North-West. The largest one is the Naroch (79.6 square kilometres). Bogs make up an integral part of Belarusian landscape. They occupy 4.4% of the area of the Republic. Low-lying bogs create unique ecosystems. There are some huge bogs in Zapadnoye Polesye that are the largest natural bogs of this kind in Europe.

50. Belarusian forests occupy 38% of its territory. The main kinds of timber are pine, fir, oak, birch, black alder and aspen. One of the oldest forest tracts in Europe is situated in Belarus and is called Belovezhskaya Puscha (Dense Forests) with stands of timber between 120 and 200 years old. Some trees are considered natural monuments and may be 350 to 500 years old. More than a thousand oaks are between 300 and 700 years old. The total timber stock in Belarusian forests is more than milliard cubic metres, increasing by nearly 25 million cubic metres every year.

51. Belarusian flora illustrates the natural and climate peculiarities of the country and has nearly 11,500 species. More than 130 rare relic types of plants grow in the Republic of Belarus.

52. The animal kingdom is one of the most significant biological resources of Belarus. Its diversity is represented by 457 species of vertebrates and more than 20,000 invertebrates. Mammals are represented by seventy-three species. A unique one is the auroch which is a kind of unique symbol of the country.

53. The total area of the natural territories of Belarus set aside for conservation is 7.6% of the country (except for Polessky radiation and ecological national park). 'Belovezhskaya Puscha' is included in the United Nations Educational, Scientific and Cultural Organization (UNESCO) list of worldwide cultural heritage sites.

54. There are 20.8 million hectares of land in the Republic of Belarus. As of 2004, 9.1 million hectares were set aside for agricultural; of which 5.6 million hectares is arable land.

Chapter 4. State Population (Demographic Data)

55. The demographic situation of the country is under constant consideration by the State. The population of the Republic of Belarus, as of 1 January 2015, was 9,480,900.

In comparison to 1995, the population figures mark a declining trend of about 713,100 people.

56. As of 1 January 2015 the urban population was 7,325,000, or about 77% of the total population of the Republic. The rural population totalled some 2,155,900 or 23% of the Republic' population. In the beginning of 2015 the male segment was 4,343,200 or 46.5% of the total population of the Republic. The female segment was 5,000,300 or 53.5%. This makes a ratio of 111 women to every 100 men.

57. According to the results of the population census in 2009, there are more than 130 nationalities who live in the Republic (83.7% of the total population of Belarus) predominant. The Russian population is 8.3%, the Polish population is 3.1% and 4.9% of the nation's population is made up of other nationalities.

58. The population of able-bodied age is 62% of the total population, population under the able-bodied age is 17% and population over the able-bodied age is 21%.

59. There is a tendency in Belarus, as well as in other European countries, of 'aging' of the population which is demonstrated by the high rate of people over 60 (22%), compared to children from 0 to 15 (16%).

60. The main aims of the demographic policy of the State are lowering the rate of mortality, the improvement of human longevity, the stabilization of the birth-rate and improvement of the process of migration. The main link in the chain in the process of population reproduction is the birth-rate. In 2014 in the Republic of Belarus 118,700 children were born.

61. Taking into account the significance of the demographic problems for the future of the country, the law on demographic security has been adopted and the Programme on demographic security is under elaboration. Implementation of this Programme shall make it possible to change the negative tendency in the birth-rate and mortality.

62. Infant mortality is the most evident indicator of the health of the population and the level of the public health care. Since 1996 there has been a declining tendency in the infant mortality rate in the Republic. In 2014 the infant mortality rate was 3.8 deaths before the age of one for every 1,000 births, compared to a rate of 13.3 per 1,000 in 1995.

63. In 2014 life expectancy was 72.5 years. The average life expectancy for men is 68 years and 78 for women.

64. In 2014 there were approximately 83,942 registered marriages, 5,942 more than in 2009. The amount of divorces was 34,864. In 2014 the proportion between marriages and divorces improved: in 2014 there were 415 divorces per 1,000 married couples, compared to 561 per 1,000 in 2002. The most active marriageable age among men and women, both from urban and rural localities, is between 20 and 29 years old.

65. Birth-rate and mortality demographic processes are greatly influenced by migration. Since 1996 the Republic of Belarus has kept a favourable balance of migration with all the CIS and Baltic countries. From 1996 to 2003 the number of people migrating to the Republic was 201,000 while those who left the Republic were 71,000. The main inflow of migration is from Russia, Ukraine and Kazakhstan. The number of people arriving from those countries in 2003 was 86% of the total number of immigrants from the CIS and Baltic countries. In 2009 19,892 people arrived in the Republic of Belarus and 7,643 left. In 2014 40,000 people arrived the Republic of Belarus, including 13,500 from the Ukraine.

66. The population of working people in the Republic of Belarus in 2009 numbered 4,643,900. The employable population of able-bodied age was 4,337,000. The number of people over and under the able-bodied age is 240,000. The employable population of able-bodied age is 94.5% of the human resources pool. The number of people who are over and under the employable age and employed in economic sector is 5.5%. The number of economically active people in 2009 was 4,686,100.

67. Of the population of able-bodied age, 4.3 million, or 72%, were employed in the economic sector of the Republic in 2009. Of the employed population, circa 80% worked in cities and urban settlements, circa 20% in rural areas. The specific proportion of all persons employed in the non-governmental sector increased from 40% in 1995 to 51% in 2009.

Part I. Sources of Constitutional Law

Chapter 1. Treaties

68. According to Article 8 of the Constitution, the Republic of Belarus shall recognize the supremacy of the universally acknowledged principles of international law and ensure that its laws comply with such principles. The conclusion of international treaties that are contrary to the Constitution shall not be permitted. This fundamental standard signifies an aspiration of the law maker to build an independent state on legal democratic principles. Putting a priority on the universally acknowledged principles of international law means there is a certain desire for the positive development of the legal system. In this sense, one shall understand the wording, 'ensure that its laws comply with such principles'. In view of the universally acknowledged principles of international law 'filling' the constitutional norms, the definition of their content should be realized.

The Republic of Belarus is a party to a number of interstate organizations: the CIS, the Union State, before the EurAsEC Customs Union/EAEC, as from 1 January 2015 the Eurasian Economic Union (EAEU). That is, it is an active participant in integration processes in the former Soviet Union. The constitution of the EurAsEC Member States, now EAEU, allow them to engage in interstate organizations or determine the higher place of international treaties in relation to acts of national legislation. The Constitution of the Republic of Belarus, in particular Article 8, stipulates that opportunity right on condition that these kinds of agreements are not contrary to the Basic Law.

69. In our legislation, until recently, there was no general wording according to which the international treaties should be concluded according to constitutional procedure, which constitutes an integral part of Belarusian law and national legislation. Certain legal sources (codes, laws) sometimes underline the supremacy of the international treaty in relation to the concrete normative act. However, it was not enough for a direct application of international treaties. The law of 23 July 2008 'On international treaties of the Republic of Belarus' stipulates a definite procedure for implementation of international treaties into the national legislation. It is important to bear in mind that according to Article 33 of the law, the norms of law contained in effective international treaties of the Republic of Belarus shall be an integral part of the legislation applied within the territory of the Republic of Belarus, shall be subject to direct application, except for cases when it follows from the international treaty that applications of such standards need the adoption (issuing) of a domestic normative legal act, and have the force of that normative legal act, by which the Republic of Belarus expressed consent to the binding nature of the relevant international treaty.

Chapter 2. Constitution of the Republic of Belarus

70. Distinctive features of the new Basic Law of Belarus are: (1) an ideologically neutral nature; (2) a variety of forms of ownership as economic base; (3) the establishment of equality of the State and the citizen with their mutual obligations; (4) the priority of the universal principles of international law as a vector for development of current legislation; (5) the rule of law; (6) the separation and interaction of powers; (7) the direct effect of the norms of the Constitution.

71. 'Democracy in the Republic of Belarus under Article 4 of the Constitution shall be exercised on the basis of diversity of political institutes, ideologies and views. The ideology of political parties, religious or other public associations and social groups may not be made mandatory for citizens'. If Article 6 of the Constitution of 1978 fixed a leading and directing role for the communist party, now the same Article speaks about the functioning of the State mechanism on the grounds of the principle of separation of powers. The Basic Law, no longer based on a specific ideological orientation, like Constitutions of other civilized countries, says nothing about the building of a socialist, communist or capitalist state. It emphasizes (Article 13) the equality of all forms of ownership and their protection. The new Constitution reflects these political, social and economic changes, and enshrines the programme of improvement of democracy, the guarantee of rights and freedoms.

72. The Constitution is the main source of national law. It has supremacy over all the other legal acts adopted at the national level. The Constitution differs from a law in terms of its legal force, form and content. The Constitution regulates the main aspects of the State, public life, supporting and directly leading the legal process, stimulating and directing legislative regulations.

73. The analysis of the content of the Constitution of Belarus helps to inspire the law maker to consider it as having direct effect, which may be subject to application without needing to pass special legislative acts.

74. The Constitution shall fix the State system, basic rights and freedoms. The Constitutional principles and norms shall predetermine the construction of the whole national legal system.

75. The Constitution enjoys increased protection. Thus, there is a differentiation of the constitutional norms as regards their stipulation and hierarchy. The most important norms enjoy special protection: correction of some of them needs a more complex procedure (e.g., they may not be amended by the Parliament, but only as a result of a referendum). This applies to sections I, II, IV and VIII.

76. Article 137 of the Constitution stipulates directly that the Constitution has supreme legal force. The laws, decrees, ordinances and other instruments of state bodies are promulgated on the basis of, and in accordance with, the Constitution of the Republic of Belarus. Where there is a discrepancy between a law, decree or ordinance and the Constitution, the Constitution shall apply. Where there is a discrepancy between a decree or ordinance and a law, the law shall have supremacy when the powers for the promulgation of the decree or ordinance was provided by the law.

77. Thus, the Constitution is the main Basic Law of the State. It lays the groundwork for all current and future legislation and the competences of state bodies will be defined in it. For this reason the Constitution is quite often considered to be the heart of the legal system. Frequently, the Constitution underlines and lays the basis for the adoption of laws for further development of the provisions it contains. For example, the Belarusian Constitution has about 100 references to laws. The Constitution has an impact on the development of the legal system, specifies law-making powers of state bodies and defines both objects and limits of legal regulation. The Constitution enshrines the different types of normative acts and the hierarchy of these acts.

78. Due to the legal status of public authorities fixed by the Constitution, it is possible to define the hierarchy of the normative acts they adopt. In addition, the supremacy with respect to all the other legal acts is the major legal feature of the Constitution. The relevant rules (about the supremacy of the Constitution) shall be fixed in the Basic Law. The priority of the Constitution in relation to other acts is also supported by the specific nature of its adoption, amendment or termination. Admittedly, the history of the Belarusian State has borne witness to cases when another normative act was given higher legal weight than the Constitution. On 25 August 1991, the Declaration of the Supreme Soviet of the Republic of Belarus on State Sovereignty was given the status of a constitutional law with a higher legal force than the Constitution: in case of any discrepancy between the norms of the Declaration and the Constitution, the priority was given to the first document.

79. Owing to the fixing in the Constitution of the principle of its priority in relation to the laws, decrees, ordinances and edicts, it is undoubtedly possible to draw a conclusion about the supremacy of the Constitution in relation to the acts of the Government (they should be based on the Constitution, laws, legal acts of the President) and other state bodies.

80. The isolation of the Constitution from real life is a characteristic from the country's history. It was necessary then that the constitutional norm could be effective only when another normative act was adopted in elaboration of it. Such an approach devalued the Constitution and made no contribution towards strengthening its supremacy and authority in the consciousness of citizens. Nowadays the situation should have been changed. Many of the norms of the Basic Law have been formulated in a wording that should have inspired direct application. Unfortunately, there is still a strong influence on certain officials to fall back on the conservative approaches of the past. This results in infringements of the principle of direct application of constitutional norms. Usually the refusal to realize this right is motivated by the absence of the relevant right in this or that concrete normative legal act (code, law, decree, etc.). Such gaps in the legislation give reasons for the refusal in the realization of this or that right. The similar position of the officials (judges) is explained not so much by intentionally ignoring constitutional orders, but by long-held conservative attitudes toward the relations to the Basic Law, according to which the norms of the Constitution would have been applied only when they have found a basis in current legislation, for example, codes (Criminal, Civil, Criminal Procedure, Civil Procedure, Labour Codes, etc.). However, in all modern civilized countries, when we speak about the rights, freedoms and duties of citizens, the accepted wisdom is not only that of the supremacy of the constitutional norms, but also their direct effect. The principle of the supremacy of the law and direct action of the Constitution shall be the grounds for law making and the application of legal practice.

81. In some cases the law maker really is late in adopting laws where the references are available in the Constitution, or as a result of omissions by the authors of the draft laws, and, perhaps, as a result of lobbying by interested subjects impeding the development of constitutional norms.

82. Directly effective norms are those constitutional standards that may be carried out with the use of constitutional remedies called mediate norms (those that require preliminary concrete definition). However, if the law maker fails to perform the duties of the legislative development of the constitutional norms in good time, then the law maker, but not the citizen, must suffer negative consequences.

83. The Constitution of the Republic of Belarus provides no indication on the direct effect of the Constitution; however, by virtue of the principle of supremacy of the Basic Law fixed in Article 137 of the Constitution, the constitutional norms shall have advantage not only in case of any discrepancy between the Constitution and the norms of by-constitutional acts, but also in connection with the gaps they contain and signify about the oversights of legal regulation. The State is also obliged to execute constitutional standards in cases when the physical or legal person makes appeal for the protection of their constitutional rights and freedoms, without reference to the norms of legislation emanating from the branches of government. A sign of direct action of the constitutional norms is their real application by courts.

84. The Constitution of the Republic of Belarus has created a new concept of the mutual relations between an individual and the State. At present, there are no class interests, but a person is judged of supreme value to the society and the State. Prior to the new Constitution, each and every person was subordinated to the interests of the State or the collective. It is time to understand the necessity for the optimization of relations between the individual and the State. The further improvement of clauses dedicated to the rights and freedoms of citizens shall be the task of all the State bodies, including the courts.

85. Amendments to the Constitution may be carried out by two subjects: the people and the Parliament. Under Article 140 of the Constitution sections I, II, IV, and VIII of the Constitution may be changed only by means of referendum. A decision to amend the Constitution by means of referendum is deemed to have been adopted where a majority of citizens on the electoral roll vote in favour of it. Constitutional amendments and instruments on the interpretation of the Constitution shall be deemed to have been adopted when not less than two-thirds of elected deputies of both chambers of the Parliament vote in favour of them. Amending the Constitution is considered by the chambers of the Parliament on the initiative of the President or of no fewer than 150,000 citizens of the Republic of Belarus who have the right to vote.

86. The procedure for creating draft laws on amending the Constitution is basically similar to that of making the drafts laws. According to Article 167 of the Rules of Procedure of the House of Representatives, if the proposal on amending the Constitution is made to the House of Representatives by the citizens of the Republic of Belarus, it shall be subject to consideration according to the Rules of Procedure, except for approval, in coordination with the subject of the right of the legislative initiative.

87. Under Article 139 of the Constitution, a Law on amending the Constitution may be adopted after it has been debated and approved twice by the Parliament with at least a three-month interval. The amendment of the Constitution by the Parliament is inadmissible during a state of emergency, as well as within the last six months of the current session of the House of Representatives.

88. The provision that the amendment of the Constitution may take place only after two discussions and votes with an obligatory interval between them, is common in international constitutional practice. Such a procedure of amending the Constitution is known as 'the double vote'. The basis for this procedure is that the deputies should think once again whether the amendments are necessary, whether they are tactical, or insufficiently balanced. The interval between the termination of the first and the beginning of the second reading of the draft law, which shall amend the Constitution, should be of no less than three months. The given rule shall be considered to be observed, if the draft at both the first and the second discussions is identical. Otherwise it will be considered an infringement of the specified constitutional demand.

89. According to the Rules of Procedure of the House of Representatives the draft law on amending the Constitution prepared for consideration should be forwarded to the deputies of the House of Representatives and other subjects entitled to legislative initiative no later than twenty days before the consideration at the session of the House of Representatives.

90. The draft law on amending the Constitution shall be reported at the House of Representatives by the President of Republic of Belarus or by his representative. If the draft is made by the citizens of Republic of Belarus, then according to the Law of 26 November 2003 'On the procedure of realization of the right to legislative initiative by citizens of the Republic of Belarus' (Article 18) shall be presented in the House of Representatives by the Chairperson of the initiative group. A decision on the end of discussion of the draft law shall be adopted by a majority of not less than two-thirds of votes of the full composition of the House of Representatives.

91. To exclude any undue pressure on the will of the deputies, it is impermissible to amend the Constitution during a state of emergency. Special conditions (military threat, natural disasters, etc.) should not be an influence on constitutional stability. The prohibition of amendment of the Constitution within last six months of the authority of the House of Representatives prevents the adoption of decisions that serve ephemeral interests (e.g., proceeding from evaluations of a pre-electoral situation in the country).

Chapter 3. Legislation and Equivalent Legislative Rules

92. The Law 'On Normative Legal Acts of the Republic of Belarus' of 10 January 2000 with further amendments has determined the concept of 'legislation'. This is a system of normative legal acts that regulates public relations. Thus, the normative legal acts of all the State bodies including local representatives (Councils of Deputies), as well as executive and administrative bodies (Executive Committees, local administrations) shall be referred to as acts of legislation. Among the texts that are considered to be part of this concept, there are legislative acts voted by Parliament, together with the Constitution. These are the laws of the Republic of Belarus, directives, decrees and edicts of the President of the Republic of Belarus.

93. In accordance with current practices in the Republic of Belarus, all legal acts are divided into normative legal acts and law enforceable enactment. Article 1 of the Law 'On Normative Legal Acts of the Republic of Belarus' specifies the concept of the normative legal act: it is an official document of a definite form adopted within the competence of the authorized state body or by referendum with the observance of the procedure established by the legislation of the Republic of Belarus that defines the common binding rules of conduct intended to ensure that it is applicable. A law enforceable enactment is the act that resolves a certain situation, conflict and there is the application of common rules to particular subjects of relations.

94. One of the main and less stable groups of legislative acts in comparison with the Constitution shall be ordinary laws. Generally, they regulate certain public relations, are not always complex and include rules applied to different spheres of public life. Ordinary laws shall be subject to adoption by the Parliament by a simple majority of the sitting members of each chamber.

95. The aim of laws is to govern public relations in order to secure the rights of the citizens and the correct functioning of state institutions. Each law has a special subject to regulate, from the political sphere to the social one.

96. The laws differ from each other by their legal force and may be ordinary or constitutional. Constitutional laws are specified by the Constitution (Article 140). These are laws on amending the Constitution and laws on the enforcement and interpretation of the Constitution. They are considered to have been adopted when not less than two-thirds of the elected deputies of both chambers vote in favour of them. Moreover, the law on amending the Constitution may only be adopted after it has been debated and approved twice by both chambers of the Parliament with at least a three months' interval between these two votes.

97. Codes should be mentioned among other ordinary laws and described as the codified acts that provide the integral regulation of a relevant field. Codes are of higher validity than other laws. The practical activities of the Belarusian Parliament signify that the law maker in certain directions strives to adopt acts that would be the basis for other ordinary laws in the relevant field. In some cases laws fix the wordings that make them stable, sound and predominant in comparison with analogous laws or by-laws. Unfortunately, there still exist the partial remains of a type of law in the form of a declaration that comes from the past when the law was considered to be a common act and an abstract norm covering the most human relations. Owing to the abstract nature of many norms of laws, the law enforcement bodies, including the courts, first of all, strived to study by-laws as those notable for their concrete nature. This is the basis for the lack of judicial rulings in our recent history with references only to the Articles of the Constitution.

98. The Constitution of the Republic of Belarus determines the spheres of relations that are subject to legislative regulation. Articles 84, 97 and 98 of the Constitution determine the scope of the norm creation activities between the President and the Parliament. The new edition of the Constitution of 1994 more accurately defines the spheres where the Parliament may make legislation.

99. The main function of any Parliament is a law-making one (even if it also has regulatory and administrative duties). It should be noted here that both chambers shall adopt laws, but it is the House of Representatives where the law-making process usually starts. According to Belarusian legislation, any draft law, unless otherwise specified by the Constitution, shall be considered in the House of Representatives and then in the Council of the Republic. As a rule, many other powers for each chamber are exclusive and require no participation of another chamber.

100. According to Article 97.2 of the Constitution, the House of Representatives has the power to consider draft laws, including the guidelines of the domestic and foreign policy of the Republic of Belarus; military doctrine; the ratification and rejection of international treaties; the fundamental rights, freedoms and obligations of its citizens; citizenship issues, the status of foreigners and persons without citizenship; ethnic minorities' rights; approval of the budget of the republic and the following-up of its implementation; introduction of national taxes and dues; principles of ownership; the basis of social security; the principles regulating labour and employment; marriage, family, childhood, maternity, paternity, education, upbringing, culture and public health; environmental protection and the rational utilization of natural resources; determination of the procedure for resolving issues relating to administrative and territorial structure of the State; local self-government; administration of justice and status of judges; criminal liability; amnesty; declaration of war and conclusion of peace; martial law and a state of emergency; institution of state awards; interpretation of laws.

101. Due to a specification in Article 97 of the Constitution of the list of draft laws for their consideration by the House of Representatives, it is possible to make certain conclusions. First, the House of Representatives (meaning the Parliament as a whole) has the authority to adopt normative acts as laws in the public sphere; second, this specification means that public relations in the given context are subject to regulation only by the law. Thereby, the activity of the legislative body is secured and any interference in its sphere on behalf of another branch of power is inadmissible. The list of draft laws that may be considered by the House of Representatives is not an exhaustive one. It is entitled to adopt laws also as regards other issues if, according to the Constitution, they are not under the authority of other state bodies. In other words, I may speak about the Parliament as the body of the national representation. A special place amongst the acts adopted by the Parliament is held by the Rules of Procedure of the Chambers. They are normative legal acts (in spite of the fact that they are subject to adoption in the form of resolutions) but unlike the laws they are signed, not by the President of the Republic of Belarus, but by the Speakers of the chambers of the Parliament. The chambers can pass resolutions on administrative and controlling issues.

102. In terms of executive power, the President of the Republic of Belarus has the right to issue decrees and orders by force of special necessity or by delegation to him by the Parliament, to issue edicts. The choice of the very form of an edict means that the act concerns problems that, under standard conditions, are subject to solutions proposed by the Parliament. There is a peculiarity here: temporary edicts are to be sent to the Parliament (House of Representatives) in a three-day period of time from the date of their issue and they shall keep their legal force, if they are not repealed by a majority of no less than two-thirds of the elected deputies of both the chambers. The Law 'On Normative Legal Acts of the Republic of Belarus' stipulates the right of the President of the Republic of Belarus to adopt directives – acts of normative and programme nature. Their provisions have direct nature of action, and the aspects of programme nature shall be subject to realization in the laws, decrees, resolutions of the Government, in resolutions of other state bodies.

103. The Government issues also normative legal acts: Resolutions. The Prime Minister issues acts of an administrative nature: Regulations.

104. The National Bank of the Republic of Belarus adopts decisions on issues of monetary and credit policy.

105. More active is departmental norm creation. In the Republic of Belarus there are twenty-four Ministries, seven State Committees, eight State Organizations that are subordinated to the Council of Ministers and can issue normative legal acts concerning the realization of their own competences.

106. The structure of normative legal acts in the Republic of Belarus was once subject to modification. Nowadays, the Constitution is the base of the national legal system. It is interesting to recall in this respect the way in which Belarusian legislation has developed over time. From 1990 to 1994 there were about 400 adopted legislative acts, i.e., the amount equal to the quantity adopted by the Supreme Council from 1938 to 1990. The law-creating activities of the Parliament became even more intensive after the adoption of the Constitution: for the period from 1994 to 2003; more than 709 laws were adopted (including more than twenty-two Codes), 199 edicts, 2080 decrees of the President, about 16,000 resolutions of the Government, as well as 256 acts of the Constitutional Court, 118 rulings of Plenum of the Supreme Court, 75 rulings of Plenum of the Supreme Economic Court, more than 10,000 departmental enforceable enactments.

107. The intensive law-creating activities fount its further development. For example, in 2010 there were adopted 130 laws, 10 decrees, 337 edicts, 916 resolutions of the Government. At the present moment, there are twenty-eight effective codes of normative nature.

108. In the course of the development of the law we have formed a kind of law application, and law reform where it has become necessary to enlarge the legislative area. Indeed, legal regulation gaps have to be filled, especially in the sphere of fundamental rights and freedoms. However, the coordination of legal acts and their validity should be given special consideration.

109. Restrictions are necessary, but the legislator should choose a course that does not entail a restriction of rights. The principle of proportionality shall be deemed to be the grounds of such possible interferences into the rights and freedoms that are constitutionally necessary. Article 23 of Belarusian Constitution, as well as other international acts on the rights and freedoms of citizens are the grounds for the specification of the legality of actions.

Chapter 4. Jurisprudence

110. Certain countries consider legal doctrine: the competent opinions of well-known scientists or lawyers on legal issues as a source of law. In English speaking countries, for instance, the works of eminent scientists are used by judges to justify their decisions. Belarusian practice is rather different.

111. Doctrine, of course, has an influence on the formation and the realization of the law and shall be the source for other forms, first of all, for normative legal acts. Moreover, it shall not perform the independent function of regulation of public affairs.

112. In Belarusian practice very often the views of eminent scientists find their acknowledgement in practice (courts, administrative bodies, state, etc.). The ideas expressed in legal literature may find their realization only after the lapse of some time. However, for a school of legal doctrine to develop it must be efficient, acceptable, authoritative, widespread and influential in public affairs so as to allow this phenomenon to gain greater credence. The recommendations of legal experts in the field of constitutionalism should specify the object of legal regulation for the benefit of the legislative and other law-making bodies.

113. The science of constitutional (state) law has run through several stages in its development. The science of state law originated in the pre-revolutionary period. Among well-known state legal scientists at the end of nineteenth century and the beginning of the twentieth century were I. Ilyin, N. Korkunov, N. Lazarevsky, L. Tikhomirov, N. Polijenko, B. Chicherina and others. They elaborated and made definitions of the basic notions of state law, including ideas of popular sovereignty and forms of government (monarchy, republic), etc.

114. The development of the science of constitutional law in the Republic of Belarus may be divided into several stages. During the soviet period the science of constitutional law and its representatives proceeded from the necessary acknowledgement of Marxist-Leninist theory as the main instrument for the solution of all the problems in society. The class approach was the dominant one.

115. In the eighties and nineties many scientists in the field of constitutional law changed their views radically by taking the position of considering the objective appropriateness of the development of the State and society. In addition, there were attempts to disagree with all that was done during the Soviet period, and not only the negative aspects of these developments.

116. In the modern period the science of constitutional law is developing around the concept of the universally acknowledged idea of the supremacy and the triumph of Constitution as the basis of the legal system. Scholars and practical workers argue (this is their right, which signifies the presence of the freedom of speech and opinion) about the content of the Basic Law and about the democratic nature of its norms. Specialists in legal science strive to react objectively to the needs of public progress and to express their own recommendations. Scientific research is directed towards the development of a political system for society, constitutional order, civil society, the legal status of the individual and finding an optimal balance of interests between the State, the society and the individual. The science of constitutional law is faced with vast tasks that are predicated by the predominant place that constitutional law holds among the other branches of law.

117. In case of any ambiguity in a normative legal act, as well as contradictions in the practice of its application, the law enforcement body that adopted this act or, unless otherwise stipulated in the Constitution of the Republic of Belarus, the body it authorized thereto shall carry out the official interpretation of those norms by way of adoption of the relevant normative legal act.

118. By interpreting a normative legal act, the content of its legal norms should be explained or clarified and should be specified in legislation, as well as functional and other links with other norms that regulate different aspects of the same type of public relations. The interpretation of normative legal acts does not assume their amendment.

119. The interpretation of acts may be classified by different features. Interpretation shall be differed by its legal obligation: (a) official (has powerful nature and is binding for execution); (b) unofficial (has no binding legal force). The official and unofficial nature of interpretation shall depend on the subject that gives interpretation.

120. The official interpretation is the explanation of the true sense of the norms of law by the State bodies in question. Official interpretation shall be divided into normative and casual. Normative interpretation shall have a common nature, i.e., it is obligatory for the definite type of public relations (categories of cases); casual interpretation shall be binding for concrete situations (specific cases).

121. Normative interpretation is the explanation that has for its purpose the removal of errors in understanding the act and ensuring its unique application. Normative interpretation shall have several types: authentic and legal (delegated) interpretation.

122. Authentic interpretation is the explanation of a normative legal act by the body that adopted it. ('authentic' means 'genuine', 'based on original'). All the law-making bodies shall have the right to authentic interpretation.

123. Legal and delegated interpretation shall presuppose the explanation of a normative act by another authorized body that did not adopt the act under interpretation.

124. Delegated interpretation may be carried out by different subjects (Council of Ministers, ministry, etc.).

125. The act of interpretation, regardless of the time period of its adoption, shall coincide with the time period of effect of the act under interpretation. In the event of a recall of normative acts, their force in full or partially shall lose the relevant norms of the act under interpretation. Acts under interpretation and the act of interpretation must coincide as regards their scope, but the latter may also be adopted in order to introduce elements of novelty in understanding the former with an allowance for new political, social and economic relations. Use of the norms of law contrary to interpretation shall stand for violation of the law.

126. The act of interpretation shall be carried out with all the procedures of the law-making process taken into account. The interpretation that is given by different bodies as regards the same issue shall be differentiated in their legal force depending on the status of the relevant body.

127. According to Article 62 of the Law 'On Normative Legal Acts of the Republic of Belarus', normative legal acts of the Republic of Belarus shall be subject to official publication. Official publication of normative legal acts is carried out in the State language in which they were adopted. (In Belarus, there are two state languages: Belarusian and Russian). Publication of a normative legal act in other languages is admissible only with the presence of its official translation into the relevant language approved by the relevant state body in accordance with the procedure prescribed for the adoption of the act in question. The date of official publication of a normative legal act should be the day of its official appearance. In the event of promulgation, at different times and at different places, in several official publications, the date of the official publication of the normative legal act and the time period of its enforcement should be determined to be the date of original publication. Normative legal acts or certain provisions thereof that contain state secrets or other information protected by the legislation of the Republic of Belarus, unless otherwise stipulated in the legislation of the Republic of Belarus, shall not be subject to publication. The decision that the normative legal act or certain provisions thereof may not be published shall be adopted in accordance with the legislation of the Republic of Belarus by the authorized state body and the original normative legal act shall be subject to the relevant mark. Normative legal acts shall be subject to publication with specification of their obligatory requisites: type of act, dates of its adoption, ordinal number and name. The official publication of normative legal acts in brief is inadmissible, except for the instances of publication of normative legal acts with certain provisions that are subject to no publication.

128. The law shall specify the terms and conditions for official publication of the normative legal act. 'Immediate' publication of laws and decrees must be of first priority, i.e., in the first issues of newspapers and magazines after the receipt of the decree or the law.

129. Decrees of the President of the Republic of Belarus, as well as resolutions of the Council of Ministers of the Republic of Belarus of normative nature shall be also subject to official publication, unless otherwise, as it is specified in Article 63.3 and in Article 63.4 of the Law, stipulated in the acts of the President or the Government. Decrees and resolutions of the Government shall be subject to immediate official publication within a five-day period of time from the date of their receipt by the official editions (except for the National Register of Legal Acts of the Republic of Belarus). According to Article 63.4 of the Law, other normative legal acts shall be subject to official publication after their inclusion in the National Register of Legal Acts of the Republic of Belarus. There is a five-day period of time for publication of normative legal acts from the day of their receipt by the bodies of official issuing. An exception is made for the decrees and laws that are subject to immediate official publication. Furthermore, there are acts that must be included in the National Register of Legal Acts of the Republic of Belarus and there are those that are subject to no inclusion. Article 63 contains an exception for publication of the National Register of Legal Acts of the Republic of Belarus where normative acts may be published also after expiration of five days period of time. In addition, I deem that exceeding the fixed time period shall be possible only due to technical reasons. On the legislative level one must specify that the publication of the normative acts received by the National Register must be carried out as soon as possible.

130. Normative legal acts may be published in editions that are not official, as well as brought to general notice through the means of broadcasting, as well as by way of other means of dissemination of information. Normative legal acts may be published in their incomplete version with the mark 'Abstract'. Publication of normative legal acts in unofficial editions shall be unofficial publications. The unofficial publication of a normative legal act shall be carried out only after its official publication with the observance of the requirements in the activities on dissemination of legal information. In addition, each normative legal act shall have the source of its official publication specified, with the number and date of the issue of license for dealing with dissemination of legal information, if this license is required in accordance with the legislation of the Republic of Belarus.

131. Decrees of the President of the Republic of Belarus and laws of the Republic of Belarus shall have legal force in a ten-day period of time after their official publication, unless those acts fix another time period.

132. Edicts of the President of Belarus, Resolutions of the Council of Ministers of the Republic of Belarus and other normative legal acts shall enter into legal force from the date of their inclusion in the National Register of Legal Acts of the Republic of Belarus, unless those acts specify another time period.

133. Resolutions of the chambers of the Parliament – the National Assembly of the Republic of Belarus – shall enter into legal force from the moment of adoption, unless otherwise specified in the resolutions.

134. Normative legal acts related to the rights, freedoms and obligations of citizens shall enter into legal force only after their official publication. In addition, normative legal acts shall be subject to publication after their inclusion in the National Register of Legal Acts of the Republic of Belarus, unless otherwise specified in the present Law.

Chapter 5. Customary Law, Unwritten Law, General Principles of Law

135. Legal custom is sanctioned by the State rule of conduct formed previously as a result of multiple repeated acts. Historically custom precedes the law: before written acts (enforceable enactments) there existed multiple rules of human conduct given from one generation to another. The attitude towards the institute of customary law of lawyers – scientists who studied at the institute during the Soviet period – was primarily negative. I deem that ideology was dominant in that case. Customary law and changes in political, social and economic systems in a revolutionary way are incompatible phenomena. While custom 'preserved' the situation, it also maintained and strengthened traditions of the past. Therefore, the preservation of customary law could prevent the destruction of all the pre-revolutionary system. Legal customs were almost totally excluded from the USSR legal system. It was admitted, in limited circumstances, only in international legal relations. In this vein, the USSR Code of Merchant Navigation was subject to frequent references.

136. Article 1 of the Constitution defines the Republic of Belarus as a democratic welfare state based on the rule of law and that shall impose certain obligations not only on law-making bodies and those executing norms of acts (state bodies, officials, citizens), but also on the Constitutional Court. The grounds for this change shall be the principles of a democratic state ruled by law that are formed by the text of the Constitution of the Republic of Belarus, as well as international instruments devoted primarily to the status of an individual and a citizen. The Constitutional Court of the Republic of Belarus puts them into practice. The enforceable nature of the constitutional principles shall affect, in addition, the entire legal system; all legislative and executive bodies should be guided by them.

137. Legal literature shall define the notion of 'principle' as the beginning, basis, leading idea and starting point. Principles of law are considered to be the leading legal ideas that are the grounds of the law and that shall express its essence and form the general direction of legal regulations.

138. As to the types of fixation, the principles of the legal system may be divided into 'principle-ideas (existing in the form of sense of justice) and principle-norms or norm-principles, i.e., principle-ideas stipulated in the sources of law'. Norms of law usually include initial norms and norms of conduct. The first variant includes basic norms, norm-principles and norm-definitions.

139. A special role in interstate relations, domestic policy, and especially legal policy, is assigned to universally acknowledged principles of international law that are defined as 'historically stipulated, basic, generally accepted norms that express the essence of international law, its distinguishing features and have a supreme imperative legal effect'. According to this doctrine, the notion of 'universally acknowledged principles' has a unique international legal nature. Due to that, the topic of admission or non-admission by different states of these ideas or standards may be discussed here.

140. Constitutional norms and principles form a legal paradigm, because they reflect and create conceptions of the legislative development of the State and the society. As the supreme judicial organ resolving legal disputes, the Constitutional Court states in its decisions whether a conception is true or not. For that reason, it does not have the right to make mistakes.

141. The principle of proportionality should be applied in criminal and administrative spheres with more significance. The measure of responsibility should comply with the gravity of the violation. This includes both the terms of imprisonment and administrative responsibility. For instance, while having preserved their punitive function, administrative fines should not be of a 'ruinous' nature. Criminal procedure relations involve the problem of taking a decision on placing a person in custody until trial under the condition that the restriction of freedom will be a proportionate measure to an alleged crime and to the punishment that the crime in question entails.

142. For a state ruled by law it is characteristic to create operative mechanisms for the restoration of violated rights. Certainly, the majority of the judges and Public Attorneys are trying to perform their functions properly. Courts are generally independent, impartial and competent. The unlimited term of office, supported by the Constitutional Court of the Republic of Belarus, shall promote this. At the same time, an excessive analysis of reasons behind so-called court bureaucracy (red tape) often results in passing by the solution of the most important problem – the administration of justice in a proper way. One should be afraid of unjust court rulings rather than the reversal of court rulings. There is no doubt that until a court ruling is reversed, it is subject to execution. All statements to the contrary are wrong.

143. One of the most important principles is the non-retroactivity of acts that establish or increase liability. Although Article 104 of the Constitution of the Republic of Belarus talks about laws, this principle is of universal character and may be applied to all the acts of legislation, i.e., decrees, edicts, resolutions of Government, acts of ministries, departments, local Councils of Deputies, executive and administrative bodies.

144. Undoubtedly, the Constitution and international acts containing not only legal norms but also principles (leading ideas defining the main directions of activities) shall be the basis of all legislative activities. By making an analysis of the Constitution of any country, one may find principles of a democratic state ruled by law. To follow them is the primary condition of rational legal regulation, ensuring a legal influence on public relations that contributes to progressive social development in an objective and regular manner.

145. These legal principles shall include:

(1) The principle of constitutionality, i.e., the supremacy of the Constitution, its direct effect, and the creation of legal acts and formation of all the hierarchy of legal acts and practice in accordance with Constitution.

(2) The correlation of state bodies by the adopted decisions, including their own decisions, and the inadmissibility of retroactivity for acts that establish or increase liability, as well as those acts that worsen the legal status of economic entities and citizens. At the same time, it is admissible when it enlarges benefits for all. When taking decisions on the economic level, it is admissible to give retroactivity only in the case of a state of emergency, circumstances when it is necessary to solve unexpected questions of vital importance that could not be expected beforehand.

(3) The deviation from the principle of the inadmissibility of giving retroactivity to laws that aggravate the legal status of participants of public relations results in the violation of the principles of a state ruled by law, as well as the rights and freedoms of citizens. In this case there is a violation of the principle of confidence of a citizen in the State. The State infringes arbitrarily upon already acquired and guaranteed rights.

(4) State bodies shall be consistent in legal regulation by securing the predictability of the actions of organs of power. Therefore, the efforts of the legislature and the executive, as well as the constitutional courts shall be directed to both approving the major principles such as prohibiting the retroactivity of the law and to maintaining the confidence of the citizen in the State through the legislative functions of its bodies, as well as to the protection of acquired rights.

(5) The legislative stipulation of the rights of citizens and their implementation shall be stable. A citizen should be confident, that he/she will not be subject to the legal consequences that he/she could not have foreseen at the moment of taking his/her decision. We hardly have a reason to speak about effective administration, if legislation itself is not stable and is influenced by the short-term concerns. Acts shall not be 'preserved' artificially or unchanged by artificial prohibition on their correction such as, for instance, by fixing the period of time for the act to remain unchanged.

(6) The major principle is to inform citizens about the adopted legislative acts. Establishment of the relevant transitional periods of time for the enforcement of the new legislative acts shall be a rule and not an exception.

(7) Normative acts shall be clear for the law enforcer and shall not be legal puzzles. It is vagueness that makes it possible to challenge normative acts before the Constitutional Court. When the rule of law is unclear, one should be careful with questions of responsibility of concrete persons. Legislation should be stable not as regards its conservation, but as regards the adoption of legal acts that anticipate the needs of the future. Stable contemporary law is the guarantor of a stable state and social development of the State and the society.

(8) Law shall be based on the aims enshrined in Preamble to the Constitution. The Parliament as a legislative body shall provide the basic principles of legal regulation. The priority of law is not in the mechanical increasing of the specific weight of the amount of laws in the legal system but in its ability to solve the major questions of society.

(9) The choice of the form of the act shall also be of a great importance. The result of legislative requirements is the clearness of its content and definition, and the ability to understand legislation. Otherwise, it will be difficult to make its administration effective.

(10) Law making and law applying activities shall be carried out with the principle of adequacy (proportionality) of restriction of rights to the goals under achievement. This principle has its own meaning. If restrictions shall be necessary, the legislator should choose the least restrictive measures possible. The principle of adequacy is considered to be the allowance for this interference into the rights and freedoms that is constitutionally necessary. Article 23 of the Constitution and provisions of international acts on the rights and freedoms of citizens are fundamental in determining the legitimate nature of actions. The issue of unreasonable 'advantaging' some categories of citizens or economic entities is also connected with the given problem.

(11) Undoubtedly, the law shall not be 'all-penetrating'. Legal regulation shall apply the prohibitive rather than positive procedure, i.e., not to enumerate what is permissible but to point out what is forbidden.

(12) For a state ruled by law it is characteristic to create operative mechanisms for the restoration of violated rights. Certainly, the majority of the judges and public Attorneys are trying to perform their functions properly. Courts are generally independent, impartial and competent. The unlimited term of office, supported by the Constitutional Court of the Republic of Belarus, shall promote this. At the same time, an excessive analysis of reasons behind so-called court bureaucracy (red tape) often results in omitting the solution of the most important problem – the administration of justice in a proper way. One should be afraid of unjust court rulings rather than the reversal of court rulings. There is no doubt that until a court ruling is reversed, it is subject to execution. All statements to the contrary are wrong.

Chapter 6. Administrative Regulations and Orders (By-Laws, Ordinances, Local Acts)

146. By-laws are acts of the Government, departmental acts, decisions of the bodies of local government and self-government, and local acts.

147. Decisions of the Council of Ministers of the Republic of Belarus shall be adopted by the majority of the members of the Government of the Republic of Belarus, present during the vote. In case of a tie vote, the decision is considered to be adopted if the presiding officer has voted for it. The law shall define which questions should be considered solely by the Council of Ministers; consequently, they are adopted in the form of resolutions taken by the Government, but not by the orders of the Prime Minister. These are: the issues of preparation and execution of the national budget; the use of the State's non-budgetary funds; drafts of programmes of the economic and social development of the Republic of Belarus; the main issues of domestic and foreign policies of the Republic of Belarus.

148. Analysis of legislation shows that resolutions of the Government may also be issued on questions of a regulatory and control nature, but these acts may have no normative nature.

149. According to the law for the operative solution of the issues on matters that are within the competence of the Council of Ministers of the Republic of Belarus, its standing body shall be the Presidium of the Council of Ministers of the Republic of Belarus composed of the Prime Minister and his Deputies. Other members of the Government may be included in the composition of the Presidium by the President of the Republic of Belarus.

150. Sittings of the Presidium of the Council of Ministers are considered to be lawful in case of the presence of more than half of the total number of the members of the Presidium. Decisions of the Presidium of the Council of Ministers shall be taken by an absolute majority of its members, and shall have the form of resolutions of the Council of Ministers and must be in line with acts adopted at sittings of the Council of Ministers of the Republic of Belarus. In case of a tie vote, the decision is considered to be adopted if the presiding officer has voted for it.

151. The law shall allow the possibility on urgent issues or questions that do not require discussion to adopt resolutions by the Council of Ministers questioning the members of the Presidium of the Council of Ministers of the Republic of Belarus (without consideration at the sittings). The law shall also stipulate the cases where the Prime Minister may issue orders. They shall be adopted on the issues that are within the competence of the Prime Minister of the Republic of Belarus, as well as with the presence of instruction of the Government as regards the issues that are within its competence but that are not related to the constitutional authorities of the Council of Ministers, if their regulation does not require adoption of decisions of normative character. Thereby, on the grounds of the law, the Prime Minister may be delegated certain competences by the Government.

152. Resolutions of the Government must be in conformity not only with the Constitution, laws and decrees, but also with the edicts of the President of the Republic of Belarus. The analysis of Article 84.25 and Article 116 of the Constitution shall confirm this principle.

153. Resolutions of the Government may be annulled by the edicts of the President, and can be found null and void (completely or partly) by the Constitutional Court when a motion is brought to its consideration about the verification of the constitutionality of the resolution. The National Assembly does not have the right to abrogate the acts of the Government; however, the chambers of the Parliament may submit the relevant motion to the President or to the Constitutional Court.

154. In the Republic of Belarus there are 1,328 effective local Councils of Deputies and approximately the same amount of local executive and administrative bodies. Each of them realizes its own functions by means of adoption of relevant legal acts in the form of decisions. The law 'On local government and self-government in the Republic of Belarus' stipulates the procedure for the adoption of decisions of local Councils of Deputies (Article 17) and local executive and administrative bodies (Articles 9 and 11), including the quorum of sitting members of these bodies and the quorum for decision making. Regrettably, there is no mentioning in this law about the procedure of publishing and enforcing of these acts. In general, these issues find no solution in the acts of legislation, including the law 'On Normative Legal Acts of the Republic of Belarus'.

155. Official editions of decisions of regional councils, the Minsk City Councils of Deputies, oblast Executive Committees, and Minsk City Executive Committees shall be published in the National Register of Legal Acts of the Republic of Belarus, as well as periodicals determined by the specified Councils of Deputies and Executive Committees. It is important to bear in mind that the normative legal acts of the specified bodies, from the authorized state bodies to the organs of official publishing (except for the National Register of Legal Acts of the Republic of Belarus) must be published on or before five days period of time from the day of their receipt. The law shall not fix this time period for their publishing in the National Register of Legal Acts of the Republic of Belarus. However, the time limits must be fixed.

156. In accordance with Article 65 of the Law 'On Normative Legal Acts of the Republic of Belarus' decisions of the regional and Minsk City Councils of Deputies, as well as oblast and Minsk City Executive Committees shall be legally enforced from the day of their inclusion in the National Register of Legal Acts of the Republic of Belarus, unless otherwise fixed in these acts. In this connection we underline that the stipulation of 'another period' may be possible when the legislative provision on retroactivity of enforceable enactments is taken into account. We also deem that the 'inclusion' of decision in the National Register shall not be enough for its enforcement. Both citizens and legal entities shall have the constitutional right to know the contents of the relevant normative legal act that may introduce new rights and duties. Moreover, the practice signifies that sometimes we may observe a time period of one, two and even more weeks between the registration of an act and its publishing.

157. The legality of decisions of local Councils of Deputies, and executive and administrative bodies, shall be secured by the bodies of the Public Attorney's Office, the Constitutional Court, and other competent bodies. There is not only the possibility of their abrogation, according to the Public Attorney's reaction, but also the verification of the constitutionality of acts in the Constitutional Court. So, according to Article 122.4 of the Constitution the decisions of local Councils of Deputies, executive bodies and administrative bodies that restrict or violate civil rights and liberties and lawful interests of citizens, as well as in other instances specified in law, may be challenged in a court of law. If we speak about normative legal acts, then according to Article 116.1 and Article 122.4 of the Constitution citizens shall have the right to apply to the Constitutional Court.

158. The most important system of state bodies shall be the structures of executive power – ministries, state committees, and some other organs, subordinated directly to the central administrative body – the Government. Each of the specified executive bodies possesses its own scope of authority within which legal acts may be published.

159. For departmental legal acts the following features are typical: they have a sub-legislative nature; must be adopted in accordance with the Constitution and acts of the bodies on a national level (Parliament, President, Government); they are notable for their enormous variety both as regards contents and form; amongst departmental legal acts there is another hierarchy: the priority of acts is predetermined by the status of the executive body in question.

160. Resolution No. 1244 of the Council of Ministers of the Republic of Belarus of 23 September 2006 shall stipulate the obligatory legal expertise of legal acts of the National Bank, the National Academy of Sciences, ministries and other national organs of state administration, region (oblasts), Minsk city Councils of deputies, region (oblasts) executive committees, Minsk city executive committee, local Councils of deputies, executive and administrative bodies of the base level. There have been approved the Instruction on the procedure of realization of the legal expertise.

161. The Government by its Resolution shall entrust the Ministry of Justice to exercise its legal expertise on legal acts issued by the mentioned bodies, except for the acts of local Council of deputies, executive and administrative bodies of the base level — their acts shall be subject to legal expertise by chief departments of justice of region (oblasts) executive committees. Legal acts of the National Bank, ministries and other republican organs of state administration, with the exclusion of legal acts of individual internal usage, shall be subject to legal oversight.

162. The procedure of drafting and adopting of legal acts within ministries and other national state bodies, as well as accounting and systematization of the specified acts and legal acts of the National Bank, the National Academy of Sciences, except for legal acts of individual usage, shall be defined by the rules adopted by the Ministry of Justice. An act is considered to be adopted from the moment of its approval by the head of the National Bank, ministry or other national state body. The normative act is brought under legal review three days from the date of signing by the head of the National bank, the National Academy of Sciences, ministry or other national state body. The normative act must be accompanied by the reference with the reason for its publishing, and information about earlier adopted legal acts on the given legal sphere. The Ministry of Justice shall carry out a review of the normative acts within ten days from the date of their reception. Legal review of acts that in view of their importance or urgency shall be subject to immediate enforcement and shall be conducted no later than the working day of reception of them for review. If the time period of finishing the legal review falls on a public holiday or weekend, the day for finalizing the consideration of legal acts submitted for legal review shall be the next working day. If it is necessary to make an all-round analysis of the normative act, as well as clarifications of questions that require special knowledge and involvement of experts (requiring additional, financial, environmental, economic and other specialized expertise), the time period for a review may be prolonged by the Ministry of Justice, but not more than for ten working days. Legal oversight of normative acts is finalized by the preparation of an opinion containing a motivated conclusion about the conformity or inconsistency of the normative act to the requirements specified in the Instruction, as well as about the admissibility of the inclusion of this act in the National Register of Legal Acts of the Republic of Belarus.

163. For consideration of the most important questions the Ministry may form a board, the composition of which shall be decided by the Council of Ministers. According to the Provision on the Minister, in case of discrepancy of opinions that may appear between the Minister and the members of the board while discussing the questions and decision making, the Minister shall put into effect his/her decision and report about it to the Government of the Republic of Belarus. Thereby, the combination of principles of collective nature and undivided authority in decision making are secured, as well as control on behalf of the Government over the activities of the Ministry.

164. Legal acts must have the required elements stipulated for the relevant documents by legislation on office work, i.e., they shall indicate: the form of the act (order, resolution, rules, etc.); the body that adopted the act; the date and registration number; the signature of the head of the ministry officially authorized to sign the respective act, or a person acting on his/her behalf.

165. The form for preparing the act is defined as proceeding from the competences of the body that must elaborate and approve the given legal act. Ministries shall issue legal acts in the form of orders, resolutions, instructions, rules, provisions, explanations, instructions and other acts. If necessary, ministries shall prepare joint legal acts. The National Bank shall issue legal acts within its powers, granted by the law, by the acts of the President and by its own Statute.

Chapter 7. Codification, Interpretation and Publication

166. Codes usually contain greater a (in comparison with an ordinary law) number of norms. They are different enough as regards their complex structure, and may consist of several parts (for instance, General and Special).

167. At present the Republic of Belarus has twenty-five effective Codes: Administrative Code, Tax Code of the Republic of Belarus, Code on Internal Water Transport of the Republic of Belarus, Bank Code of the Republic of Belarus, Forest Code of the Republic of Belarus, Electoral Code of the Republic of Belarus, Criminal Code of Executions of the Republic of Belarus, Code of Trade Navigation of the Republic of Belarus, Labour Code of the Republic of Belarus, Criminal Code of Procedure of the Republic of Belarus, Family Code of the Republic of Belarus, Criminal Code of the Republic of Belarus, Housing Code of the Republic of Belarus, Air Code, Civil Code of Procedure, Land Code of the Republic of Belarus, Economic Procedural Code of the Republic of Belarus, Civil Code of the Republic of Belarus, Water Code of the Republic of Belarus, Customs Code of the Republic of Belarus, Code of the Republic of Belarus on Mineral Wealth, Economic Procedural Code of Belarus, Code of the Republic of Belarus on Education, Budget Code of the Republic of Belarus, Code of the Republic of Belarus on the Judicial System and Status of Judges.

168. Certainly, the tendency of the law maker to codify the complexity of normative acts is conditioned by a number of reasons, for instance, a desire to put legal regulations in proper order, avoid contradictions in current legislation or duplication and to simplify the application of regulations.

169. In practice there are questions about the correlation of norms in codes and in ordinary laws. This question is not a simple one and it is very important to solve it in a proper way. Regrettably, our legislation (codes) has a lack of coordination in approaches to the solution to the problems, though Article 10 of the Law 'On Normative Legal Acts of the Republic of Belarus' shall stipulate that the code has a higher legal force in respect to other laws, but the Civil Code has higher legal force in respect to other codes and laws that contain the norms of civil law. A great deal depends on how the law maker defines the place of the code amongst other acts; and whether they are given priority (one shall bear in mind here that the code, in our opinion, may not 'tower' above programme laws). There are questions here about the correlation of the norms of the codes and the norms of the decrees. In our opinion, the *following* principle must exist: a new law abrogates the regulations of an old act.

170. According to Article 2 of the Criminal Code, the given Code is a single criminal law for the Republic of Belarus. This is quite a reasonable approach because of the special character of relations regulated by the specified Code. In turn, the Administrative Code of the Republic of Belarus (Article 2) envisages that legislative acts and resolutions of the Council of Ministers before their inclusion in accordance with the procedure established in the Code shall be subject to direct application on the territory of the Republic of Belarus. In addition, provisions of the Code shall cover administrative offences, the liability for committing of which is envisaged by legislation that is not yet included in the Code.

171. The Civil Code of Procedure (Article 1) also envisages that civil proceedings in the courts of common law of the Republic of Belarus are stipulated in this Code, as well as in other acts of legislation of the Republic of Belarus.

172. The New Housing Code (Article 2) envisages that housing legislation is based on the Constitution and consists of the specified Code, decrees and edicts of the President, resolutions of the Council of Ministers and other acts of legislation of the Republic of Belarus which regulates housing relations. It is interesting that the text of the Code (Article 3) solves the issue about the correlation of civil and housing legislation in the *following* way: it is provided that civil legislation is applied to housing relations so far as these relations are not regulated by housing legislation in the Republic of Belarus.

173. More systematically this issue is solved by the new Civil Code (Articles 3–8). This Code shall more strictly and entirely define the sources of civil legislation, its action in a time period, the procedure of application of the civil legislation by analogy, and the relation between civil legislation and the norms of international law.

174. The direction towards the extension of a number of codes shall also impose certain obligations on the law maker: if the code exists, it is necessary to reduce to a minimum the adoption of other independent laws that regulate the same public relations as the norms of the code.

Part II. Form of Government

Chapter 1. General

§1. Introduction

175. Under Article 6 of the Constitution the State power in the Republic of Belarus shall be carried out on the principle of the separation of powers among the legislative, executive and judicial branches. State bodies within the confines of their powers shall be independent: they shall cooperate with each other by acting on the principle of checks and balances.

176. Thus, each body of a branch of power shall be a state body (e.g., a court, an Executive Committee, a district administration). Therefore, one should not use in legal acts and in literature the phrase 'bodies of state power and governing bodies'.

177. The President shall take a special place in the system of state power as the Head of State. He shall ensure, in particular, the continuity and the interaction of state bodies, and maintain intermediation among the State bodies (Article 79 of the Constitution). In fact we may speak about one more stronger branch of power.

178. The legislative body is the Parliament – the National Assembly of the Republic of Belarus. Simultaneously, it also acts as a representative body (Article 90 of the Constitution). The head of State and local Councils of Deputies shall also be referred to as representative bodies.

179. Together with the Parliament, legislative power is also exercised by the President of the Republic of Belarus, who, under the Constitution, shall have the right to issue special types of normative acts – decrees that shall have the same level as laws (Article 101 of the Constitution).

180. Bodies of executive power are notable for their variety. However, they have in common the exercise of executive and administrative activities, i.e., they execute or organize the execution of legislative acts (laws, decrees), decisions of higher state bodies (President, Government) as well as executing administrative activities with respect to lower bodies by way of the issuance of legal acts that are binding for execution.

181. Bodies of the executive may be classified according to the scope of activities as national and local. The Government – the Council of Ministers of the Republic of Belarus – is the central state body. National state bodies are the ministries and state committees of the Republic of Belarus. Local bodies of the executive are the Executive Committees and local administration. The principle of undivided authority is more typical for bodies of executive power. Unlike representative bodies, they are usually established and appointed, not by elections, but by higher power structures.

182. According to the nature of powers, the bodies of the executive may be classified as bodies of common competence (those that are in charge of many sectors) and of special competence (those that are in charge of certain sectors). Organs of the first group are the Government and Executive Committees; the second group is comprised of ministries, state committees and certain departments. Bodies that belong to the second group shall also be grouped by branches (in charge of a sector of management) and interdepartmental (those that carry out interdepartmental management, such as state committees).

183. As to how they exercise their powers, the bodies of the executive can be divided into two groups: collective (adoption of decisions by a required majority of votes of the members of the specified body, such as the Government or an Executive Committee) and those of undivided authority, where one person acts on behalf of the body in question (such as the Minister).

184. Bodies of the executive have their own organizational structure. They are divided into multiple sections and collaterally subordinated to higher bodies and a chain of management (e.g., the Chairperson of the Executive Committee and his/her Deputies, collective body – Executive Committee and personnel of the body of the executive).

185. The courts exercise judicial power in the Republic of Belarus. The judicial system is based on the principles of territorial delineation and specialization. The Constitution prohibits the formation of special courts. In administering justice judges are independent and subordinated to the law alone. Any interference in a judge's activities in the administration of justice is impermissible and liable to legal action. Judicial power is exercised by the Constitutional Court, as well as by courts of general jurisdiction and other courts stipulated by the laws of the Republic of Belarus.

186. In accordance with the Code of the Republic of Belarus on the Judicial System and Status of Judges, Presidential Decree 29 November 2013 No. 6 'On improving the judicial system in Belarus', the courts of general jurisdiction are the Supreme Court of the Republic of Belarus, oblast, City of Minsk, the economic courts of oblasts (City of Minsk), and district (city) courts. A further system of courts of general jurisdiction with specialized divisions may be established.

187. The system of courts of general jurisdiction shall be divided into the relevant specialized jurisdictions, as well as specialized courts: juvenile, family, administrative, land, tax and other courts. After the referendum of November 1996, the Constitutional Court was included in Chapter 6 'Courts'.

188. Under Article 125 of the Constitution the Public Attorney's Office shall be entrusted to supervise a strict and unified implementation of the laws, decrees, regulations and other enforceable enactments of ministries and other bodies subordinated to the Council of Ministers, as well as by local representative and executive bodies, enterprises, organizations, establishments, public associations, officials and citizens. The Public Attorney's Office shall exercise supervision over the implementation of the laws determining the execution of verdicts of the courts in civil, criminal and administrative cases in instances determined by the law, as well as carry out preliminary investigation and support state charges in the courts. The Attorney-General heads the unified and centralized system of bodies of the Public Attorney's Office and is appointed by the President with the consent of the Council of the Republic. The subordinate Public Attorneys are appointed by the Attorney-General.

§2. Political Parties, Lobbies and Interest Groups

189. At present, in the Republic of Belarus there are fifteen political parties that are registered and effective. Among them are the Agrarian Party, the Belarusian Green Party, Belarusian Patriotic Party, Belarusian Social Democratic Party, Belarusian Social and Sporting Party, Communist Party of Belarus, Conservative and Christian Party, Liberal and Democratic Party, Joint Civil Party, Belarusian Social and Democratic Party (Gramada), the BNF Party and so on.

190. All the parties are not strong. In the Belarusian Parliament in 2004, from among 174 members there were only six communist and one liberal democrat representatives. In 2008 the Belarusian Parliament held six members of the Communists Party of Belarus and one representative of the Agrarian Party. The weakness of parties is revealed in the number of existing organizational structures. At the present moment, after the parliamentary elections in late 2012, the Belarusian Parliament has only four members of the Communists Party of Belarus.

191. According to the data of the Institute of Social and Political Studies under the Administration of the President of the Republic of Belarus, the most widely supported party is the Belarusian Communist Party, which supports the President of the Republic of Belarus, and which garners 8.2% of popular support. The BNF is supported by 1.4% of population, the Joint Civil Party 1.2%. At the same time, more than half of inhabitants of the country (53.5%) give no preference to any of political parties.

192. Parties that form opposition to the current power-holders are the following: the Greens, the Belarusian Social and Democratic Party, the Conservative and

Christian party, the BNF, Liberal and Democratic Party, Joint Civil Party, and Gramada.

193. Parties that support the current government and President: Agrarian Party, Belarusian Patriotic Party, Belarusian Social and Sporting Party, Communist Party of Belarus, Republican Party, Republican Party of Labour and Equity.

§3. Miscellaneous (Referendum, Popular Initiative, Delegation of Powers, Etc.)

194. Citizens of the Republic of Belarus shall have the right to take part in solution of state matters both directly and through freely elected representatives.

195. Direct participation of citizens in administration of affairs of society and the State shall be safeguarded by the holding of referenda, the discussion of draft laws and issues of national and local significance, and by other means specified by law.

196. Under the procedure specified by the legislation, citizens of the Republic of Belarus shall take part in discussion of issues of national and public life at national and local meetings.

197. Among the forms of exercising state power in the hands of Belarusian citizens, the main ones are referenda, the discussion of draft laws and issues of national and local significance, rural gatherings, meetings of citizens, etc.

198. Referenda and public discussions, the most important institutes of direct democracy, are not the same. They have in common citizen participation in law-making activities by state bodies and the fact that they shall be the expression of public attitudes towards the problem in question. However, in the case of the former, the decision as a rule is binding, in the second (in case of holding of public discussions) there is only an opinion expressed that is not legally binding to the power structures of the State.

199. Article 74 of the Constitution shall specify the subjects that are authorized to organize and to initiate the organization of referendum. National referenda shall be called on the initiative of the President of the Republic of Belarus, as well as on the initiative of the Council of the Republic or the House of Representatives by a majority of the full membership of deputies of each chamber, or on the initiative of no fewer than 450,000 citizens eligible to vote, including no fewer than 30,000 citizens from each of the regions (oblasts) and the City of Minsk.

200. The President shall call a national referendum after submission to him of the proposals of the Council of the Republic and the House of Representatives in accordance with the law or of the citizens themselves. The date for holding a referendum shall be fixed no later than three months after the President issues the decree on holding a referendum. The decisions taken by the national referendum shall be signed by the President of the Republic of Belarus.

201. The issue on making a submission to the President for a proposed national referendum may be considered initially at a session of any of the chambers. It is important to hold the sessions separately and their positions shall be coincided therein, and for these purposes it is possible to create a conciliatory commission.

202. A decree of the President of the Republic of Belarus on calling a referendum as a rule shall specify: the date for holding a referendum; the legal force of the decision taken by referendum; the wording of the issue (issues) proposed in the referendum; other organizational measures on the securing of the referendum.

203. If the subject of the referendum is a draft law, it must be appended to the decree made by the President of the Republic of Belarus for calling the national referendum. The date for holding a referendum shall be fixed no later than three months from the date the decree was issued by the President of the Republic of Belarus on the calling of the referendum.

204. The decree of the President of the Republic of Belarus on the calling of a referendum, and the text of the draft law or a draft decision proposed for referendum shall be subject to publication in the press and promulgated in other mass media in accordance with the procedure prescribed by the President of the Republic of Belarus.

205. The President of the Republic of Belarus shall have the right to reject a proposal to hold a referendum, if it is not in conformity with the relevant acts of legislation of the Republic of Belarus. The decision of the Republic of Belarus on the rejection of a referendum shall be drawn up by the decree.

206. Local referenda shall be called by relevant local representative bodies on their initiative or on the recommendation of not less than 10% of the citizens who are eligible to vote and are residents in the area concerned.

207. The procedure governing the holding of referenda shall be specified by the Electoral Code of the Republic of Belarus.

208. The Law of 12 July 2000 'On National and Local Meetings' stipulates the procedure for initiating, calling, holding meetings as well as the competences of national and local meetings in the Republic of Belarus.

209. Citizens of the Republic of Belarus who have reached the age of 18 and live permanently in the Republic of Belarus in the relevant territory may take part in national and local meetings. The Law specifies certain restrictions concerning the categories of persons who have the right to take part in elections (Article 3).

210. Legislation shall specify the procedure for forming public committees and their competences (Law on Local Government and Self-government). Federation of Trade Unions of Belarus is the national trade union centre. It unites thirty-one republican branch trade unions, six region (oblasts), Minsk city association of trade unions and trade unions of big enterprises. The strength of the Federation of Trade Unions of Belarus is more than 4 million members. Other twenty-five registered trade unions are not in the composition of the Federation of Trade Unions of Belarus. Their overall strength is 120,000 members. In the Republic there are 212,444 public associations, including 243 international and 721 republican – Belarusian Confederation of Industrialists and Entrepreneurs (Employers), Belarusian Children Fund, Belarusian Republican Youth Union, Belarusian Women Union, Belarusian Union of Entrepreneurs, Belarusian Red Cross Association etc.

Chapter 2. Head of State

§1. Appointment

211. The President of the Republic of Belarus, according to the Constitution, is elected on the basis of universal, equal, direct, free elections and secret voting. The legal grounds for the elections of the President of the Republic of Belarus shall be the Constitution, the Electoral Code of the Republic of Belarus, as well as some other legal acts.

212. In accordance with Article 81 of the Constitution, elections of the President are called by the House of Representatives no later than five months and shall be held no later than two months prior to the expiration of the term of office of the previous President. If the post of the President is vacant, then elections shall be held not earlier than thirty days and not later than seventy days from the day of the opening of the vacancy. Reduced time periods for holding a pre-election action in this event is stipulated by the Central Commission on Elections and Holding of National Referenda.

213. In accordance with Article 60 of the Electoral Code of the Republic of Belarus, recommendations for candidates to the post of the President when holding of next elections begins eighty days and ends fifty days prior to elections.

214. The Constitution determines the requirements to accede to the presidency of the Republic of Belarus. The candidate for the election to the post of President must be a citizen of the Republic of Belarus by birth, at least 35 years of age, is eligible to vote and has been a resident in the Republic of Belarus for at least ten years directly before the elections (residence qualification).

215. It is important to note that Belarusian legislation does not provide requirements of the nationality of a candidate.

216. Legislation of the Republic of Belarus does not establish any restrictions for a candidate for the post of President as a civil servant or as a regular military serviceperson; there is no requirement to have an ecclesiastical capacity.

217. The Electoral Code gives more concrete specifications for the procedure for the collection of signatures of citizens. It is stipulated that the nomination of the candidate for President of the Republic of Belarus by the citizens is achieved by an initiative of not less than 100 voters.

218. The list of the members of the initiative group with the consent of their leader, together with an application for registration of the group, shall be submitted to the Central Commission at least eighty-five days before the elections in order for their nominee to be slated as a presidential contender. The list shall indicate the surname, name, patronymic name, date of birth, profession, occupation, place of work and place of residence, party membership of the person proposed for the presidency, as well as surname, name and patronymic name, date of birth and place of residence of each member of the group and its leader.

219. The Central Commission, within a five-day period of time, considers the application, registers the initiative group and gives the members of the initiative group proper certificates and subscription lists for the collection of signatures of voters in support of the aforementioned person for the presidency of the Republic of Belarus. The collection of signatures of constituents can be realized only by members of the initiative group.

220. Subscription lists shall indicate the surname, name, patronymic name, date of birth, profession, position, place of work and place of residence, party membership of the presidential contender, as well as surname, name and patronymic name of each member of the initiative group, who shall collect the signatures and the registration number of the initiative group. The subscription list must have the signatures of the electorate living within one settlement only and in cities with district divisions – within one district.

221. The subscription list shall indicate the surname, name, patronymic name, date of birth, place of residence, passport or identity card series and number of each constituent. Data about a constituent shall be included in the subscription list. A constituent puts down on the subscription sheet the date of their signature and signs it. Signatures are numbered.

222. The Code stipulates that the personal signature of a member of the initiative group who collected signatures of constituents shall be put down on each subscription sheet in the presence of the Chairperson or the Deputy Chairperson of the town (city of oblast and district subordination), village, rural Executive Committee, head or deputy heads of the district administration in the city where the collection of signatures took place, in Executive Committees of cities and villages, in the presence of the Chairperson or the Deputy Chairperson of the regional Executive Committee and is subject to certification by a seal immediately.

223. Subscription lists shall be returned at least fifty days before elections in regional, town, district or city electoral commissions constituted for elections of the President of the Republic of Belarus which within a ten-day period of time shall check the validity of signatures of constituents in the subscription lists made by the members of the initiative group and secure the validity of the number of signatures. At least 20% of the signatures of the constituents in the subscription lists shall be subject to a check by the relevant commission.

224. If necessary, oblast and Minsk City Commission on the Election of the President of the Republic of Belarus within five days period of time may check the validity of the signatures of the constituents in subscription lists.

225. The member of the initiative group who collected the signatures shall bear liability for the validity of the data in the subscription lists. Subscription lists with fictitious signatures or signatures of one and the same constituent or two or more constituents or signatures of people who do not have electoral rights, as well as subscription lists that are not duly signed by the member of the initiative group or not certified by the seal of the local executive and administrative body, are considered to be invalid.

226. Registration of the candidates for the post of the President of the Republic of Belarus is carried out by the Central Commission on Elections and Holding of National Referenda.

227. Registration of a presidential contender of the Republic of Belarus starts thirty-five days and ends twenty-five days prior to elections.

228. The decision on registrations of the presidential contenders of the Republic of Belarus shall be taken with the presence of the following documents: protocols of the regional, Minsk City Commissions on Elections of the President of the Republic of Belarus that confirm the presence of not less than 100,000 signatures of constituents of the Republic of Belarus for the nomination of the presidential contender, applications of candidates expressing their consent to stand for elections, as well as biographical personal data of the nominated person for the presidential contender of the Republic of Belarus and declarations about income and property.

229. Any number of presidential contenders of the Republic of Belarus may be submitted for registration.

230. The Central Commission on Elections and Holding of National Referenda must give the presidential contenders the relevant certificates within two days following registration.

231. Elections of the President of the Republic of Belarus are universal: citizens of the Republic of Belarus above the age of 18 have the right to elect their President. Moreover, the law underlines that any direct or indirect restrictions of electoral rights on the grounds of origin, social and property position, race and national identity, sex, education, language, religion, political views, type and nature of occupation are prohibited.

232. The Constitution and the law stipulate that citizens found by the court to be incapable, and individuals who are incarcerated may not take part in the elections. Persons, who, in accordance with the criminal legislation of procedure, were taken into custody for a suppression measure, may not take part in voting. Thus, in principle, those individuals who are remanded in custody have a passive right, but are deprived an active electoral right.

233. Another important principle is the free character of elections: the elector shall decide individually whether to participate in the elections as well as who to vote for. Moreover, the preparation and holding of elections shall be free and open. Freedom of pre-election agitation shall serve the same goal – to secure the free character of the elections. So, the citizens of the Republic of Belarus, political parties, other public associations, labour groups, and people close to the presidential contenders are given the right to have free discussions about the electoral platforms of the presidential contenders and the political, economic and personal qualities of the presidential contenders, to demonstrate their support or opposition for presidential contenders at meetings, mass-meetings, in the media, on television and radio and during meetings with constituents.

234. The equality of elections reveals itself in the fact that constituents' votes have equal value, and candidates for state posts shall participate in elections on equal terms.

235. Belarusian legislation shall also specify the other aspects of the electoral process. According to Article 70 of the Constitution, expenditures incurred in the preparation and holding of elections are covered by the State within the funds assigned for that purposes. In instances determined by the law, the expenditure for the preparation and holding of elections may be carried out at the expense of public associations, enterprises, institutions, organizations, and citizens. The Electoral Code shall to a certain extent build upon these constitutional provisions. Thus, Article 48 stipulates that the order of distribution and use of the funds shall be determined by the Central Commission. It is stipulated that the funds that are used for holding pre-election campaigning must be divided equally between all presidential contenders and be spent upon their requirements under the procedure stipulated by the Central Commission. The Law of 4 January 2010 stipulates creation of electoral funds of candidates for the post of the President of the Republic of Belarus and deputies of the House of Representatives. Thus, according to Article 48^1 of the Electoral Code of the Republic of Belarus the specified above candidates shall have the right to create their own electoral funds for financing additional expenses on election agitation. Electoral funds may be formed for the cost of the following means: (1) own money resources of a candidate with maximum rate of not more than fifty base units for holding elections of the President of the Republic of Belarus and twenty base units for holding elections of the deputies of the House of Representatives; (2) voluntary donations of citizens of the Republic of Belarus with maximum rate of not more than ten base units for holding elections of the President of the Republic of Belarus and five base units for holding elections of the deputies of the House of Representatives; (3) voluntary donations of legal entities with maximum rate of not more than 9,000 base units for holding elections of the President of the Republic of Belarus and 1,000 base units for holding elections of the deputies of the House of Representatives. It is prohibited to make donations for foreign state and organizations, foreign citizens and stateless persons, international organizations, organizations with international investments, citizens of the Republic of Belarus under the age of 18, state bodies and bodies of local self-government, organizations with full or part budget financing, charitable and religious organizations, anonymous donors. Candidate for the President of the Republic of Belarus, for the deputy of the House of Representatives shall open a special account in a division of open joint-stock association 'Savings Bank "Belarusbank"'. The payment for banking services is not stipulated and the bank pays no interest for the use of money resources that are on a special electoral account. A citizen, in case of making donation on a special electoral account, shall specify in a payment document the following personal information: first name, family name, date of birth and place of residence, passport data of the citizen of the Republic of Belarus. Voluntary donation of legal entities shall be made by a written order on a special electoral account with specification of the following information in a paysheet: registration numbers of a tax-payer, name, banking requisites, legal address. The candidates who created electoral funds shall have the right to dispose the means thereof. The means of electoral funds may be used for the payment of: (1) broadcasting time period and printing area in mass media; (2) rent of building and premises, equipment, transport expenses, communication services; agitation printing materials; (3) consultation and agitation works (services); stationary and other expenses related directly to electoral agitation. A candidate shall have the right to return a donor a donation to the electoral fund, except for the donation made by an anonymous donor. In case a voluntary donation to the electoral fund is on behalf of a donor who has no right to make it or a donation is of a rate that increases the rate envisaged by part two of the given Article, a candidate shall be obliged within seven days from the day of receipt of the donation on the special electoral account to return it in full or the part of it that increase the fixed maximum rate of the donation for the donor with specification of the reasons of return. Control over the entrance and use of the means of electoral funds shall be carried out by the Central Electoral Commission, district electoral committees and by financial bodies. Bank division where the special electoral account is opened shall inform weekly the registered commission of a candidate about the entrance and expense of means that are on the account of the relevant candidate for the President of the Republic of Belarus, for the deputy of the House of Representatives. The relevant commission within the time period of two days after receiving the information shall inform mass media for publication about the total sum of means entered the electoral fund and the total sum of expended means.

Candidates shall be obliged to submit to the commission they registered thereof the financial reports within the following time periods: the first financial report – no early than before fifteen days and no later than ten days before elections; the concluding financial report – no later than within five days period of time from the date of elections. In case of abolition of decision on registration of a candidate or in case of withdrawal of one's candidature, the relevant commission shall inform about that to the division of the bank which shall terminate all transactions on a special electoral account of a candidate. All banking transactions on a special electoral account, except for the return of non-expended means into the electoral fund and entering in the specified account of the means transferred before the date of elections, shall be terminated at the date of elections. A candidate of the President of the Republic of Belarus, of the deputy of the House of Representatives shall be obliged to transfer non-expended means that are on the special electoral fund no later than within three days period of time since the date of elections to the citizens and legal entities who made donations to his/her electoral fund in proportion to the means invested. After expiration of the time period in question the division of the bank where the special electoral account is opened shall be obliged to transfer the means remain on the account to the republican budget. Under the application of a candidate to the Central Commission, the relevant district electoral commission may prolong the time period of making transactions on a special electoral account. A candidate of the President of the Republic of Belarus, of the deputy of the House of Representatives shall be obliged within the time period fixed by part 14 of the given Article to submit to the commission he/she had registered the financial report about the amount and all resources of creation of one's electoral fund, as well as about all the expenses. The report shall be attached with primary financial documents that confirm entering, return and expenditure of the means of the electoral fund, certificates of the means remain and (or) about closing of the special electoral account of a candidate. The procedure in question shall cover also the persons with respect to whom decisions on registering them as candidates, as well as persons who withdrew their candidates before the day of elections were subject to repeal. In case of the second round of elections the transactions on payment from special electoral accounts of candidates who are in the second round of elections shall be subject to revival at the day fixed by the Central Commission and district electoral commission of the second round of elections and shall be subject to termination at the day of the second round of elections.

It is very important that publicity is secured in the sphere of spending of the funds: the Central Commission is obliged to report the scale of funds allotted to the election campaign of each candidate, through mass media, no later than within three days following the expiry of the period of registration of the presidential contenders.

236. Speaking about the possibilities of financing of the elections on the part of organizations and citizens, it is important to note that there is a statutory prohibition regarding any direct or indirect participation of foreign organizations and foreign citizens for providing financing and other material help for electoral campaigns of contenders.

237. The list of constituents shall include all the citizens of the Republic of Belarus that have reached the age of 18, who reside constantly or temporarily at the moment of drawing up the list in the territory of the given area and eligible to participate in voting.

238. According to the law, the elector may not be included in the list of constituents at other polling stations.

239. Lists of constituents are subject to general review fifteen days before the elections, and at the polling stations in sanatoriums, rest homes, hospitals and other stationary medical institutions two days before the election.

240. Citizens may review the list of constituents and check the correctness of the District Commission on Elections of the President of the Republic of Belarus.

241. Each citizen is given the right to appeal against their failure to appear on the list, or the incorrect inclusion on the list or withdrawal from the list, as well as against inaccuracies in the list and in the data about the given constituent. Motions about errors in the list are considered by the District Commission, which is obliged no later than in two weeks period of time, and on the eve of the day of election to immediately examine the motion, make the necessary corrections in the list or give the petitioner a copy of the motivated decision declining of his/her motion. The decision may be appealed at least five days before the elections to the district court that is obliged to consider the complaint within three days period of time.

242. The law shall stipulate the guarantees of activities of presidential contenders of the Republic of Belarus and their fiduciaries.

243. A presidential contender in the Republic of Belarus may have up to thirty people who render assistance in his/her electoral campaign, carry out publicity for his/her election as President, represent the interests of the candidate in his/her relations with state and public bodies, constituents, as well as in the commissions on elections of the President of the Republic of Belarus.

244. The presidential contender defines these individuals at his/her own discretion and reports them for registration in the Central Commission on Elections and Holding of National Referenda, which shall give them the necessary certificates after registration. A presidential contender in the Republic of Belarus has the right at any time before elections to substitute these assistants for others.

245. Presidential contenders in the Republic of Belarus, after their registration by the Central Commission, shall participate in the electoral campaign on equal terms and have equal rights on the use of mass media in the Republic of Belarus.

246. All registered presidential contenders are given equal opportunities to material, technical and financial coverage of their electoral campaign.

247-248. Registered presidential contenders, during the election campaign, have the right to waive service or routine duties without reservation and still receive the average salary at their place of working.

249. Presidential contenders, fiduciaries of presidential contenders may not be dismissed from work, as well as transferred to other work or another position without their consent during the electoral campaign.

250. The election of the President of the Republic of Belarus shall take place, on the date of elections, from 8:00 a.m. to 8:00 p.m. At least ten days before the elections, the electorate shall be informed by the District Commission of the time and place of voting.

251. Voting shall be conducted in special premises that must be equipped with a sufficient number of booths or rooms for secret voting, a place to issue ballots and installed ballot boxes. Ballot boxes should be places so that voters who approach them do not pass through other voting booths, so as to assure the secrecy of the voting process.

252. On the day of the election prior to the beginning of voting, the ballot boxes shall be checked, stamped or sealed by the chairperson of the District Commission and witnessed by not less than two-thirds of the commission.

253. Each constituent shall vote personally. Voting on behalf of other persons is not allowed. The ballot is given to the constituent of the relevant District Commission on the basis of his/her inclusion in the list of constituents, after presentation of the passport or other identity cards. The reception of the ballot shall be endorsed by the voter in the list in front of his/her surname.

254. The ballot for election of the President of the Republic of Belarus is filled in by the voter in a booth or secret voting room. The presence of anybody else in the booth or secret voting room is forbidden. However, a constituent who cannot fill the ballot their self has the right to invite into the booth or room another person of his/her choice, except for a member of the District Commission.

255. When a constituent votes under conditions that exclude control over his/her will, they shall delete in the ballot the surnames of the candidates against whom he/she votes. The constituent places the completed ballot into a ballot box.

256. On the election day, a constituent who cannot to be at the polling place has the right, not earlier than five days before the election, to fill in a an absentee ballot that is placed in a separate absentee ballot box.

257. When a constituent, due to their state of health or other legitimate reasons, cannot go to the polling place may request the District Commission in written or oral form to entrust not less than two members of the commission to organize voting at the domicile of the constituent on the election day.

258. On the basis of the protocols of the Regional and Minsk City Commissions on Elections of the President of the Republic of Belarus, not less than ten subsequent to the vote, the Central Commission shall determine and release the following data in the protocols: the entire number of constituents; the number of constituents who obtained ballots for the election of the President of the Republic of Belarus; the number of constituents who took part in voting; the number of votes for and against each presidential candidate; the number of ballots that were found null and void and the number of clean ballots.

259. This protocol shall be signed by the Chairperson, Deputy Chairperson, secretary and members of the Central Commission.

260. The President of the Republic of Belarus is considered to be elected, if he/she gained more than half of the votes cast by citizens of the Republic of Belarus in the election.

261. Elections are found void if less than half of citizens on the list of constituents took part in the elections, or if there was a withdrawal of all registered presidential contenders of the Republic of Belarus.

262. Elections of the President of the Republic of Belarus as a whole within the republic or in the separate areas for voting, regions, cities, regions in cities, areas, City of Minsk may be found void because of breaches committed in the course of elections or at the stage of counting of votes and if they have influenced elections in the Republic as a whole. The decision about finding the elections void shall be taken by the Central Commission and it may be subject to appeal to the Supreme Court of the Republic of Belarus within ten days. The right to appeal against the decision on finding the elections void is the right of the presidential contenders of the Republic of Belarus. In the opinion of the author, the right to check the constitutionality of elections shall belong to the Constitutional Court. Internationally, usually just the bodies of constitutional control check the constitutionality of elections and referenda.

263. The report on the results of the elections of the President of the Republic of Belarus shall be forwarded by the Central Commission to the mass media for proclamation and publishing no later than three days from the date of signing of the protocols on the results of the elections. The law shall stipulate that if the ballot contains more than two presidential contenders of the Republic of Belarus and none of them obtained necessary number of votes, then within two weeks period of time the Central Commission shall hold a second round of voting for the two candidates who received the greatest number of votes. Information on the second round of voting shall be published in the mass media the day after appointment of the second round of voting. The President is considered to be elected, if he/she in the second round of voting obtained more than half of the votes of the constituents who took part in voting. If, due to the withdrawal of all the other candidates, only one candidate remains in contention, a second round of voting is held with respect to his/her candidacy. In this case more than half of constituents who took part in voting must cast their votes for his/her election. Elections are considered valid if more than half of constituents that are on the list of citizens eligible to participate in the elections cast ballots. If not more than two presidential contenders at the elections of the President of the Republic of Belarus stood for elections and none of them was elected, as well as in the event of withdrawal of all presidential contenders or finding the elections of the President ineffective or void or, if the second round of voting did not legally elect a President, the Central Commission on Elections and Holding of National Referenda shall solve the problem by calling further elections with the repeated nomination of the presidential contenders. Moreover, it may take a decision about holding of elections by the territorial and District Commissions in a new composition. According to the law, further elections are held three months after the first election. Voting is conducted at the same polling place with the same voter registration lists from the first election and elaborated on the eve of the further election. The Constitution and effective legislation of the Republic of Belarus stipulate the procedure for the inauguration of the President.

264. The key moment of the inauguration is the Oath of the newly elected President. With the Pronouncement of the Oath, the power of the previous President is ended. The Oath is pronounced in a solemn occasion in the presence of the Deputies of the House of Representatives and members of the Council of the Republic, Judges of the Constitutional Court, Supreme Court and Supreme Economic Court, no later than two months after the election of the President. The President takes the following Oath: 'Assuming the office of the President of the Republic of Belarus, I solemnly swear to faithfully serve the people of the Republic of Belarus, to respect and safeguard the rights and liberties of its citizens, to abide by and protect the Constitution of the Republic of Belarus, and to discharge strictly and conscientiously the lofty duties that have been bestowed upon me'. The President of the Republic of Belarus shall be the Head of State, the guarantor of the Constitution of the Republic of Belarus, and of human rights. The separation of the branches of power into legislative, executive and judicial (Article 6 of the Constitution) does not at all mean an absence of the necessity for interaction. In this connection, internationally it is usually the post of the head of the State (the monarch, president) who is the official who occupies the highest place in the system of the State bodies. An analysis of the Constitutions of many foreign countries shows that the head of state participates in all the branches of power or is included in the legislative and executive branches of power or in the executive only.

265. A lot of Constitutions do not directly mention the term 'head of state'. In literature we usually take this to mean the monarch or the president of the country. The head of state shall secure official representation of the country, often he/she is a state symbol: a symbol of unity of the nation.

266. Charles de Gaulle formulated his doctrine of constitutional construction in the following words: 'To my mind, it is necessary for the State to have the head, a leader, whom the nation can see as the person standing above arguments and disputes, who is empowered to solve the principal problems of the country, and who is the guarantor of their destinies'. This doctrine was enshrined in the Constitution of France, adopted by referendum in 1958. The Constitution of Belarus in its new edition is highly similar to the Constitution of France.

§2. Legal Status

267. The President of the Republic of Belarus occupies special place in the system of state bodies. According to Article 79 of the Constitution, he is the Head of State, the guarantor of the Constitution and of the rights and freedoms of its citizens. The President shall personify the unity of the nation, the implementation of the main guidelines of domestic and foreign policy and shall represent the State in its relations with other states and international organizations. The President shall provide the protection of the sovereignty of the Republic of Belarus, its national security and territorial integrity, shall ensure its political and economic stability, the continuity and interaction of bodies of state power and shall maintain intermediation among the bodies of state power.

268. Thereby, the Constitution of the Republic of Belarus entrusts the Head of State with the most important functions and goals.

269. Charging the President of the Republic of Belarus with the duty to be the guarantor of the Constitution and of human rights and civil liberties is conditioned by the goal of securing stability of the constitutional system, guaranteeing of rights and liberties of man and citizens. With those purposes, the President is charged with the functions of an arbitrator between the powers.

270. In the opinion of the author, the mediation of the President has more of a political, rather than a purely legal nature: after all, the Constitutional Court of Belarus in legal respects shall have extensive rights, including those concerning the settlement of disputes about competences by means of verification of the constitutionality of normative acts.

271. There is a single superior who controls the President – the people. This is the source of state power and of sovereignty. Where discords between branches of power may not be resolved, the people shall solve the relevant question through a referendum.

272. A distinctive feature of the status of the President of the Republic of Belarus is in the fact that he acts, on the one hand, as an arbitrator in conflicts between institutions and, on the other hand, he may actively control the Government and subordinated bodies.

273. The President has solely individual powers, where there is no requirement for countersigning or some other participation of another state body (for instance, filing a motion, coordination, etc.). These powers of the President of the Republic of Belarus will be mentioned *below*.

274. The President has a certain inviolability; his honour and dignity are protected by the law. Public insults of the President or slander with respect to him, including with the help of press or other mass media, leads to a liability stipulated by the law.

275. According to Article 367 of the Criminal Code, to slander the President of the Republic of Belarus in a public appearance or in printed or in publicly demonstrated materials or in the mass media shall be punishable by a fine or correctional work for a term of up to two years or incarceration for a period of up to four years, or deprivation of liberty for the same period. The same action committed by a person who has earlier been convicted of slander or insult, or connected with the accusation of the commission of a grave or a particular grave crime shall be punishable by the restriction of liberty for a period of up to five years or incarceration for the same period. Liability for an insult to the President shall be envisaged in Article 368 of the Criminal Code. Public insults to the Head of State are punishable by a fine or correctional work for up to two years, or arrest for a period of up to six months, or restriction of liberty for a period of up to two years, or incarceration for the same period. The same action, committed by a person who has earlier been convicted for insult or slander, or connected with the accusation of the commission of a grave or a particularly grave crime is punishable by a fine, or correctional labour for the period of up to two years, or restriction of liberty for the period of up to three years, or incarceration for the same period.

276. Criminal cases concerning public insults to the President or slander with respect to him, including the use of the press or other mass media, shall be brought under the procedure prescribed by the Criminal Code of Procedure of the Republic of Belarus.

277. Suits concerning the protection of the honour and dignity of the President shall be brought before the court under the procedure prescribed by the Civil Code of Procedure of the Republic of Belarus: petitions concerning the protection of the honour and dignity of the President of the Republic of Belarus shall be brought before the court by the Attorney-General, or by Public Attorneys of oblasts and of the City of Minsk, or Public Attorneys chosen with the consent of the President of the Republic of Belarus.

278. The new edition of the Constitution does not contain direct instructions on the fact that the Head of State is simultaneously the head of the executive. The President is officially *above* all the other powerful structures. Here is his potential as a subject of rule making.

279. The Constitution of the Republic of Belarus envisages the following types of legal acts of the President: decrees, edicts, and orders. The Law 'On Normative Legal Acts of the Republic of Belarus' stipulates the possibility of issuing directives – decrees of programme nature that the Head of State shall issue for the purposes of system solution of questions that are of prior political and social significance.

280. Decrees shall be one of the new types of acts of the President. In their contents they are acts of normative nature.

281. The Constitution and the Law on the President of the Republic of Belarus stipulate the cases where the Head of State has the right to issue decrees.

282. According to Article 101 of the Constitution, on the proposal of the President, the House of Representatives and the Council of the Republic may adopt a law supported by the majority of the full composition of the chambers, delegating to him legislative powers to issue decrees which have the power of a law. This law must determine the subject of the regulation and the term of the powers of the President to issue such decrees.

283. It is not admissible to delegate powers to the President to issue decrees that provide for the amendment of the Constitution, its interpretation; amendment of programme (policy) laws; the approval of the national budget and its implementation; alterations with regard to the elections of the President and

Parliament; restrictions of constitutional rights and freedoms of citizens. Laws on delegation of legislative powers to the President neither shall permit him to alter these laws, nor shall it permit him to adopt retroactively enforceable regulations.

284. By virtue of special necessity, the President may personally initiate or as a result of the proposal of the Government may issue temporary decrees with the legal force of law. If these decrees are issued on the initiative of the Government, they shall be signed by the Prime Minister. Temporary decrees shall be submitted for further approval within a three-day period of time of their adoption by the House of Representatives, and then to the Council of the Republic. These decrees shall be valid if they are not rejected by a majority of no less than two-thirds of votes of the full composition of both chambers. The chambers may regulate through legislation relations that have emerged on the grounds of decrees that were subject to abolition.

285. Thus, decrees of the President may be of two types: decrees issued on the grounds of a law delegating legislative powers to the President of the Republic, and temporary decrees issued by the Head of State on the basis of special necessity.

286. Previously, Acts with the force of law, could be issued only by the Supreme Soviet, which according to the Constitution of 15 March 1994 was the highest representative and single legislative body of state power in the Republic of Belarus. Now the President of Belarus in instances provided by the Constitution may also issue acts that have the force of a law.

287. In practice, so far there have no laws that directly delegated these or those powers to the President on the issue of decrees.

288. The practice of the issue of decrees after the request of the opinion of the Government and higher judicial authorities will be well-grounded.

289. It will be useful, if the necessity for the issue of temporary decrees will be motivated by the Government and other state bodies and meaningful arguments shall be presented for this. In this case, the blame shall be entrusted exactly to these bodies who are responsible for possible negative consequences of the adoption of those acts.

290. It is impossible to forget that transfers by the Parliament of a part of its own power to the President shall be a restriction of the rights of the National Assembly. Often this may be conditioned by the unwillingness of the President for the Parliament to fulfil its legislative activity in one or another sphere. At the same time, an argument about the efficiency and flexibility for the adoption of decrees by the President may be crucial.

291. The distinctive feature of the Constitution of Belarus, with respect to the constitutions of other countries, is that its text stipulates original approaches to the registration and conservation of the effect of temporary decrees of the President that on the grounds of Article 101 of the Constitution may be issued by the President both on his own initiative and as a result of a proposal of the Government. In the last case, decrees must be countersigned by the Prime Minister. Thereby, here the principle of countersigning on the part of the head of the Government is effective. In the rest of the cases the Constitution and the legislation do not provide any joint authorities of the President and other bodies related to countersigning of temporary decrees.

292. Besides, internationally decrees usually preserve their force if they are confirmed by a parliamentary majority; but in our country they keep their authority until they are rejected by no less than two-thirds of the votes of the Deputies.

293. If decrees are always of a normative nature, the situation is more complicated when it comes to edicts (ukaz). In some cases they include provisions of both a normative and a non-normative nature. If decrees, in the opinion of the author, always have a normative nature, then as regards edicts, it is impossible to say the same thing. Regrettably, neither the Constitution nor the law define clearly what relations are to be adjusted by edicts; this may be specified by the order of the President. Edicts that have a normative nature are acts that establish general rules of behaviour issued for multiple uses.

294. The clarification of the nature of an edict (is it normative or not?) has not only theoretical, but also practical importance. According to Article 116 of the Constitution the Constitutional Court has a control over the constitutionality of normative acts. This is a general provision that predetermined the status of the Constitutional Court. At the same time, the given Article among the list of acts that may be verified by the Constitutional Court talks about edicts of the President with no reference to their normative nature.

295. The new edition of the Constitution of 1994 provides for two types of edicts: (1) edicts issued on the basis of a constitutional norm; (2) edicts specified in law.

296. In the first case it is possible to affirm that an edict has no by-law nature because it is based on a constitutional norm. The question resides only in the matter of who has the final word in any possible dispute. In the opinion of the author, in case of a dispute about competences (where the competence is already subject to realization through the adoption of the acts) the Constitutional Court, as it was already noted, as a result of the suggestion of the authorized subjects, must give its judgment. As a whole, it would be useful to authorize the Constitutional Court with the right to consider disputes about competences.

297. The second kind of edicts in the hierarchy of normative acts shall obviously tag along with laws. This way of thinking confirms, once again the conclusion that has already been repeatedly expressed by the author in the press about the necessity when publishing normative acts to make references in the preamble to the act of higher legal force, i.e., Constitution or the law.

298. Any legal decision of the President must be given a form stipulated by the Constitution (decree, edict and order). Even if there is an imperative need to operatively inform the different subjects about the decisions of the President (sometimes this is carried out by telegram), nothing prevents the developers of such a document (moreover, this is necessary to do) to 'wrap' it in the form of a decree, edict, order and to forward it through the same channels, as those employed when the telegram was sent. This will allow the occasional excluding of remarks related to the normative activities of the Head of State.

299. It is necessary to emphasize one more peculiarity of the edicts of the President. Usually, they are not subject to approval by the Parliament. An exception is a decision on a State of Emergency, or about the declaration of a full or partial military mobilization. We think that, as for this question, it is inadmissible to adopt decrees in lieu of edicts because this will bring about a breach of balance envisaged by the Constitution.

300. Orders of the President are not acts of a normative nature. They shall be issued in solution to organizational and personnel issues.

301. According to the Law 'On the President of the Republic of Belarus', decrees, edicts and orders of the President shall be subject to publication or brought to public light by some other means stipulated by the law.

302. Decrees, regardless of their type, shall be immediately officially published after their signing and shall be enforced within a ten-day period following their official publication, unless some other period of time is stipulated. The same procedure for legal enforcement applies to temporary decrees of the President and they are effective until adoption by the National Assembly in the manner envisaged by Article 101.3 of the Constitution. Edicts and orders of the President shall be subject to legal enforcement in accordance with the procedure determined by the President.

303. According to Article 86 of the Constitution, the President may not hold any other office or receive any monetary remuneration other than his salary, apart from royalties for works of science, literature and art. The President shall suspend his membership in political parties and other public associations of a political nature during the whole term in office.

304. Accordance to Article 87 of the Constitution, the President may tender his resignation at any time. The resignation of the President shall be accepted by the House of Representatives.

305. The procedure for the acceptance of the resignation of the President is regulated by the Rules of Procedure of the House of Representatives of the National Assembly of the Republic of Belarus.

306. The retirement of the President shall be accepted by the House of Representatives and shall have the form of a resolution of the House of Representatives adopted by a majority of its full composition.

307. The President is not obliged to report to the House of Representatives about the reason for his retirement. Regulations do not cover the question about a possible discussion of the reasons for the resignation of the President.

308. The President of the Republic of Belarus may be prematurely removed from the office where he is persistently incapable to discharge his duties on account of the state of his health. The issue of removing the President shall be taken by a resolution of the House of Representatives adopted by a majority of not less than two-thirds of the elected deputies as determined by the Constitution and a majority of not less than two-thirds of the full composition of the Council of the Republic as determined by the Constitution on the grounds of the findings of an ad hoc Commission formed by the Chambers of the Parliament. The President may be removed from office for acts of state treason and other grave crimes. Decisions to file charges against the President shall be supported by a majority of the full composition of the House of Representatives on behalf of not less than one-third of the number of deputies. The investigation of the charges shall be organized by the Council of the Republic. The President is considered to be removed from office if the decision is adopted by not less than two-thirds of the full composition of the Council of the Republic, as well as not less than two-thirds of the full composition of the House of Representatives. The failure of the Council of the Republic and the House of Representatives to take a decision to remove the President from office during the month following the initiation of the procedure shall make the move invalid. The motion about the removal of the President from his office may not be initiated in accordance with the Constitution in the process of hearings on prior termination of the powers of the Parliament. In case of removal of the President in connection with the commission of a crime, the case shall be examined on the merits of the charge by the Supreme Court.

309. Legislation shall not determine the period within which the President is not capable to perform his own duties on the ground of disease, i.e., it may be even shorter than four months, as it is stipulated in labour legislation. It is important that the removal from office is possible only in the event of the continuing inability, under the President's state of health, to perform his duties, and thus the question is most probably about some irreversible processes.

310. Apart from retirement and removal from office on account of the state of health, the office of the President may be vacant in the event of dismissal of the President. However, this is possible only for the acts of state treason or other grave crimes. The definition of state treason or other felonies is given in Articles 356, 12 of the Criminal Code. In addition, the specified Code divides crimes depending on their nature and degrees of social danger into crimes of little social danger, lesser crimes, grave crimes and particularly grave crimes. In this context, the dismissal of the President from office is possible for both grave crimes and particularly grave crimes.

311. The Constitution and regulations of the chambers quite precisely determine the procedure for dismissal of the President from office by this reason, as well as guarantees of the rights of the Head of State.

312. The history of the Belarusian State has borne witness to attempts to dismiss the President from office on the initiative of seventy-three deputies of the Supreme Soviet of the Republic of Belarus. What is significant is the fact that, contrary to all effective legal rules, notwithstanding the entire complexity of the problem, the proceedings on the case were brought on the same day of reception of the motion in the Constitutional Court, on 19 November 1996, and consideration of the case was set for 22 November 1996. Before 22 November six deputies recalled their signatures to dismissal of the President from office, but after the holding of a referendum of 24 November 1996 on the issues suggested by the Head of State, a few more deputies, having seen the support of people, considered it impossible to demand the dismissal of the President from the office.

313. In this respect the recent impeachments of the Presidents of the USA and Lithuania shall be considered very significant. They lasted several months. Heads of state, just like any other person, have a possibility to make proper preparation for a case, to have contacts with constituents and to prove their faultlessness. Against this background, the actions of deputies and the Constitutional Court who had a desire to finish this process within three days received a negative response from a legal point of view. Without rejecting the right to such an initiative, we shall notice that all requirements of a law are binding to all the participants in the procedure of the impeachment of a Head of State from office. In Lithuania the President was consequently dismissed from office, which was the first case of such an event in European history. In Korea, owing to the judgment of the Constitutional Court, the President of the country was rehabilitated, in spite of the decision of the Parliament.

314. According to Article 89 of the Constitution, whether the office of the President falls vacant or the President is unable to discharge his duties in the manner enshrined by the Constitution, the powers of the President shall be transferred to the Prime Minister until the President-elect is sworn in.

315. The Prime Minister shall therefore have second place in the hierarchy of officials of the State. The Prime Minister shall be called to temporarily perform the duties of the President only in instances specified in the given Article. It is unconstitutional to allow a temporary transfer of power to the second person in the State, for instance, due to Presidential vacation, or an illness that does not prevent the President from performing his duties. The relevant historical examples (1994–1995) had only aroused opposition between the branches of power and were probably aimed exactly at this, if we exclude the legal idiocy of people who brought forth those ideas.

§3. COMPETENCES

316. Powers of Belarusian President are mainly enshrined by Article 84 of the Constitution. However, other Articles thereof, the law on the President and other normative acts contain the norms dedicated to the rights and duties of the President. Let us consider the most important of these.

317. The calling of national referenda. The President is the only single person who may call a referendum.

318. The calling of regular and extraordinary elections to the House of Representatives, the Council of the Republic and local representative bodies. The Constitution has divided the powers of the President and the Parliament in regards to the issue of holding of elections. If it concerns collective representative organs, the decision on calling elections shall be taken by the President (Article 84.2), but if it comes to the election of the Head of State, the decision shall be taken by the House of Representatives (Article 97.3). Such an approach shall allow us to avoid the situation of the violation for the terms of holding elections that, regrettably, has already taken place in our modern history, when the election of 1995 was held.

319. Dissolution of chambers of the Parliament. The premature termination of powers of the chambers of the Parliament, i.e., their dissolution, is one of the ways to solve a conflict between the branches of power, that is to say, between the legislative and the executive. The arbitrator in this case shall be the Head of State.

320. The powers of the chambers of the Parliament may be terminated ahead of schedule only according to the procedure specified in the Constitution. First, they may be terminated in advance in the event of a vote of no-confidence in the Government. Thus, under Article 106 of the Constitution, the Prime Minister may request from the House of Representative a vote of confidence with regard to a governmental programme or any other issue. If a no-confidence vote is passed by the House of Representatives, the President shall have the right, within ten days, to accept the resignation of the Government, or dissolve the House of Representatives, and call for new elections. In the event of a rejection of resignation of the Government, the latter shall continue to discharge its duties.

321. It is necessary to note that under Article 97.7 of the Constitution, the issue of the responsibility of the Government may not be discussed during a year after the approval of the programme of governmental policy. I deem that the given norm shall also cover instances of raising the question of confidence in the Government by the Prime Minister. During the specified period of time, such an initiative on the part of the Prime Minister shall be inadmissible.

322. Second, the powers of the houses of Parliament may be terminated in the event of a no-confidence vote in the Government. A no-confidence vote in the Government may be expressed on the initiative of not less than one-third of the full composition of the House of Representatives (Article 97.7 of the Constitution). In the particular case of the expression of a no-confidence vote in the Government, we must also consider the repeated refusal by the House of Representatives of the agenda of the Government (Article 97.5 of the Constitution). In the case of the expression of no-confidence therein, the Government must declare its resignation to the President.

323. Third, the powers of the House of Representatives may be terminated in advance as a result of a double refusal of consent for the appointment of the Prime Minister. The relevant decision must be adopted by the House of Representatives within two weeks period of time from the day of the proposed candidacy of the Prime Minister. If the House of Representatives give its second rejection of consent for the appointment of the Prime Minister, the President shall have the right to appoint an acting Prime Minister, to dismiss the House of Representatives and call for new elections.

324. Fourth, the powers of the House of Representatives or of the Council of the Republic may be terminated in advance, on the grounds of the judgment of the Constitutional Court, that there are instances of systematic or flagrant violations of the Constitution by the chambers of Parliament. Consideration by the Constitutional Court on the issue of systematic or flagrant violations of the Constitution by the chambers of the Parliament of the Republic of Belarus is carried out as a result of a proposal by the President. Its consideration may not be denied on the initiative of the Constitutional Court. In the opinion of the author, the law should give an interpretation to the notion of what is a 'systematic' or 'flagrant' violation of the Constitution, as well as to fix a time period, in the course of which the President shall have the right to bring the constitutional motion before the Constitutional Court (e.g., one to two years), since the day of adoption by the chamber of the Parliament of the relevant legal act (law, resolution).

325. Taking into consideration the important nature of the specified problem, evidently, it is inadvisable to make an analogy to norms of law that refer to other branches of law, for instance, labour law.

326. Thus, the President shall have all the grounds for making a request to the Constitutional Court on the evidence of systematic or flagrant violation(s) by the chambers of Parliament of the Constitution if, for instance, he imposed a veto on the adopted law(s), and, contrary to the norms of the Constitution, the veto(s) was overturned by a Parliamentary vote. In cases where the chamber of the Parliament adopted other acts (resolutions) and violated (systematically or flagrantly) the Constitution, there are also grounds to put the relevant question before the Constitutional Court.

327. The Constitution stipulates that, as a result of the termination of the powers of the House of Representatives or the Council of the Republic upon the decision of the President, he may also terminate the powers of the other house in question, i.e., it is admissible to dissolve one or two chambers simultaneously.

328. International legislation contains both similar and other rules which specify the premature termination of the powers of only the chamber of the parliament that was involved in the decision in question – the expression of a vote of no-confidence, refusal of confidence in the Government, etc.

329. The decision on the dissolution of the chambers of the Parliament must be taken by the President within two months after official consultations with the Chairpersons of the chambers (Article 94 of the Constitution).

330. There are restrictions on the dissolution of the chambers: their powers may not be terminated during a state of emergency or martial law, in the last six months of the terms of office of the President, or in the course of proceedings taken by both chambers on the premature removal of the President from office. Both chambers may not be dissolved in the course of the first year after the first sittings were held.

331. Appointment of members of the Central Commission on Elections and Holding of National Referenda. According to Article 84.4 of the Constitution, the President shall appoint six members of the Central Commission on Elections and Holding of National Referenda. The other six members of the Central Commission on Elections and Holding of National Referenda shall be elected by the Council of the Republic. Thus, equal representation is secured by both the Head of State and the Parliament in the body that solves issues on the holding of elections of both the President and the Parliament. Candidacies for membership of the commission are recommended respectively to the President and to the Council of the Republic by joint representations of the presidiums of regions and Minsk City Councils of Deputies and regional and Minsk City Executive Committees.

332. Formation, dissolution and reorganization of the Administration of the President and some other bodies. The Constitution explicitly stipulates the right of the President to form, dissolve or reorganize the Administration of the President, other bodies of state administration, as well as consultative advisory councils, and other bodies attached to the President.

333. Appointment of the Prime Minister. Issue about granting consent for the appointment of the Prime Minister of the Republic of Belarus shall be solved at the session of the House of Representatives by secret voting and shall be executed by a resolution.

334. Deputies of the House of Representatives shall have the right to put questions to the President of the Republic of Belarus on candidatures for the office of the Prime Minister, express their opinions with respect to the proposed candidature, and agitate 'for' or 'against' the candidature.

335. A candidature for the office of the Prime Minister of the Republic of Belarus is considered to be approved if a majority of the full composition of the House of Representatives votes in his/her favour.

336. The decision as regards granting consent to the appointment by the President of the Republic of Belarus of the Prime Minister shall be taken by the House of Representatives within two weeks after the day of making the proposition on the candidature of the Prime Minister.

337. In the event of double refusal by the House of Representatives of consent for the President's appointment of the Prime Minister, the President shall have the right to appoint an acting Prime Minister, to dismiss the House of Representatives and call for new elections.

338. It is natural to expect that the President shall propose the candidature who shares the political course of the Head of State for the office of the Prime Minister.

339. Determination of the structure of the Government, appointment and dismissal of the members of the Government and their resignation. The President is independent in his determination of the structure of the Government. For these purposes the President may create ministries and departments within the structure of the Government.

340. Appointment of Chairpersons of higher judicial bodies. According to Article 84.8 of the Constitution the President, with the consent of the Council of the Republic shall appoint the Chairperson of the Constitutional Court, the Chairperson of the Supreme Court and the Chairperson of the Economic Courts from among the judges of these courts.

340.1. Appointment of judges of higher judicial bodies, the Chairperson of the Central Commission on Elections and Holding of National Referenda, the Attorney-General, the Chairperson and members of the Board of the National Bank. According to Article 84.9 of the Constitution the President shall appoint the judges of the Supreme and Economic Courts, the Chairperson of the Central Commission on Elections and Holding of National Referenda, the Attorney-General, the Chairperson and members of the Board of the National Bank with the consent of the Council of the Republic.

341. The procedure of appointment of the specified persons is similar to the appointment of the heads of the higher judicial bodies specified in Article 84.8 of the Constitution.

342. Appointment of the judges of the Constitutional Court. As regards equal participation of the President and the Parliament in forming the Constitutional Court, the President shall independently solve the issue of the appointment of six of the twelve judges of the Constitutional Court.

343. In addition, the President must be guided, first of all, by the requirements of Article 116.2 of the Constitution, according to which the Constitutional Court shall be comprised of the most highly qualified specialists in the field of law, who, as a rule, have a scientific degree.

344. Indication in the Constitution of the presence of a scientific degree means, in the opinion of the author, that at least the majority of the members of the Constitutional Court must have a scientific degree. It should be also pointed out that the Constitution specifies no particular field of scientific knowledge.

345. Dismissal of the Chairperson and judges of higher judicial bodies, the Chairperson and members of the Central Commission on Elections and Holding of National Referenda, the Attorney-General, the Chairperson and members of the Board of the National Bank. According to Article 84.11 of the Constitution, dismissal of the Chairperson and judges of the Constitutional Court, the Chairperson and judges of Supreme Court, the Chairperson and members of the Central Commission on Elections and Holding of National Referenda, the Attorney-General, the Chairperson and members of the Board of the National Bank shall be made by the President on the grounds specified by the law, with notification made to the Council of the Republic.

346. In accordance with the Code on the Judicial System and Status of Judges, the Chairperson of the Constitutional Court of the Republic of Belarus may be dismissed from office on grounds specified by that Code. These grounds are the following: request for resignation, loss of citizenship, age limit for the office of judge, continuation of activities incompatible with the office of judge, in spite of warnings by the Constitutional Court, and so on (Article 124 of the Code). Premature termination of the office of judge of the Constitutional Court shall be admissible under similar grounds.

347. The Code on Judicial System and Status of Judges stipulates the grounds for termination of office for the judges. They may be deprived of their powers for intentional breach of legality or committing a vicious action that is not compatible with their high rank, upon the decision of the body which elected or appointed them, as well as due to enforcement of the Verdict of Accusation delivered by the court. Judges may be discharged under other grounds specified by the law (state of health, election or appointment to another office or transfer with their consent to other work in accordance with their own will, etc.).

348. Grounds for the dismissal of judges of economic courts shall be specified by the Code on Judicial System and Status of Judges.

349. Terms of office of the Central Commission on Elections and Holding of National Referenda shall be five years. The Chairperson, Deputy Chairperson, secretary and members of the Central Commission, may be dismissed from their offices before the expiration of their term by the President of the Republic of Belarus in the case of a written application to leave office; loss of citizenship; systematic failure to perform their duties; committing actions that are a discredit for the Central Commission; enforcement of a Verdict of Accusation delivered by the court (Article 32 of the Electoral Code).

350. According to the Law 'On the Public Attorney's Office in the Republic of Belarus', the dismissal of the Attorney-General of the Republic of Belarus during his term of office may take place only in the case that a crime was committed by the Attorney-General, or he/she is unable to perform official duties because of his/her state of health or at his/her own will, as well as under certain grounds stipulated by the legislative acts (Article 18 of the Law).

351. The Procedure for the appointment and dismissal of the Chairperson and members of the Board of the National Bank shall be stipulated by the Law 'On the National Bank of the Republic of Belarus'.

352. Appointment and dismissal of the Chairperson of the State Supervisory Committee. The State Supervisory Committee of the Republic of Belarus is a state body formed by the President of the Republic of Belarus for monitoring the implementation of national budget policies, the use of public property and implementation of the acts of the President, Parliament, Government and other state bodies governing public property relationships and economic, financial and tax relations.

353. In accordance with the Rules of Procedure on the State Supervisory Committee of the Republic of Belarus approved by the Republic of Belarus Law 'On the State Control Committee of Belarus and its territorial bodies', the structure and staff of the bodies of the Committee shall be approved by the President and its structure – by the Chairperson of the Committee. The Chairperson of the State Supervisory Committee shall be appointed and dismissed by the President and is accountable to the President. Grounds for dismissal are stipulated by the specified Rules of Procedure.

354. Messages to the people. Messages of the President to the people of the Republic of Belarus on the State of affairs and on the guidelines of domestic and foreign policy are essential for the explanation of the policies followed by the Head of State. By means of these messages, the President may state the tasks and goals that he strives to solve at the present moment.

355. The Constitution and current legislation shall not specify the frequency of the messages of the President to the people. Identification of the frequency and time period for those messages proceeding from diverse situations shall be the right of the Head of State.

356. Annual messages to the Parliament; participation in the work of the Parliament. The right of the President to address the Parliament is common in a number of other countries. Traditionally, as is enshrined in the Belarusian Constitution, the addresses of the President may be annual. However, there is no exclusion of the right of the President to make addresses to the Parliament because of specific circumstances. The addresses of the President may contain his vision of domestic political and foreign political situations, proposals of lists of the normative acts that shall be adopted by the Parliament, i.e., proposals of his agenda of laws to be drafted, and his opinion about the activities of the Parliament.

357. According to the Rules of Procedure of the Chambers of the Parliament, annual messages may be heard separately by each chamber or jointly.

358. The Constitution stipulates that the President of the Republic of Belarus shall have the right to participate in sessions of the Parliament and its organs, deliver speeches and addresses at any requested time with a speech or a message. Thereby, there is an implicit exclusion to hold closed sessions of the Parliament, where the presence of the President is inadmissible. This is an important guarantee of the interaction of the Head of State and the Parliament.

359. Chairmanship of meetings of the Government. Due to the fact that the President is the Head of State, Article 84.15 of the Constitution quite soundly stipulates that the President shall have the right to chair meetings of the Government of the Republic of Belarus. Usually, this takes place when the Government considers the most important issues of the day. In this case the President chairs the meeting.

360. Appointment of heads of national state bodies, determination of their status; appointment of other persons. The Constitution stipulates that the President shall independently appoint the heads of national state bodies and define their status.

361. The President as the Head of State may also appoint other officials, if their posts are determined in accordance with legislation, unless otherwise stipulated by the Constitution. There are several restrictions here: the Constitution or another Normative Act adopted on the grounds thereof shall refer the appointment of the given person to the prerogative of another body; there are restrictions of financial nature, for example, in accordance with the approved budget it is impossible to create the relevant structure and introduce the post for which the person was expected to be appointed.

362. Solution of issues related to granting citizenship, its termination and granting of asylum. Citizenship is the integral attribute of state sovereignty that determines the nationality of a person and stipulates the extent of their rights and duties and their protection on behalf of the State.

363. Applications on the issues connected with citizenship shall be filed at the address of the President with a specification of the date of application. Applicants shall enclose a questionnaire form in two copies; five photos; autobiography in two copies; copy of the birth certificate of the applicant, and in case of necessity of other persons; documents on payment of national tax or exemption from its payment; document about expatriation or non-affiliation to the nationality of another country; certificate from the place of residence with indication of family composition. Applications may also contain other relevant documents.

364. Applications on issues related to citizenship shall be made to different bodies according to the place of residence of the applicant, and persons who live abroad to the nearest diplomatic representation or consular institution.

365. There is a fixed time period for consideration of applications to local bodies, the Ministry of Internal Affairs, diplomatic or consular institutions, the Ministry of Foreign Affairs, the KGB and the Council of Ministers of the Republic of Belarus. This time period shall not be longer than one month.

366. Termination of citizenship may take place due to expatriation from the Republic of Belarus or loss of citizenship, as well as on other grounds stipulated by the law.

367. Institution of state holidays and red-letter days, bestowal of state awards, ranks and titles. State holidays may be instituted due to important historical events, or to honour a person or group of people. State holidays may be either working or non-working days.

368. The right of the President to bestow state awards, ranks and titles is directly connected with the right of the Parliament to establish state awards, ranks and titles. Thus, in this particular case, one organ shall adopt the law and another one shall implement it, and that is the realization of the concept of separation of powers.

369. Granting of pardons to convicted citizens. A pardon differs from an amnesty because it shall be realized with respect to concrete persons upon their initiative or that of other authorized persons and organs.

370. Pardons shall be applicable, as a rule, under the personal initiative of convicted persons. Motions on pardons shall be considered only after the legal enforcement of the verdicts.

371. Capitally convicted persons may ask the President of the Republic of Belarus for a pardon from seven days following the day of being presented with a copy of the sentence. If the capitally convicted person fails to make the motion for pardon or states his/her unwillingness to make this motion within the fixed period of time, the act shall be considered under the prescribed rules. The motion or the act shall be forwarded to the President of the Republic of Belarus within three days following the day of the filing of the motion.

372. Conducting of negotiations and signing of international treaties, appointment and recall of diplomatic representatives. The President as the Head of State shall represent the Republic of Belarus in relations with other countries and international organizations. This may be reflected in the right to sign international treaties, and to make declarations of the position of the country regarding international problems. The main restriction as regards signing of international treaties is that they shall be in line with the Constitution (Articles 8 and 116).

373. Another prerogative of the President as Head of State is the appointment and recall of diplomatic representatives of the Republic of Belarus to foreign states and to international organizations.

374. Receipt of credentials and letters of recall of the diplomatic representatives. The President shall receive the credentials and letters of recall of accredited diplomatic representatives of foreign states.

375. The Credential is a document that certifies the representative nature of a diplomatic representative and accredits him/her as having this quality in a foreign state. Credentials that are addressed to the Head of the hosting State shall be signed by the Head of State who appoints a diplomatic representative and shall be signed by the Foreign Minister. Credentials define the nature of general powers of a diplomatic representative.

376. The recall of a diplomatic representative on the initiative of its government is drawn up by way of presenting to the receiving Head of State a letter of recall – the document about recall of a diplomatic representative is signed by the Head of the State who appointed him/her. Letters of recall are drawn up in the same way as credentials.

377. According to standard practice, the President of the Republic of Belarus receives credentials and letters of recall of accredited diplomatic representatives of foreign states in the presence of the Minister of Foreign Affairs of the Republic of Belarus or his/her Deputy and other senior officials of the specified Ministry.

378. Declaration of a state of emergency. According to Article 84.22 of the Constitution the President shall, in the event of a natural disaster, a catastrophe, or unrest involving violence or the threat of violence on the part of a group of persons or organizations that endanger peoples' lives and health or jeopardize the territorial integrity and existence of the State, declare a state of emergency on the territory of the Republic of Belarus or in specific areas thereof and submit the decision to the Council of the Republic for approval within three days.

379. The decision adopted by the President on the declaration of a state of emergency shall be submitted for the approval of the Council of the Republic within three days. Issues about the approval of the decision of the President of the Republic of Belarus on the declaration of a state of emergency must be considered within three days following the moment of the carrying out of the relevant decision by the President.

380. If, as a result of emergency circumstances the members of the Council of the Republic are unable to arrive at their normal meeting place, and the meeting of the Council may not take place in the building, another locality for holding a session may be chosen, and the deputies must be informed thereof through the mass media or by some other way.

381. Under the decision of the Council of the Republic, the issue of a state of emergency may be subject to consideration without preliminary examination in commissions of the chamber.

382. When the Council of the Republic approves an edict of the President about a declaration of a state of emergency and measures to be taken during the period in question, only the approved provisions thereof shall be enforceable. About its approval – the Council of the Republic must notify the President and shall report through the mass media.

383. If a resolution about the approval of an edict of the President about a state of emergency fails to gain a majority of the full composition of the Council of the Republic, the decision on a state of emergency shall not be subject to approval and this is expressed in the form of a resolution of the Council of the Republic. In this particular case the edicts of the President shall have no legal force.

384. Deferment of a strike or its suspension. According to Article 84.23 of the Constitution in instances stipulated by the legislation, the President shall have the right to defer a strike or suspend it for a period not exceeding three months. Thus, the law must specify the events when the strike, the right to which is enshrined in Article 41 of the Constitution, will be deferred or will be suspended, but for no more than three months period of time.

385. A strike is a full or partial voluntary work stoppage (comprising absence from work and failure to execute labour duties) by a group of employees to achieve demands denied by the employer.

386. Strikes are prohibited in the armed forces, forces of law and order, civil defence personnel, state safety organizations, the Public Attorney's Office, state bodies, at enterprises producing energy, organs producing any kind of centralized heat or gas supply, in institutions of urgent medical aid, as well as at enterprises of which the termination of work creates a threat to the lives and health of people.

387. Signing of bills. One of the most important aspects of the interaction of powers is the adoption of the laws and their signing.

388. Signing of laws as the right to legislative initiative is a powerful and strong tool of influence of one branch of power on another. This covers not only the purely formal aspect of relations between the branches of powers, but also potential possibilities for reinforcement of the position of one or another of these branches.

389. By striving to secure the principle of separation of powers, which in many respects means not only a differentiation of competences, but also mutual checks and balances, and mutual influences of the legislative and executive powers, the Constitution envisages the rule that all laws shall be signed by the President. Moreover, the President has the right to return a law, or certain provisions thereof, with his objections to the House of Representatives, meaning that the President shall have the right to veto an adopted law.

390. Laws adopted by the House of Representatives and approved by the Council of the Republic or adopted by the House of Representatives under the procedure stipulated by Article 100 of the Constitution shall be presented to the President for his signature within ten days. If the President does not return the law within two weeks after its submission, the law is deemed to have been signed. The law is not deemed to have been signed and shall be invalid, if it failed to be returned back to Parliament due to the end of the session. Thus, the new wording of the Constitution envisages the consequences of a situation when the President is presented a law for the signature during the last days of session. After the expiration of the stipulated time period for the solution of the issue about signature, the President may not return it to the Parliament, because of the interval between the sessions. In the USA this practice is known as a 'pocket veto' that may not be overridden by Congress due to the absence of defined procedures regarding the practice. The Rules of Procedure of the House of Representatives specify another approach.

391. In case of disagreement with the text of the law, the President of the Republic of Belarus shall return it with his own objections to the House of Representatives, which must consider the law with the objections of the President within thirty days. The Council of the House of Representatives shall forward the text of the law returned by the President with his objections to the commission in charge of making its conclusion and fixing the terms for submitting the law for consideration by the House of Representatives. The commission shall organize the work on the draft law in accordance with the procedure envisaged by the Rules of Procedure for all draft laws.

392. Objections of the President of the Republic of Belarus are considered in the commission that is examining the draft law, which shall prepare its conclusions as regards the objections and submit it to the Council of the House of Representatives. The conclusion of the commission must have one of the following decisions therein: to agree with the objections of the President of the Republic of Belarus and to forward the law he returned for its completion; or to submit the returned law for the consideration of the House of Representatives and overriding of objections of the President of the Republic of Belarus.

393. The Council of the House of Representatives considers the conclusions of the commission and takes a decision about completing the law and specifies the commission which will do this, or takes a decision on putting the issue about the further consideration of the law on the agenda of the session of the House of Representatives.

394. The draft law returned by the President of the Republic of Belarus may be considered in accordance with the priority procedure.

395. After finishing the law returned by the President of the Republic of Belarus, the commission shall make a proposal about putting the issue about consideration of the law in a second reading on the agenda of the session of the House of Representatives to the Council of this chamber. When considering the law in the House of Representatives, only those positions that were altered during the process of completion shall be subject to a vote. Then there shall be a vote on the draft law as a whole.

396. If the law is subject to consideration by the House of Representatives to override the objections of the President, voting is conducted on the law as a whole. In this case, amendment of the law is not admissible. If the law is adopted by the House of Representatives with a majority of not less than two-thirds of its full membership, it shall be forwarded within five days with the objections of the President to the Council of the Republic, which also must consider it within twenty days. The law returned by the President of the Republic of Belarus may be subject to consideration under the priority procedure.

397. Together with the text of the law returned by the President of the Republic of Belarus, with his objections and considered by the House of Representatives, the resolution of the House of Representatives concerning the further consideration of the law, the objections of the President of the Republic of Belarus, a stenographic report (shorthand record) of the sitting of the House of Representatives as regards the objections of the President of the Republic of Belarus, to the Chairperson of the Council of the Republic.

398. A standing commission of the Council of the Republic, which previously gave its conclusions on the law returned by the President of the Republic of Belarus, shall consider the remarks of the President and the text of the law adopted by the House of Representatives in its formerly adopted wording and give the conclusion thereon. Conclusions shall be prepared by the standing commission under the procedure stipulated by the Rules of Procedure of the Council of the Republic.

399. As a result of the reception of the conclusions by the standing commission, the Chairperson of the Council of the Republic shall make a proposal about putting the issue of the further consideration of the law on the agenda of the Council of the Republic.

400. While reconsidering the law returned by the President of the Republic of Belarus and adopted by the House of Representatives in its formerly adopted wording, the Council of the Republic shall have the right: to open discussions on the law to put to vote the issue of the approval of the law in its formerly adopted wording without the opening of discussions.

401. After discussion the presiding officer of the Council of the Republic is obliged to put the issue of the approval of the law in its previous wording adopted by the House of Representatives to vote.

402. The law is considered to be adopted if it has been approved by not less than two-thirds from the full composition of the Council of the Republic. The law, after overcoming the objections of the President, shall be signed by the President within five days period of time. The law shall become valid also if it is not signed by the President within the fixed period.

403. Under the same procedure, the chambers shall consider the objections of the President as regards certain provisions of the law that are re-voted. In this case, before the relevant decision of the House of Representatives and the Council of the Republic, the law shall be signed by the President and shall be valid, exclusive of those provisions with respect to which there are objections of the President.

404. The right to abolish the acts of the Government. The competence stipulated in Article 84.25 of the Constitution means that the President has the right to abolish any act of any central body of state administration – the Government. In addition, the President may be guided not only by the fact that the relevant act is at variance with legislation. The President may also abolish the act of the Government under the reasons of the non-expediency of its adoption. Here is the distinguishing feature between the aforementioned competence and the right of the relevant executive and administrative bodies to abolish acts of lower level bodies contradictory to legislation (Article 122 of the Constitution).

405. Supervision of the observance of legislation by the bodies of local government and self-government. Under Article 84.26 of the Constitution, the President shall exercise supervision directly, or through specially formed bodies, over the observance of laws by local organs of government or self-government and have the right to suspend decisions of local Councils of Deputies, or abolish decisions of local executive and administrative bodies where they do not conform to the requirements of national legislation.

406. It follows from the analysis of the Constitution that control over activities of local bodies of government and self-government shall be exercised, first of all, by the State Supervisory Committee, by the Public Attorneys' Office of the Republic of Belarus and by their bodies in localities.

407. The President shall have no right to abolish decisions of local Councils; however, in case of any discrepancy between these decisions and legislation, he may suspend their effect. Legislation has not yet created any mechanism for further actions of the President. It is necessary to define the term during which the President must make an address to the Council that adopted the illegal decision with the proposal to abolish it.

408. Creation of the Security Council. For the first time the Security Council was created by the President of the Republic of Belarus by the Decree of 5 August 1994 No. 24. However, if previously the Constitution specified that the President is only the Head of the Security Council, and that was the ground for disputes about the procedure of the determination of its composition, then in accordance with the new wording of the Constitution of 1994 the President is both the Head of the Security Council and chooses its members. The Constitution shall stipulate directly that the Head of State shall appoint and dismiss the State Secretary of the Security Council. The currently effective composition of the Security Council was adopted by Decree of the President of the Republic of Belarus of 29 July 2010 No. 391.

409. The State Secretary is the head of the staff of the Security Council, who is subordinated directly to the President.

410. Leadership of the Armed Forces of the Republic of Belarus. In presidential republics the Head of State is usually the Commander-in-Chief of the Armed Forces. He appoints and dismisses the Supreme Command of the Armed Forces. Therefore, it is quite suitable here to note the stipulation of the specified competences in the Constitution of the Republic of Belarus (Article 84.28).

411. The armed Forces of the Republic of Belarus are intended for the defence of the Republic of Belarus, the safeguarding of its State borders, its sovereignty and its territorial integrity.

412. According to the Law 'On Armed Forces' of 3 November 1992 the Ministry of Defence of the Republic of Belarus shall be responsible for fighting and mobilizing readiness, training of the Armed Forces for the solution of wartime tasks, material and technical supply, development of organizational structures, armaments and military techniques, operative and fighting training, military discipline, securing of protection of secret information and counteraction to foreign intelligence, in observance of legislation.

413. The President, as the Commander-in-Chief of the Armed Forces of the Republic of Belarus, is responsible before the people for the securing of the reliable protection of the State, following international agreements on defence, and carrying out military policy and military doctrine of the Republic of Belarus. He appoints the Supreme Command of the Armed Forces of the Republic of Belarus.

414. Introduction on the national territory of a state of martial law, and the declaration of general or partial mobilization. In the event of military threat or attack, the President shall impose martial law on the territory of the Republic of Belarus and announce a general or partial mobilization with the submission of the decision taken for approval of the Council of the Republic within three days.

415. The President may realize other powers entrusted with him by the Constitution and the laws (Article 84.30 of the Constitution).

Chapter 3. The Legislature

§1. The Organ of State (Bicameral System, Composition, Electoral System, Election Process)

416. Under the Constitution of the Republic of Belarus (Article 90) the Parliament shall be defined as the National Assembly of the Republic of Belarus – a representative and legislative body of the Republic. The National Assembly shall consist of two chambers: the House of Representatives and the Council of the Republic.

417. Elections to determine the new composition of the chambers of Parliament shall be set no later than four months and held no later than thirty days prior to the expiration of the powers of the current Parliament. Extraordinary elections for the chambers of the Parliament shall be held within three months since the premature expiration of the powers of the chambers of the Parliament.

418. Each of the chambers of the Parliament shall have its own powers. The Constitution shall not stipulate issues of joint powers of the chambers.

419. The idea of a bicameral Parliament is widespread in the world. Experience shall signify that a two-chamber system exists in federal states, as well as usually in unitary states with a population of over ten million. The chief point is that such a parliament, with a well-considered differentiation of the powers of the chambers, shall make it possible to increase the representation of population in it, and (though this is a paradox) to save the means of tax-payers, enhance the efficiency of its work, ensure the interests of the bodies of territorial self-government and secure the principle of separation of powers to a greater extent – the legislative and the executive, which means an improvement in the stability of the State.

420. The following stages of the electoral process to the chambers of Parliament may be specified. Calling of elections. According to Article 22 of the Electoral Code, the President of the Republic of Belarus shall call regular and extraordinary elections to the House of Representatives and the Council of the Republic and shall determine the directorial arrangements as regards the securing of their holding.

421. Elections for a new composition of the chambers of the Parliament shall be set no later than four months and held no later than thirty days prior to the expiration of the powers of the current Parliament. Extraordinary elections for the chambers of the Parliament shall be held within three months from the premature expiration of the powers of the chambers of the Parliament.

422. Drawing up the list of the electorate of the deputies of the House of Representatives, the deputies of local Councils of Deputies. City, settlement, rural Executive Committees, and in cities with regional divisions – regional administrations, regional Executive Committees in cities and settlements of city type without city and rural Executive Committees – shall ensure the registration of the electorate and transfer the lists of citizens of the Republic of Belarus who reside in the territory of the relevant polling stations and who shall have the right to participate in elections to the Divisional Election Commissions. These lists are signed by the chairpersons of the relevant Executive Committees, and by heads of regional administrations.

423. Lists of citizens who are servicemen and who are in military units, as well as members of families of servicemen and other electors who reside in the regions of the location of military units shall be based on the grounds of the data presented by the commanding officers of the military units. Servicemen who reside outside of the military units shall be put on the lists of citizens who have the right to participate in the elections, referenda, and votes on the recall of a deputy in accordance with the place of the residence under the common grounds.

424. Lists of citizens who have the right to participate in the elections according to polling stations made in sanatoria, preventive clinics, holiday homes, hospitals and other preventive medical institutions shall be based on the grounds of the data presented by the heads of the establishments in question.

425. Lists of citizens who have the right to participate in elections, the deputies of the House of Representatives, according to polling stations set outside of the territory of the Republic of Belarus shall be made on the basis of the data presented by the heads of diplomatic missions (consular establishments) of the Republic of Belarus which are effective in the territory of the relevant foreign states.

426. Names of citizens in the list shall be specified according to the procedure that handles the holding of votes.

427. The list of citizens who have the right to participate in elections shall contain all the citizens of the Republic of Belarus who have reached the age of 18 on the date of elections, referenda and votes on recall of a deputy, who live permanently or temporarily in the territory of the particular polling station at the moment the list is composed and who have the right to take part in elections.

428. A citizen who has the right to participate in elections may be put on the list at only one polling station.

429. Lists of citizens who have the right to participate in elections shall be presented for general familiarization fifteen days before the election, and at polling stations made in sanatoria, preventive clinics, holiday homes, hospitals and other stationary preventive medical institutions, two days before the election.

430. Citizens shall be given the possibility to familiarize themselves with the list and to verify the correctness of its composition in the office of the electoral commission.

431. Each citizen shall be granted the right to appeal against non-inclusion, wrongful inclusion on the list or withdrawal from the list, as well as mistakes in the personal data information about the citizen. Appeals about incorrectness of the list shall be considered by the Divisional Election Commission which is obliged in a two-day period of time, and on the eve of and on the day of elections, referenda and votes on recall of a deputy to consider the application without delay, and to make necessary corrections in the list or to give the applicant a copy of the well-grounded decision on the dismissal of his/her application. This decision may be subject to appeal to the highest commission which is obliged to consider the appeal within two or three days, and, on the date of voting immediately. The decision of the Divisional Election Commission may be also subject to appeal up to five days before the elections, referenda and votes on the recall of a deputy in the regional or city court which is obliged to consider the complaint within three days. The decision of regional, city court is subject to no appeal or protest. The Divisional Election Commission shall immediately make corrections in the list in accordance with the decision of the highest commission or the court.

432. The electoral commission, before each round of voting, shall specify lists of citizens who have the right to participate in elections.

433. Formation of election commissions. The election commission shall carry out the organization and holding of elections. The Electoral Code envisages the relevant system of election commissions.

434. The Central Commission shall secure the preparation and holding of elections of deputies of the House of Representatives, and create election commissions on elections of deputies of the House of Representatives.

435. The Central Commission is at the head of the system of effective election commissions and commissions on referenda during the period of preparation and holding of elections and national referenda.

436. The Central Commission is a legal person, and has the stamp with design of the State Emblem of the Republic of Belarus and has an official name and bank account.

437. The preparation and holding of elections of the deputies of the House of Representatives shall be secured by the relevant election commissions: district election commissions and Divisional Election Commissions.

438. The Electoral Code shall specify the terms and procedure of formation of election commissions.

439. Formation of district election commissions. District election commissions shall be the election territorial unit. The first is for the election of one deputy, the second for the election of one or more deputies. The Electoral Code of the Republic of Belarus stipulates the creation of one-mandate district election commission.

440. There shall be 110 district election commissions in the territory of the Republic of Belarus for the holding of elections of deputies of the House of Representatives.

441. The average number of voters at a district election commission on elections of deputies of the House of Representatives shall be specified by the Central Commission no later than five months preceding the expiry of the term of powers of the current session of the House of Representatives.

442. A district election commission shall have a unique territory: it is inadmissible to form a district election commission in non-contiguous territories.

443. Lists of district election commissions with their names, numbers, borders, number of voters and locations of election commissions shall be subject to publication: for the elections of the deputies of the House of Representatives, this is done by the Central Commission on or before the fifth day after the decision to hold elections to the House of Representatives.

444. In case of dismissal of the House of Representatives, elections of the House of Representatives shall be held within district election commissions created while holding elections of deputies of the House of Representatives on the previous occasion.

445. One deputy shall be elected from each district election commission.

446. Formation of polling stations. For voting and counting votes for elections of deputies of the House of Representatives, the territory of regions, cities, and regions in cities shall be divided into polling stations. Polling stations shall be formed in sanatoria, preventive clinics, holiday homes, hospitals and other stationary preventive medical institutions. Polling stations shall be formed also in military units.

447. Polling stations shall be formed no later than two months before the elections and on or before twenty-five days before the referendum.

448. Nomination and registration of candidates. The right of nomination of candidates for the office of deputy shall belong to political parties registered by the Ministry of Justice of the Republic of Belarus within six months before the appointment of elections, for the labour collectives, as well as to the citizens by way of collection of signatures.

449. Nomination of candidates for the office of deputy shall be started seventy days before and shall be completed forty days before the elections.

450. The candidate for the office of deputy may stand for election only within one district election commission. The candidate for the office of deputy while standing for election within several district election commissions shall inform the authorities of his consent to stand for election within a particular district election commission and about his refusal to stand within other district election commissions no later than three days after ending the terms of nomination of the candidate for the office of deputy. Failure to meet this requirement shall be grounds for the refusal of registration of the candidate for the office of deputy within all the district election commissions.

451. The Central Commission and the relevant territorial election commission shall verify the conformity between the procedure of nomination of candidates for the office of deputy and the requirements of the Electoral Code and shall adopt a decision on registration of candidates for the office of deputy or a well-motivated decision on refusal in registration. The decision of the commission on refusal of registration shall be issued the day after the adoption of the decision.

452. The protocol on the registration of the candidate for the deputy of the House of Representatives shall be presented to the Central Commission.

453. Refusal of registration of the candidate for the deputy of the House of Representatives may be subject to appeal, within three days, to the Central Commission. The decision of the Central Commission may be subject to appeal, within three days, to the Supreme Court of the Republic of Belarus. The Supreme Court of the Republic of Belarus shall examine the appeal within three days and its decision shall be final.

454. The competence of a person nominated as a candidate to the deputy of the local Councils of Deputies and who is a member of the Central Commission, territorial, Divisional Election Commission shall be deemed terminated from the moment of his/her registration as a candidate for the office of deputy.

455. Election campaign. Citizens of the Republic of Belarus, political parties, other public associations, labour collectives, authorized persons working for the candidates for the office of deputy, initiative groups which carry out campaigning for election of candidates for the office of deputy shall be granted the right to freely discuss and pre-election programmes of the candidates, their political, professional qualifications and their personal qualities, and carry out campaigning for or against a candidate at meetings, in the mass media, as well as during the meetings with the electorate.

456. Foreign citizens shall have no right to participate in campaigning.

457. From the moment of registration of candidates for the office of deputy by the relevant commission, political parties, labour collectives, citizens who proposed the candidates, and the candidates for the office of deputy shall have the right to produce placards, appeals, subscriptions, leaflets, and photo materials (which hereafter is also referred to as placards). The candidate shall be granted a sum equalling fifty times the minimum wage for expenses related to the production of the placards. Placards need no special permission. Printed materials must contain information about organizations or persons responsible for their issue, as well as about their circulation. Dissemination of anonymous printed materials shall be prohibited fourteen days before the elections – there shall be stands drawn up with information about candidates at all the polling stations. Those stands shall be kept also in the premises for voting at the day of elections. In case of holding of referenda the issues (draft decisions) opened for referendum shall be put up prominently.

458. Campaigning (including appeals to boycott elections, referendum) shall be inadmissible on the day of voting. Printed materials previously put up out of the premises for voting shall be kept in their places.

459. State mass media, the mass media financed partly from the State budget, as well as the mass media where one of the founders are state bodies or organizations, shall be obliged to secure equal possibilities for pre-election speeches of the candidates, as well as the publication and promulgation of the issues or of texts of draft laws put to referendum.

460. The candidate shall have the right to publish in national or in local press his/her pre-election platform in up to two typed pages and to present the text of this programme twenty days prior to the elections.

461. Publication of pre-election programmes of candidates for the deputy of the House of Representatives shall have priority in the press.

462. Candidates for the office of deputy of the House of Representatives shall have the right to free speeches on state television, as well as radio. The national state broadcasting company of the Republic of Belarus shall grant, from ten days after the calling of elections by the Central Commission, time for speeches of the candidates on state television, as well as by radio. The fixed broadcasting time must fall on peak broadcasting hours.

463. During the last ten days before the elections, it is inadmissible to publish the results of polls related to elections, or predictions of their results.

464. Candidates for the deputy of the House of Representatives, their authorized persons, organizations and persons carrying out campaigning for election of the candidates shall not be entitled to give out money, gifts and other material objects, or to carry out preferential sale of goods, or to render for free any services and goods, except for printed materials produced specially for the election campaign or referendum observing the requirements of the Electoral Code. Pre-election agitation or agitation on referenda shall prohibit exerting influence on citizens by way of giving promises to hand them over money.

465. Voting. Voting for the deputies of the House of Representatives takes place from 8:00 a.m. to 8:00 p.m. Divisional Election Commissions shall inform the electorate about the time and the place of voting ten days before the elections.

466. As for the polling stations in sanatoria, preventive clinics, holiday homes, hospitals and other stationary preventive medical institutions, the Divisional Election Commissions may declare the voting to be completed before 8:00 p.m., if all the voters, or participants in a referendum, included in the list have cast their votes.

467. Voting shall be carried out in specially allotted premises with an adequate number of polling booths or rooms for secret voting, with specified places for issuing ballot-papers and polling boxes. They shall place ballot boxes required in the path of voters to the pooling booths or the rooms. Voting boxes must be placed in the field of vision of the members of Divisional Election Commission.

468. Divisional Election Commissions shall be responsible for the organization of voting, securing the secrecy of the will of the electorate, equipment of premises and maintenance. On the day before the voting the voting boxes shall be verified and sealed by the chairperson of the Divisional Election Commission in the presence of not less than two-thirds of the composition of the commission. Each voter, or participant of referendum, shall vote in person. It is inadmissible to vote on the behalf of other persons.

469. A ballot-paper shall be given to the voter or participant in a referendum on signature by the member of the Divisional Election Commission on the grounds of the list of citizens who have the right to participate in elections or referenda, or in voting on the recall of a deputy, on presenting their passport or their identity card. The ballot-paper shall be completed by a voter in the booth. It is inadmissible to allow the presence of any person except the voter when completing the ballot-paper. A voter, or a participant in a referendum, who has no possibility to fill in the ballot-paper independently shall be entitled to invite to the booth another person at his/her own discretion for the secret ballot, except for the members of divisional or higher election commissions, a candidate for the office of deputy, their authorized persons, as well as persons specified in part three of Article 13 of the Electoral Code. The completed ballot-paper shall be placed in the ballot box by the voter, or participant in a referendum, in the voting box.

470. A voter, or a participant of a referendum, who has no possibility at the day of election or referendum, to be at his/her own place of residence shall have the right no earlier than five days before elections under conditions excluding control over his/her will, to fill in the ballot-paper in the premises of Divisional Election Commission and to place it in the sealed box designated for the voters and referendum participants who will be absent at the day of holding of elections or referenda according to the place of their residence. There is no need for official confirmation of the reasons that it is impossible for a voter to come to the polling station at the day of the election or referendum.

471. Voting in advance shall be carried out from 10:00 a.m. to 2:00 p.m. and from 4:00 p.m. to 7:00 p.m. in the presence of not less than two members of the Divisional Election Commission.

472. A voter, by taking the ballot-paper, shall sign the list of citizens who have the right to take part in elections, referendum with his/her own hand and fix the date of voting in advance.

473. Count of votes and finding the results of elections. Direct counting of votes shall be carried out by the members of Divisional Election Commissions. If no candidate for deputy of the House of Representatives collected the necessary number of votes, then no later than two weeks period of time under decision of the Divisional Election Commission, there shall be a second round of voting for the two candidates for the office of deputy who collected the majority of votes of the electorate. The Divisional Election Commission shall inform the Central Commission and the electorate about this on the day after the proposal of the second round of voting. The second round of voting shall be carried out with the observance of the requirements of the Code in question.

474. Elections at the second round shall be found to be valid, if more than 25% of the voters on the list of citizens who have the right to participate in elections took part in voting. The candidate for the office of deputy is considered to have been elected, if he/she collected the majority of votes of those who participated in voting. If one of the candidates for deputy of the House of Representatives included in the ballot-paper in the second round of voting has withdrawn his/her candidature, the second round shall be carried out for one candidate. The candidate shall be deemed elected, if he/she collected more than half of votes of voters who took part in voting.

475. The Central Commission, on the grounds of the records from Divisional Election Commissions, shall find the results of elections of deputies in accordance with Divisional Election Commissions, and shall register the elected deputies for the House of Representatives.

§2. Legal Status

476. The National Assembly of the Republic of Belarus shall have a representative character, i.e., shall express the interests of the Republic of Belarus. A deputy of the House of Representatives must be a citizen of the Republic of Belarus who reached the age of 21. A member of the Council of the Republic must be a citizen of the Republic of Belarus who reached the age of thirty years and who has resided in the territory of the relevant oblast or in the City of Minsk for not less than five years.

477. Deputies of the House of Representatives shall carry out their functions in the Parliament on a professional basis, unless otherwise stipulated by the Constitution. The same person may not be simultaneously a member of both chambers of the Parliament. A member of the House of Representatives of the Republic may not be a member of a local Councils of Deputies. A member of the Council of the Republic may not simultaneously be a member of the Government. No person may exercise his/her duties as a member of the House of Representatives, or member of the Council of the Republic and simultaneously hold the office of President or a judge.

478. The term of the Parliament shall be four years. The powers of the Parliament may be extended by law only in the event of a war. The mandate of a member of the Parliament shall be imperative; it may be recalled in advance by the electorate. But it takes place very rarely.

479. After elections in 1995, in practice, discussion took place about the time of beginning of work of the Parliament. In order to avoid any disputes in this respect, the new wording of the Constitution stipulates that the first session of the chambers of the Parliament after elections shall be convened by the Central Commission on elections and holding of republican referendum and shall start its work no later than thirty days after elections. The counting of thirty days period of time for calling and beginning of the work of the first session of the House of Representatives shall be made from the second round of voting on elections of its new composition. If there is no second round of voting on elections for the House of Representatives, the counting out of thirty days period of time shall be made from the day of holding of the first round of common elections in the Republic of Belarus. The counting out of thirty days period of time for calling and beginning of the work of the first session of the Council of the Republic shall be made from the first day of meeting of the deputies of local Councils of Deputies of the level on elections for members of the Council of the Republic on behalf of oblasts or the City of Minsk.

480. In instances and under the procedure envisaged by the Constitution the powers of the House of Representatives or the Council of the Republic may be terminated before the fixed time. Alongside the termination of powers of the House of Representatives or the Council of the Republic according to the decision of the President the powers of the Council of the Republic or the House of Representatives may be terminated. Thus, the powers of the House of Representatives may be terminated before the fixed time in case of a refusal of confidence in the Government, in case of a vote of no-confidence in the Government or a second refusal in giving consent for the appointment of the Prime Minister. The powers of the House of Representatives or the Council of the Republic may also be subject to termination on the basis of the conclusion of the Constitutional Court for systematic or flagrant violation by them of the Constitution.

481. The President shall adopt decisions on these issues no later than two months after official consultations with the Chairpersons of the chambers. The Chambers of Parliament may not be dismissed during a period of emergency or martial law, during the last six months of power of the President and during the period of solution by the chambers of the issue of the premature removal of the President from the office. Both chambers may not be dissolved in the course of the first year since the first sittings were held. Under the Constitution the National Assembly – the Parliament – shall be the representative and legislative body of the Republic of Belarus.

482. The House of Representatives shall consist of 110 deputies. Elections of deputies to the House of Representatives shall be carried out in accordance with the law on the basis of universal, equal, free, direct electoral suffrage and by secret ballot. The majority system shall be applied.

483. The candidate shall be deemed elected in the first round within the Divisional Election Commission for the deputy to the House of Representatives, if he/she collected more than half of votes of voters who took part in voting and if the elections were found to be valid. Elections shall be found to be valid, if more than half of the voters of the Divisional Election Commission put on the list of citizens who have the right to participate in elections took part in voting.

484. If no candidate for the deputies of the House of Representatives collected the necessary number of votes, then no later than within two weeks period of time under decision of Divisional Election Commission there shall be a second round of voting in the electoral district for the two candidates for the office of deputy who collected the majority of the votes of the electorate. The Divisional Election Commission shall inform the Central Commission and the electorate about this on the day after the proposal of the second round of voting. The second round of voting shall be carried out with the observance of the requirements of the Electoral Code.

485. Elections at the second round shall be found to be valid, if more than 25% of the voters on the list of citizens who have the right to participate in elections took part in voting. The candidate for the office of deputy is considered to have been elected, if he/she collected the majority of votes of those who participated in voting. If one of the candidates for deputy of the House of Representatives listed on the ballot-paper in the second round of voting has withdrawn his/her candidature, the second round shall be carried out for one candidate. The candidate shall be deemed elected, if he/she collected more than half of votes of voters who took part in voting.

486. If, within the electoral district, the holding of the first and the second rounds of voting the elections were not found to be proper or valid, or the first round was only for two candidates and no one collected the necessary number of votes of the electorate, or if the second round of voting was only for one candidate for the office of deputy who did not collect the necessary number of votes, as well as in the case of removal of all the candidates for the office of deputy, the Central Commission shall entrust the Divisional Election Commission to hold further elections in the election district. In addition, it may take a decision on the necessity of holding elections by divisional and district election committees in new compositions. Voting shall be carried out at the same polling stations according to the lists made for holding of basic elections and which are subject to elaboration before the repeated elections.

487. The Council of the Republic is the Chamber of Territorial Representation. Elections shall be held by secret ballot at the sittings of the deputies of local Councils of Deputies of based level of each oblast and the City of Minsk. Thus, there shall be elected eight members of the Council of the Republic, and eight members of the Council of the Republic shall be appointed by the President of the Republic.

488. It should be noted that the quantity composition of the Parliament of the Republic of Belarus recently had significantly changed. Before 1990 there were 485 deputies, then 360 members, since 1995 there were 260 members, and now there are 174 members. The norm in question is optimal, and that shall make it possible, on the one hand, for the Parliament to be the body of wide representation of the people of the Republic, and, on the other hand, to be efficient. Calculation shall signify that the Parliaments of Japan, Brazil, Germany, the United Kingdom, France and Italy have ratios of 6.2; 4.3; 9.2; 11.4; 15.2; and 16.5, respectively, of elected representatives per million inhabitants. So, formally, it is typical to have wide representation in the Parliament of the Republic. However, there is one more very important aspect: the Parliament must be an operative, initiative-taking centre of state power, and what is also important is for it to be inexpensive for the tax-payers.

489. The social composition of the Parliament is one characteristic of the fact that the Parliament is a really representative body. Those features are the age of the deputies, number of women in the Parliament or their professional affiliation. Age structure usually has an indirect relation to the term of office of the same persons in the Parliament. We have not had, in practice, in particular, a tendency towards long-term participation in the work of the Parliament by the same individuals over a long period of time – the phenomenon of professional politicians is rare. There are no restrictions for deputies as regards their period of office in the Parliament. Disputes on this issue are still ongoing.

490. In comparison, it is possible to note that the Scandinavian countries have the largest representation of women in bodies that adopt important decisions. Parliaments of Sweden, Finland, and Denmark have up to 40% of women, the Parliament of Norway better still on 50%. The Government of Sweden formed in 1993 has twenty-one ministers, of which eight were women. These included the ministers of finance, foreign affairs, justice, culture, and the Speaker of the Parliament. South Africa has 25% of women in the Parliament. Now there are five women in the House of Representatives of the National Assembly of the Republic of Belarus and nineteen women in the Council of the Republic.

§3. Competences

491. The main function of any Parliament shall be the law making function (along with the control and administrative functions). Moreover, one shall bear in mind that the adoption of laws shall be the business of both chambers; although the law-making process begins in the House of Representatives. According to the legislation of Belarus, any draft law, unless otherwise stipulated by the Constitution, shall be considered first in the House of Representatives and then in the Council of the Republic. Many other powers for each chamber, as a rule, are exclusively their own powers and need no obligatory participation of another chamber.

492. Consideration of draft laws on amending the Constitution and on interpretation of the Constitution. Article 97.1 of the Constitution shall specify, in particular, the power of the House of Representatives to consider draft laws on amending the Constitution and on interpretation of the Constitution. In addition, it shall be emphasized that those drafts may be considered by the chamber in question only as a result of the proposal of the President or the initiative of not less than 150,000 citizens of the Republic of Belarus who have the electoral right. Thus, the given case needs the initiative from the specially authorized subject. Organs and persons specified in Article 99 of the Constitution that have the right to legislative initiative may not raise the issue before the House of Representatives for correction of the Constitution or its interpretation under this procedure.

493. The procedure of submitting draft laws on amending the Constitution and on interpretation of the Constitution by the President to the House of Representatives are, in principle, similar to the procedure of making draft laws. As for popular initiatives, i.e., when a relevant proposal is submitted by 150,000 citizens of the Republic of Belarus, the law should stipulate the procedure and the terms of collection of signatures for the approval of the project. Nowadays it is possible to use the procedure of collection of signatures for the preparation of holding a referendum. According to Article 167 of the Rules of Procedure of the House of Representatives, if the proposal on amending the Constitution is submitted to the House of Representatives by the citizens of the Republic of Belarus, it shall be subject to consideration in accordance with the Rules of Procedure, apart from parliamentary approval or agreement with the subject of discussion and attaching the necessary materials to the draft law.

494. Under Article 139 of the Constitution the law on amending the Constitution may be adopted after it has been debated and approved twice by both chambers of the Parliament with at least three months' interval.

495. The provision that amendments of the Constitution may be carried out only after two discussions and approvals with an obligatory interval between them is a worldwide constitutional practice. This procedure of amending the Constitution may also be known as a 'double vote'. The sense of this procedure that the deputies must think once again whether the amendments they have already voted for are necessary or merely of momentary advantage and perhaps badly elaborated.

496. The interval between the end of the first reading and the beginning of the second reading of the draft law on amending the Constitution must be no more than three months. This rule is considered to be observed if the draft is identical at both readings. Otherwise a violation of the constitutional demand in question will have taken place. According to the Rules of Procedure of the House of Representatives, the prepared draft law on amending the Constitution must be forwarded to the deputies of the House of Representatives and to other subjects who have the right to legislative initiative no more than twenty days prior to examination by the House of Representatives.

497. Laws on amending the Constitution, on enforcement of laws, and on interpretation of the Constitution shall be deemed to have been adopted where not less than two-thirds of the elected deputies of both chambers of the Parliament have voted in favour of them. This rule is only effective when the two required discussions and approvals have taken place.

498. Taking into account the specific nature of the subjects, the Rules of Procedure of the House of Representatives envisage that the draft law on amending the Constitution shall be reported in the House of Representatives by the President or by his representative. If the draft was made by the citizens of the Republic of Belarus, then it shall be reported by the Chairperson of the House of Representatives or his/her Deputy (Article 172 of the Rules of Procedure). In the latter instance it is not fully lawful to deprive a representative of the citizens, initiating a correction of the Constitution, to report the draft at the session of the House of Representatives.

499. For the purposes of exclusion of any influence on the will of deputies, the inadmissibility of amending the Constitution during a state of emergency is the norm. Special conditions (threat, natural calamity, etc.) shall exert no influence on constitutional stability.

500. A ban on amending the Constitution during the last six months of the current composition of the House of Representatives shall prevent the adoption of decisions to please short-term interests (e.g., decisions based on an evaluation of the pre-election situation in the country).

501. Practically analogous is the procedure of interpretation of the Constitution by the House of Representatives aimed at securing a unique and sound interpretation of the constitutional norms. The Rules of Procedure stipulate the forwarding of this text to deputies seven days before consideration at the session of the House of Representatives.

502. Consideration of draft laws. According to Article 97.2 of the Constitution consideration of draft laws is the competence of the House of Representatives, including the guidelines of the domestic and foreign policy of the Republic of Belarus; military doctrine; ratification and abrogation of international treaties; the fundamental concepts and principles of human rights, freedoms and duties of Belarusian citizens; citizenship issues, the status of foreigners and persons without citizenship; the rights of ethnic minorities; the approval of the budget of the Republic and its implementation; the introduction of national taxes and dues; the principles of ownership; the basics of social security; the principles regulating labour and employment; marriage, the family, childhood, maternity, paternity, education, upbringing, culture and public health; environmental protection and the rational utilization of natural resources; determination of the procedure for resolving issues relating to the administrative-territorial structure of the State; local self-government; the administration of justice and the status of judges; issues of criminal liability and amnesty; declaration of war and conclusion of peace; martial law and a state of emergency; institution of state awards; interpretation of laws.

503. Thus, the Constitution shall limit the domains of the legislative power of the House of Representatives (and of Parliament as a whole). Article 97.2 of the Constitution gives a list of draft laws that are subject to consideration by the House of Representatives, however, to my mind, it is not an exhaustive one.

504. Due to the specification in Article 97 of the list of draft laws that are subject to consideration by the House of Representatives, it is possible to make several conclusions. First, the competences of the House of Representatives (and of Parliament as a whole) shall be the adoption of enforceable enactments such as laws in the field of public and private relations; second, the fact of making this list implies that the subjects in this sphere may be regulated only by the law. Thereby, one can clearly see certain guarantees of the development of the legislative body, and on the inadmissibility of encroachment upon its sphere of influence on behalf of another branch of power. The specified list of draft laws which may be considered by the House of Representatives shall not be an exhaustive list, it shall be entitled to adopt laws on other issues, if the Constitution does not refer their settlement to other state bodies.

505. Proposals on holding of referendum. Declarations on presidential elections. National referenda shall be appointed by the President of the Republic of Belarus. The initiator of presidential elections may be the House of Representatives and the Council of the Republic. The relevant proposal shall be taken up by the chambers in separate sittings by the majority of the full membership of the deputies of each chamber.

506. Thus, in the given case both chambers must express a single (coinciding) will. According to the Rules of Procedure of the House of Representatives, its resolution on the given issue must contain the expected date of any given referendum, the type of referendum, questions posed in the referendum, and the proposal for the Council of the Republic to consider the issue on holding of referendum (Article 206; Articles 199 and 200 of the Rules of Procedure of the Council of the Republic). After adoption of the relevant resolution by the Council of the Republic the duly prepared proposal must be forwarded to the President for adoption of a decision on the holding of the referendum.

507. It will be correct to empower the Constitutional Court to verify the constitutionality of questions that are subject to referendum. This shall improve legality and the protection of the right of citizens to administer the affairs of the State.

508. The new wording of the Constitution distributes the roles for the holding of presidential and parliamentary elections. The House of Representatives shall hold elections for the Head of State. The procedure and the terms of appointment of elections of the President shall be envisaged by the Constitution (Article 81) and the law on elections of the President of the Republic of Belarus.

509. The decision on the holding of elections for the President of the Republic of Belarus and on securing the relevant organizational arrangements as regards their preparation and holding shall be the exclusive right of the House of Representatives: it shall be adopted without the participation of the second chamber – the Council of the Republic. The given decision shall be adopted in the form of a Resolution of the House of Representatives.

510. Consideration of issues on premature retirement and dismissal from the office of the President of the Republic of Belarus. The term of office of the President of the Republic of Belarus shall be five years; however, he may tender his resignation at any time subject to approval by the House of Representatives which must be fixed by the relevant resolution. The President is not obliged to indicate the reasons of his resignation. The Rules of Procedure should envisage the procedure of acceptance of resignation.

511. Under Article 88 the President of the Republic of Belarus may be prematurely removed from office when he is persistently incapable to discharge his duties on account of the State of his health. The issue of removing the President shall be taken by resolution of the House of Representatives by a majority of not less than two-thirds of the House of Representatives and a majority of not less than two-thirds of the Council of the Republic on the basis of the findings of an ad hoc Commission.

512. The President may be removed from office for acts of state treason and other grave crimes. The decision to file a charge against the President shall be supported by the majority of the House of Representatives on behalf of not less than one-third of its deputies. The President shall be deemed to be removed from office, if the decision is adopted by not less than two-thirds of the Council of the Republic, as well as two-thirds of the House of Representatives. The failure of the House of Representatives and the Council of the Republic to take a decision to remove the President from office within a month since it was initiated shall mean the dismissal of the charge. The proposal to remove the President from office may not be initiated in accordance with the provision of the Constitution in the course of hearings on the premature termination of the powers of the Parliament.

513. Delegation of legislative powers to the President. The practice of delegation by the Parliament of its powers to other state bodies is not a new one. It is a wide spread practice abroad (in France, Spain, Germany), and took place previously in our law-making activities.

514. Article 97 of the Constitution stipulates the basic powers of the House of Representatives. Among those already considered, this chamber shall grant consent to the President concerning the appointment of the Prime Minister; consider the report of the Prime Minister on the policy of the Government and approve or reject it; consider the initiative of the Prime Minister on votes of confidence; and cancel the order of the Chairperson of the House of Representatives. Certain powers were considered in other chapters. The House of Representatives may take decisions on other issues if they are determined by the Constitution.

515. Powers of the Council of the Republic. Speaking about the law-making process, first of all, the right of the Council of the Republic to approve or to decline draft laws on amending the Constitution; on interpretation of the Constitution; and drafts of other laws adopted by the House of Representatives should be noted.

516. The Council of the Republic shall have wide powers while solving personnel issues. As it was already emphasized, the Council of the Republic shall grant consent to the appointment by the President of the Chairperson of the Constitutional Court, the Chairperson and judges of the Supreme Court, Chairperson and judges of the Supreme Economic Court, the Chairperson of the Central Commission on Elections and Holding of National Referenda, the Attorney-General, the Chairperson and members of the Board of Directors of the National Bank; he shall elect six judges of the Constitutional Court; he shall elect six members of the Central Commission of the Republic of Belarus on elections and holding of national referenda.

517. Taking into account the fact that the Council of the Republic is the chamber of territorial representation, it shall have a number of powers with respect to local Councils. Thus, the Council of the Republic shall have the right to reverse decisions of local Councils of Deputies that do not conform to legislation; to adopt resolutions on the dissolution of the local Councils of Deputies where it systematically or flagrantly violates the requirements of the law and other instances determined by the law (Article 19 of the Law on local government and self-government).

518. The Council of the Republic shall be the second instance, which, following the House of Representatives, considers charges of treason or of other grave crimes against the President and takes decisions on its investigation. Given the presence of substantial evidence, the Council of the Republic shall take a decision to remove the President from office with not less than two-thirds of the full composition of the chamber; consider Presidential decrees on the introduction of a state of emergency, martial law, general or partial mobilization no later than three days after their submission and take the appropriate decision; the Council of the Republic may take decisions on other issues determined by the Constitution.

§4. Legislative Process in Parliament

519. Stages of legislative process. Acts of Parliament of the Republic of Belarus shall be subject to adoption under a specific procedure, i.e., by way of gradual actions that are stages of the legislative process. The legislative process in Belarusian Parliament has several stages. The first stage in the legislative process shall be analysis and planning of future legislation.

520. Unfortunately, previous practice signifies that this aspect of the legislative process was paid no due attention. The preparation of draft laws and their adoption contain no analysis of the situation created as a result of the adoption of a law, the effects of its adoption on the living standards of people, or possible infringements of this law, crimes included. Parliamentary hearings on execution of laws in any given sphere may improve work on the effectiveness of Belarusian legislation.

521. The Parliament, and the President of the Republic of Belarus, deal regularly with the problem of prospective and current legislative activities. However, the plan of legislative activities is conditioned often by the content of the adopted law, where the relevant bodies are charged with bringing legislative acts into line with the adopted law.

522. The new Constitution shall specify relations that are subject to regulation by the law. This shall also exert an influence on the planning of future laws. It is quite correct that the adoption of acts further elaborating the Constitution shall be of first priority. Plans of preparation of draft laws must take the principle needs of Belarusian society into account. This is the way that the pertinence of future acts shall be decided. The current Constitution shall predetermine the necessity of approval of the programmes of legislative works that would contain the preparation of laws by the Parliament, the adoption of which is justified by the Constitution, as well as new laws and improvement of existing legislative acts. Preparation of this programme should not include at all the whole list of legal acts (except for those specified in the Constitution); they must contain at least the main legislative acts.

523. Regrettably, work on planning legislative activities is not always effective; there are instances where plans contain no drafts to be adopted, under the priority procedure included. However, that shall not prevent legislators from submitting these drafts according to the procedure of legislative initiative for consideration by the legislative body.

524. The second stage of legislative process – legislative initiative. The notion of the right to legislative initiative arouses the interest of both scientists and practical workers in the field of law. Certain researchers deem that the right to legislative initiative is none other than the possibility to submit draft laws for the consideration of the Parliament; other researchers included additionally the right to make proposals on the elaboration or adoption of new laws, and reversing or developing of the current laws.

525. The Constitution defines which bodies shall possess the legislative initiative (Article 99). This right shall belong to the President, members of the House of Representatives, the Council of the Republic, the Government, as well as to the citizens who are eligible to vote, in a number of not less than 50,000. Moreover, it is necessary to take the following peculiarities into account. The Constitutional Court is entitled to make proposals to the Parliament on the necessity of amending acts of effective legislation, and the adoption of new enforceable enactments. The Basic Law points out a special level of the legislative initiative as regards amending the

Constitution (Article 138). The circle of these subjects is significantly smaller than that specified in Article 99 of the Constitution.

526. The draft laws aimed directly at the realization of provisions of the Constitution of the Republic of Belarus shall be subject to consideration of the House of Representatives. The draft law or the draft resolution of the House of Representatives drawn up according to the law and the rules established by the Rules of Procedure shall be subject to obligatory consideration by the House of Representatives. Several subjects may realize the right to legislative initiative simultaneously. The legislator shall be entitled to recall the introduced draft before consideration in the House of Representatives in the second reading. The legislator shall be entitled to recall his/her signature before the consideration of the draft law or the draft resolution of the House of Representatives in the second reading, if the draft law or draft resolution of the House of Representatives was made by several legislators.

527. The draft law must contain exhaustive unique information about the aims and the essence of issues to be placed under regulation: their subjects and objects must be in line with the principles of the construction of the legal system. The draft law may contain information on special notions and terms used in the text. Draft laws of the Republic of Belarus shall be presented by legislators for consideration of the House of Representatives with the addendum of the following materials: covering letter; reasons for the necessity of adoption of the given decision; financial reasoning for the draft law and information on the anticipated expenses related to the realization of the draft law. The materials in question may be drawn up as a single document. The draft law may include information about preliminary expert examination by scientists and specialists (if such expertise took place), as well as conclusions of the interested state bodies, their remarks and proposals.

528. Under the Constitution and according to practice in the Republic, each deputy shall have the right to legislative initiative. Very often the deputy is proceeding from populist and local interests. The introduction of the rule under which submission of the draft law to the Parliament needs the support of at least five deputies would eradicate such a practice. This approach would make it possible on the first stage to carry out approbation of those drafts, to study the possibility of their positive consideration in the Parliament.

529. The third stage is a preliminary consideration of drafts. The draft laws and draft resolutions received by the House of Representatives according to the Rules of Procedure shall be forwarded by the Chairperson of the House of Representatives, and in his/her absence by the Deputy Chairperson to the Department of the Secretariat of the House of Representatives which shall carry out expert legal activities for the preparation of conclusions on the conformity between the draft law and the requirements of the Rules of Procedure. If the presented draft law or the attached materials do not meet requirements, this draft, with the consent of the Chairperson of the relevant standing commission, may be returned by the Chairperson of the House of Representatives or by his/her Deputy to the legislator that introduced the draft with the proposal to fulfil the requirements. The Chairperson of the House of

Representatives or his/her Deputy shall appoint a commission for the preliminary consideration of the draft and for preparation of the opinion thereupon.

530. If the leading commission states its incompetence as regards the draft or there are disputes between two or among more commissions, the Chairperson of the House of Representatives or his/her Deputy, after consultations with the Chairpersons of those commissions in case of the failure to find consent, shall submit the proposal on the formation of a special commission for the consideration of the Council of the Republic. The Council of the House of Representatives shall approve the Chairperson and the composition of the special commission. The commission on the draft law shall forward the draft law to the standing commissions and to the necessary subdivisions of the Secretariat of the House of Representatives, shall define other subjects engaged in the preliminary consideration of the draft, and time limits for remarks and proposals on the draft of not less than ten days, unless otherwise stipulated in the Rules of Procedure. The commission may create a working group on a draft law.

531. According to the requirements of the Rules of Procedure of the House of Representatives the work of commissions on a draft law must be carried out openly and in public. The commission shall have the right to propose to carry out preliminary discussion of the draft law in the form of parliamentary hearings or to submit the draft to national discussion in accordance with the procedure specified by the legislation. In instances of necessity according to the decision of the leading commission the draft law shall be forwarded to examination by scientific experts, requests of the ministries and administrations and opinions of different organizations may also be made. The leading commission may ask the legislator for the necessary additional materials and information.

532. Remarks and proposals in the process of discussion of the draft law shall be considered at the sittings of the leading commission and shall be agreed with the legislator that introduced the draft law or by the person it authorized. The draft law shall include only those observations and proposals under which the consent was found with the legislator that introduced the draft law or by the representative thereof.

533. The draft law with the remarks and proposals under which the consent was found with the legislator that introduced the draft law or with the authorized representative thereof must be signed by the aforementioned person. The Chairperson of the House of Representatives shall carry out the settlement of disputes among the standing commissions of the House of Representatives as the elaborators of the draft law. Issues which were given no consent shall be subject to consideration of the House of Representatives. Equally, with the draft law on amendment of current laws, the House of Representatives must present the table or the information with the current article or other structural part of the draft and the new wording (with alterations and addenda). The Chairperson of the commission or the Deputy thereof shall sign the table or the information.

534. After the completion of the work the commission shall forward the opinion and the draft law with all the necessary materials to the Council of the House of Representatives for the preliminary consideration of the issue on the inclusion of the draft law in the agenda of the session of the House of Representatives for consideration in its first reading. In addition, the draft law must be signed by the legislator that introduced the draft law or the representative authorized thereof; by the Chairperson of the commission; by the heads of the structural subdivisions of the Secretariat of the House of Representatives which carry out expert legal and editorial activities, and in their absence by their deputies. In case of disagreement with the provisions of the draft, the signing shall be made with the attachment of the relevant remarks and proposals. The time period for the signing shall be not less than three days, unless otherwise stipulated by the Rules of Procedure.

535. The negative opinion of the commission on the usefulness of adoption of the given draft law shall not repeal the necessity of an obligatory examination by the House of Representatives of the draft in the author's wording, if the draft is not recalled by the legislator.

536. The important guarantee of the right of legislative initiative shall be fixed in the Rules of Procedure with the rule that, in instances of disagreement of the legislator that introduced the draft law with alterations and addenda and the draft law proposed by the commission, or other legislators, the draft law shall be considered in the author's wording. In those cases signing envisaged by Article 132.2 of the Rules of Procedure shall be carried out only by the legislator.

537. The fourth stage is consideration of the draft at the sitting of the House of Representatives. Consideration of draft laws submitted to the House of Representatives shall be carried out in two readings, unless otherwise stipulated by the Rules of Procedure.

538. The text of the draft law prepared for the first reading and included in the agenda of the session, materials thereof, and the opinion of the commission on the draft shall be forwarded by the Secretariat of the House of Representatives to the deputies of the House of Representatives, to the legislator that introduced the draft law, as well as the interested bodies no later than three days before its consideration in the first reading, unless otherwise specified by the Rules of Procedure.

539. While considering the draft law in the first reading, the House of Representatives shall hear the report of the legislator that introduced the draft law or the representative thereof and co-report of the commission. Consideration in the first reading through shall be given to the orientation and structure of the draft law, as well as the basic elements and usefulness of the adoption of the law. In the presence of alternative draft laws, the House of Representatives shall decide which of the drafts shall be taken as a principle for the preparation for the second reading.

540. According to the results of discussion, the House of Representatives, by voting, shall adopt or reject the draft law. A decision as regards the draft law considered in the first reading shall be adopted, if the majority of the full composition of the House of Representatives voted for it, and this decision shall be drawn up by resolution of the House of Representatives.

541. If, according to the results of voting the draft law was not adopted by the House of Representatives, the House of Representatives may adopt a decision on the rejection of the draft law. The decision on the rejection of the draft law shall be deemed to be adopted if the majority of the full composition of the House of Representatives voted for it. In case of adoption of such a decision, examination of the given draft law is possible only after its repeated submission to the House of Representatives under the procedure of the deputy's legislative initiative. Moreover, it shall be considered as a new draft law. If there was no decision taken as regards the rejection of the draft law or if there was no proposal made as regards the rejection of the draft law, the draft law shall be sent for completion to the relevant commission and the relevant protocol note shall be made. The House of Representatives may increase the number of commissions for finishing the draft law or entrust the special commission to finish it. After it is finished, the draft law shall be subject to consideration in the first reading.

542. After adoption of the draft law in the first reading, the House of Representatives shall refer it for finishing to the same or to another commission, or increase the number of commissions or entrust the special commission with finishing the draft law, fix the terms for finishing and presentation of the draft for the second reading. According to the decision of the House of Representatives, the draft law may be forwarded for proposals and remarks to the President of the Republic of Belarus, to the Council of the Republic, to the Council of Ministers and to other state bodies.

543. According to decision of the House of Representatives the draft law between the first and the second reading may be submitted for national discussion. The commission shall examine the amendments and prepare the draft law for the second reading. The finished draft law, according to the decision of the Council of the House of Representatives, shall be submitted for inclusion in the agenda of the session.

544. The draft law prepared for consideration in the second reading must be signed by the Chairperson of the leading commission, heads of subdivisions of the Secretariat of the House of Representatives that carry out expert legal and editorial activities, and in their absence by their deputies. In case of disagreement with the provisions of the draft law, signing is carried out with attachment of the relevant remarks and proposals. The term for signing must be not less than three days, unless otherwise specified by the Rules of Procedure.

545. The draft law prepared for the consideration in the second reading must be forwarded by the commission to the deputies of the House of Representatives and to the legislator that introduced the draft law no later than seven days before the examination of the draft law in the second reading, unless otherwise stipulated by the Rules of Procedure. The draft shall be forwarded with specification of the adopted amendments and enclosure of the table of the rejected amendments.

546. If, in the course of the first reading the House of Representatives finds the draft to be good without amendments, then, under decision of the House of Representatives, it may be considered in the second reading without finishing in the standing commissions. If, while finishing the draft for the second reading, the concept of the draft has been changed, the House of Representatives may adopt a decision on repeal of the previously adopted resolution and on the repeated consideration of the draft in the first reading according to the proposal of the standing commission. This decision shall be drawn up by a resolution of the House of Representatives. Repeated examination of the draft in the first reading shall be carried out according to the Rules of Procedure. While considering the draft law in the second reading, the report shall be made by the Chairperson of the commission or his/her Deputy.

547. Discussion of the draft law in the second reading shall begin with adoption of its name and after that the preamble shall be discussed. Afterwards, according to the decision of the House of Representatives the draft law shall be discussed by paragraphs, chapters, sections, or by other structural parts of the draft or as a whole. During discussion it is possible to adopt a decision on returning certain parts or the whole draft law for the finishing.

548. The fifth stage is the adoption of the law. Each article, chapter, section or other structural part of the draft shall be put to a vote separately. If there are no remarks or proposals on the draft law, the House of Representatives may adopt a decision on voting on the draft as a whole. Amendments rejected by the commission shall be subject to voting while discussing the relevant article, chapter, section and other structural parts of the draft. Only the amendments of the deputies of the House of Representatives and other legislators produced in written form shall be put to voting. A deputy of the House of Representatives, a legislator or his/her representative shall be asked to speak and give reasons for the amendment.

549. Each amendment shall be discussed and voting on it shall be held separately. At first, it shall be the amendment that will be discussed, after that, if a decision has not been taken, the article in the wording proposed by commission will come under scrutiny. In case of several amendments within one article of the project, then the priority for discussion and voting is given to the amendment whose adoption or rejection will make allow solutions to issues on other amendments.

550. After the voting on all the articles, chapters, sections or other structural parts of the draft, as well as on all the amendments, the draft law shall be put to a vote as a whole. If, in the process of the second reading the draft law has been amended, the voting on the draft as a whole shall be held only after printing the final text of the draft law with the adopted amendments. At the same time, the leading commission must make the opinion on the lack of contradictions in the draft. After hearing the opinion of the leading commission the voting on the draft law as a whole shall be held without discussion.

551. The Constitution confirms that, on the demand of the President or with his consent, the Government, the House of Representatives, in its session, shall adopt a decision by voting as a whole for the draft of the President or the Government or its part preserving only those amendments proposed or adopted by the President or the Government.

552. The Rules of Procedure of the House of Representatives specifies that the President or the Government may put this requirement forward in the second reading before consideration of the draft law by the House of Representatives or at any stage of consideration, but before the adoption of the draft law as a whole.

553. As a result of the second reading the House of Representatives may take a decision on adoption of the draft law or its rejection. The specified decision shall be drawn up by resolution of the House of Representatives. The draft law shall be deemed to have been adopted by the House of Representatives under the condition that the majority of the full composition of the House of Representatives voted for it, unless otherwise stipulated by the Constitution of the Republic of Belarus.

554. Under the Constitution the draft programme laws on basic lines of domestic and foreign policy of the Republic of Belarus, and on military doctrine of the Republic of Belarus, shall be deemed to be adopted under conditions that not less than two-thirds of the full composition of the House of Representatives voted for it. The decision on the adoption of the draft law on demand of the President or on behalf thereof by the Government under Article 100.5 of the Constitution of the Republic of Belarus (i.e., without the Council of the Republic) shall be deemed to be adopted if the majority of the full composition of the House of Representatives voted for it.

555. If as a result of voting the draft law has not been adopted by the House of Representatives, the House of Representatives may adopt a decision on the rejection of the draft law. A decision on rejection of the draft law shall be deemed to be adopted if the majority of the full composition of the House of Representatives voted for it. In case of the adoption of this decision consideration of the given draft law is possible only after its repeated submission to the House of Representatives according to normal legislative procedures. In addition, it shall be considered as a new draft law. If a decision on rejection of the draft law has not been adopted or if there was no proposal made on rejection of the draft law, the draft law shall be referred for its finishing to the relevant commission: and a protocol note shall be drafted about this. The House of Representatives may broaden the number of commissions for finishing the draft law or to charge the special commission to finish it. After finishing the draft law shall be considered again in the second reading.

556. The adoption of a decision very often needs the clarification of two aspects: the quorum of persons who must take part in voting and the number of persons who expressed their opinions in favour of this or that decision. Each sitting of the chamber of the Parliament shall begin with the determination of their competence.

557. The Constitution establishes the obligation of the Parliament to examine draft laws in a fixed period. Under Article 99 of the Constitution of the Republic of Belarus the President or, by appointment by him, the Government, shall have the right to forward proposals to the House of Representatives on the urgent consideration of a draft law. The House of Representatives must consider it in the course of ten days after the date of its submission.

558. In case of this urgency procedure, the Chairperson of the House of Representatives and, in the absence thereof, his/her deputy shall appoint the commission in charge of this procedure, specify the concrete reduced terms for preparation and consideration of the draft, and measures on the acceleration of this process.

559. According to the Rules of Procedure of the House of Representatives the draft law must be brought to the notice of the deputies of the House of Representatives no later than two days after its arrival in Parliament, and the proposals and remarks of the deputies of the House of Representatives shall be forwarded to the leading commission no later than twenty-four hours before consideration of the draft.

560. Draft laws for urgent consideration shall be finished, submitted and discussed at the session of the House of Representatives according to the procedure specified by the Rules of Procedure for all the draft laws. Draft laws adopted by the House of Representatives during these five days shall be referred for the consideration of the Council of the Republic during a period of twenty days and not longer, unless otherwise stipulated by the Constitution (while declaring the draft law to be urgent, it must be considered by the Council of the Republic within ten days from the date of its submission for consideration). Together with the draft law adopted by the House of Representatives the Council of the Republic shall also be forwarded all the materials which were presented while submitting the draft law to the House of Representatives, as well as the resolution of the House of Representatives on the adopted draft law, a stenographic report (verbatim) of the sitting of the House of Representatives, amendments rejected in the course of finishing the draft law, texts of non-specified remarks and proposals, opinions of experts, specialists and of the expert legal department of the Secretariat of the House of Representatives on the given draft law, opinions of interested state bodies and officials, and the original text of the draft law presented by the legislator.

561. A draft law which would result in reduction in the revenue of the State, the creation or the increase of expenses, should be enclosed by the document confirming the consent of the President of the Republic of Belarus or his assignment for the Government to submit this draft law. The absence of the aforementioned document shall be grounds for rejection of the draft law by the Council of the Republic.

562. The sixth stage is consideration and approval (rejection) by the Council of the Republic of the adopted draft laws. According to the Rules of Procedure of the Council of the Republic the term during which the Council of the Republic shall consider the draft law from the House of Representatives shall be calculated from the date following the day of registration of this draft law in the Secretariat of the Council of the Republic. If the last day of the term is a day off, then the day of the end of the term shall be the next working day.

563. The draft law from the House of Representatives shall be registered in the Secretariat of the Council of the Republic and shall be submitted to the Chairperson of the Council of the Republic who shall determine one or several standing commissions that are to study the draft law in question. In addition, a time limit for consideration of the draft law shall be fixed and the commission responsible for its consideration shall be determined.

564. During the five days from the moment of registration of the draft law, the House of Representatives should forward the necessary documents and materials to all the members of the Council of the Republic. In the presence of remarks and proposals on the draft law, the members of the Council of the Republic will refer them to the commission responsible for examination of the given draft law.

565. Standing commissions shall discuss the draft law at their sittings and shall adopt opinions on it which are forwarded to the commission responsible for examination of the given draft law. This commission shall generalize the opinions, remarks and proposals on the draft law and make an opinion thereon.

566. Standing commissions shall consider openly the draft law adopted by the House of Representatives. Initiator or the representative thereto, scientists and specialists as experts, as well as representatives of the mass media may be invited at the sittings of the commission. The opinion on the draft law under consideration shall be taken by way of open voting by the majority of the voters present at the sitting of the members of the commission. Opinion of the standing commission that is responsible for examination of the adopted by the House of Representatives draft law shall give the estimation of the draft law under consideration and one of the following decisions shall be adopted: to recommend the Council of the Republic to approve the draft law adopted by the House of Representatives; to recommend the Council of the Republic to reject the draft law adopted by the House of Representatives by giving in the opinion the reasons according to which the standing commission deems it necessary to reject it. The opinion of the standing commission that is responsible for consideration of the draft law adopted by the House of Representatives shall be submitted to the Council of the Republic.

567. If the standing commission that is responsible for consideration of the draft law proposes the Council of the Republic to approve the draft law adopted by the House of Representatives without discussion, then the Council of the Republic shall adopt by the majority of the voters present at the sitting of the members of the Council of the Republic the decision on holding of a vote related to approval of the draft law without discussion. If the proposal of the commission does not collect a necessary number of votes, as well as in all the other instances after pronouncement of the opinion of the standing commission that is responsible for consideration of the draft law, the Council of the Republic shall discuss the draft law. The Council of the Republic shall specify the procedure of discussion of the draft law.

568. As a result of consideration of the adopted by the House of Representatives draft law, the presiding officer shall put to vote the issue on approval of the draft law by the Council of the Republic. In an instance of inadequate preparation of the draft law for its consideration, the Council of the Republic shall have the right to adopt a decision on moving its consideration to the next session. The specified decision shall be taken by the majority of the voters who are present at the sitting of the members of the Council of the Republic. If the specified decision has not been taken, the chairperson is obliged to put the issue on approval of the draft law.

569. Resolution of the Council of the Republic on approval of the draft law shall be adopted by the majority of the votes from the full composition of the Council of the Republic, unless otherwise stipulated by the Constitution. Resolutions of the Council of the Republic on approval of draft laws on amending the Constitution, on enforcement of the specified laws, acts on interpretation of the Constitution, as well as draft laws on main directions of domestic and foreign policy, on military doctrine shall be deemed to be adopted under condition, if not less than two-thirds of the full composition of the Council of the Republic voted in favour of them. A decision on approval or rejection of the adoption by the House of Representatives draft law must be made within the time periods specified by the Constitution.

570. If the draft law has not been subject to consideration by the Council of the Republic within the terms fixed by the Constitution, then it shall be considered to be approved and shall be forwarded to the President of the Republic of Belarus for signature. The draft law shall be considered to be rejected, if the necessary number of members of the Council of the Republic has not voted for its approval. The decision on rejection of the draft law shall be drawn up by Resolution of the Council of the Republic.

571. Resolution of the Council of the Republic on a rejection of a draft law may contain the list of sections, chapters, articles, as well as parts and points of the articles of the specified draft law, the disagreement on which must be overcome between the Council of the Republic and the House of Representatives, as well as a proposal on creation on an common ground for the conciliation commission for elaboration of the conciliatory text of the draft law. Text of the draft law elaborated by the conciliation commission shall be submitted for the approval of both chambers.

572. Resolution of the Council of the Republic on the rejection of the draft law adopted by the House of Representatives, together with the draft law or resolution of the Council of the Republic on approval of the adopted by the House of

Representatives draft law in five-day period of time shall be forwarded to the House of Representatives.

573. In case of repeated consideration by the House of Representatives of the draft law rejected by the Council of the Republic, the House of Representatives shall adopt it taking into account all the proposals of the Council of the Republic, the relevant standing commission of the Council of the Republic shall confirm this by its opinion and make the proposal on approval by the Council of the Republic of the draft law adopted by the House of Representatives. In case of repeated discussions of the draft law rejected by the Council of the Republic, the House of Representatives adopted it in the wording while taking into account the part of proposals of the Council of the Republic or the wording containing any exceptions or new proposals as regards the previously adopted wording, the draft law shall be considered by the Council of the Republic as a new one.

574. The law adopted by the House of Representatives and approved by the Council of the Republic together with resolution of the Council of the Republic during ten days period of time shall be submitted to the President of the Republic of Belarus for signature.

575. The last stage of the legislative process shall be the signing and proclamation of the law. The law adopted by the House of Representatives and approved by the Council of the Republic or adopted under the Constitution only by the House of Representatives shall be submitted within ten days period of time for the signature of the President of the Republic of Belarus. The Chairperson of the Council of the Republic shall certify the authenticity of the adoption by the House of Representatives and the approval by the Council of the Republic of the law submitted to the President for signature.

576. If the President does not agree with the text of the bill, he shall return it together with his objections to the House of Representatives that shall consider it with the President's objections within thirty days.

577. The Council of the House of Representatives shall forward the text of the law returned by the President with the objections to the leading commission on the draft law for an opinion and shall fix the time limit for submitting the draft law for consideration by the House of Representatives. The leading commission shall organize the work on the draft law according to the procedure specified by the Rules of Procedure for all the draft laws.

578. Objections of the President of the Republic of Belarus shall be considered by the leading commission on the draft law. The commission shall prepare the opinion on the objections and submit it to the Council of the House of Representatives. The opinion of the commission must include one of these responses: to agree to the objections of the President of the Republic of Belarus and to forward the draft law returned them for its completion; to submit the returned law for consideration to the

House of Representatives to override the objections of the President of the Republic of Belarus.

579. The Council of the House of Representatives shall consider the opinion of the commission and shall adopt a decision on finishing the law, as well as determine the leading commission or adopt a decision on the inclusion of the issue on repeated consideration of the law by the House of Representatives in the agenda of the session of the House of Representatives. The law returned by the President of the Republic of Belarus may be subject to primary consideration.

580. After finishing the law returned by the President of the Republic of Belarus, the commission shall submit to the Council of the House of Representatives the proposal on inclusion of the issue on consideration of the draft law for the second reading in the agenda of the session of the House of Representatives.

581. While considering the draft law in the House of Representatives, only those provisions that were amended in the process of finishing shall be subject to voting. Consequently, a vote shall be held on the draft law as a whole.

582. If the law is subject to consideration by the House of Representatives for overcoming the objections of the President, the vote shall be on the law as a whole. In this instance it is inadmissible to amend the law. If the law is adopted by the House of Representatives by a majority of not less than two-thirds of votes of the full composition, then it shall be forwarded within five-day period of time to the Council of the Republic together with the objections of the President. If the objections of the President have not been overcome, the law shall be forwarded for finishing or shall be rejected.

583. According to the same procedure the House of Representatives shall consider the objections of the President on certain provisions of the law that shall be returned for repeated voting. In this instance, prior to the relevant decision of the House of Representatives and the Council of the Republic, the law shall be signed and enforced without the provisions where there are objections emanating from the President.

584. If the law returned by the President with his objections to the House of Representatives has been forwarded by the House of Representatives for the approval of the Council of the Republic, the Council of the Republic must consider it within twenty days. The law returned by the President of the Republic of Belarus may be subject to consideration under the priority procedure.

585. The resolution of the House of Representatives about the repeated consideration of the law, the objections of the President of the Republic of Belarus, a verbatim record of the sitting of the House of Representatives on the objections of the President of the Republic of Belarus, and the opinion of the standing commission of the House of Representatives on the objections of the President of the Republic of Belarus shall also be forwarded to the Chairperson of the Council of the Republic together with the text of the law returned by the President of the Republic of Belarus with his objections and considered by the House of Representatives.

586. The standing commission of the Council of the Republic which previously passed the opinion on the law returned by the President of the Republic of Belarus shall consider the remarks of the President and the text of the law adopted by the House of Representatives and give its opinion thereupon. The standing commission shall prepare an official opinion according to the procedure specified by the Rules of Procedure.

587. The Chairperson of the Council of the Republic shall make a proposal on the inclusion of the issue under consideration in the agenda of the Council of the Republic after receiving the opinion of the standing commission. In the event of consideration of the law returned by the President of the Republic of Belarus and adopted by the House of Representatives in the previous wording, the Council of the Republic shall have the right to open discussion of the law without opening a hearing which includes voting the issue on approval of the law in the wording previously adopted by the House of Representatives.

588. After the discussion the presiding officer of the Council of the Republic is obliged to put the issue on the approval of the law in the previous wording adopted by the House of Representatives to a vote. The law shall be considered to be adopted if it has been approved by a majority of not less than two-thirds of the full composition of the Council of the Republic. The law shall be considered to be rejected if less than two-thirds of the full composition of the Council of the Republic cast their votes.

589. The Council of the Republic shall draw up a decision on rejection or approval of the law returned by the President of the Republic of Belarus and adopted by the House of Representatives in the previous wording. The law approved by the Council of the Republic together with the resolution of the Council of the Republic on the approval of the law shall be forwarded by the Chairperson of the Council of the Republic for the signature to the President of the Republic of Belarus within five days.

590. Under the same procedure the Council of the Republic shall consider the objections of the President to certain provisions of the law that have been returned for repeated voting. In this instance, prior to the relevant decision of the House of Representatives and the Council of the Republic, the law shall be signed and enforced without the provisions where there are the objections of the President.

591. In case of repeated consideration by the House of Representatives of the law returned by the President of the Republic of Belarus, it is adopted in the new wording, and then the draft law shall be considered by the Council of the Republic as a new one.

§5. PARLIAMENTARY HEARINGS AND OTHER FORMS OF CONTROLLING ACTIVITIES

592. The Parliament shall have the right to hold parliamentary hearings with invitation of the officials whose field of activities will be involved during the hearings. According to the Rules of Procedure, the parliamentary hearing is a form of activity of the House of Representatives which comprises the presentation of information and opinions of the deputies of the House of Representatives, representatives of the State bodies and public associations, experts and specialists in concrete problems or other issues related to the competences of the House of Representatives.

593. Parliamentary hearings shall be held following a decision of the House of Representatives. Proposals with specifications of the topic in question and motivation of the necessity of holding of parliamentary hearings shall be made in written form by any given legislator, by the Council of the Republic, by standing commissions, or by groups of deputies.

594. The issue of holding parliamentary hearings shall be put to the consideration of the House of Representatives at the next plenary session. The initiator of the proposal on holding of parliamentary hearings shall demonstrate the necessity of holding them in the House of Representatives. The Council of the House of Representatives shall give its opinion by considering the given issue.

595. The decision on holding parliamentary hearings shall be taken in the form of resolution. The resolution on holding parliamentary hearings shall specify their date, time, place, topic (opening or closing), as well as the bodies of the House of Representatives that are charged with the organization and holding of parliamentary hearings. The bodies that organize the hearings shall specify the composition of the group invited for the parliamentary hearings.

596. Parliamentary hearings, as a rule, shall be open to representatives of the mass media and the public. They have special seats in the public hall of the House of Representatives. Secret parliamentary hearings shall not allow for the representation of the mass media. Parliamentary hearings shall be conducted by the Chairperson of the House of Representatives or the Deputy thereof or, according to decision of the Council of the House of Representatives, by the chairperson of the standing commission that is in charge of the issues under consideration. If the organization and holding of the parliamentary hearings are entrusted to several commissions, then the control of the parliamentary hearings may be given to the chairperson or the deputy chairperson of the leading commission on the issue under consideration. The presiding officer shall give the floor to the deputies of the House of Representatives and those invited, shall organize discussions, and shall provide information on the issue. Parliamentary hearings shall be started with the opening remarks of the presiding officer who shall inform those present about the essence of the issue under discussion, its significance, the procedure of the holding of parliamentary hearings, and the composition of the group of participants. Consequently, the floor shall be given to the rapporteur on the issue under discussion. The rapporteur may put questions both in written form and orally. After the replies given by the rapporteur the floor shall be given to the deputies of the House of Representatives and the persons invited. The time limit for the reports and appearances shall be granted according to the procedure specified by parts two and three of Article 68 of the Rules of Procedure, unless otherwise specified by the House of Representatives in its decision.

597. The persons invited and presented at the parliamentary hearings must observe the procedure of parliamentary hearings. The presiding officer shall be entitled to remove those causing disturbances from the hall. Parliamentary hearings shall be recorded and taken down in shorthand by the Secretariat of the House of Representatives. The presiding officer shall sign the record of parliamentary hearings. Recommendations of open parliamentary hearings may be published and referred to the mass media. Materials of parliamentary hearings in secret sessions shall be provided to the participants and nobody else. Similar rules are also fixed in the Rules of Procedure of the Council of the Republic (Article 129–137). Due to its specific nature the Parliament shall have the right to control activities concerning the execution of the adopted acts (laws, resolutions).

598. Hearings on the report of the Prime Minister about the programme of activities of the Government and approval or rejection of it shall also be considered as an instrument of control over the executive, as well as exerting the influence on the development of the national economy and the economic system (Article 97.5 of the Constitution).

599. The approval of the budget of the republic and its implementation (Article 97.2) shall also signify that Parliament shall have both legislative and control functions. It is possible to study the process of implementation of the budget during the year in question in commissions of the chamber of the Parliament for the purpose of preparing debates in the House of Representatives.

600. The Council of the Republic as the chamber of territorial representation shall also have the relevant controlling powers. As a sound display of this function one may highlight the right to repeal decisions of the local Councils of Deputies that are not in line with legislation (this is possible only as a result of the examination of the legality of a decision); and the adoption of decision on dismissal of the local Councils of Deputies where it systematically and flagrantly violates the requirements of the law and other instances determined by the law (points 5 and 6 of Article 98).

601. The current wording of the Constitution (Article 103) is the origin of the norm under which one sitting a month shall be reserved for questions of the deputies of the House of Representatives and members of the Council of the Republic and replies of the Government. The Rules of Procedure of the chambers of the Parliament shall specify the norm in question in detail. Thus, according to Article 239 of the Rules of Procedure of the House of Representatives the term for the holding of this sitting shall be put on the agenda of the session. Decisions on joint sessions for questions of the deputies of the House of Representatives and members of the Council of the Republic shall be adopted according to the procedure specified by the Rules of Procedure.

602. Deputies of the House of Representatives shall forward their questions for their referral to the Government in written form to the Secretariat of the House of Representatives no later than seven days before the beginning of the work of the session. Questions must contain brief requests about information or decisions as regards the issues within the competence of the Government. The list of questions and their order of priority shall be approved by the Chairperson of the House of Representatives or by his/her Deputy and shall be referred to the deputies of the House of Representatives before the beginning of the work of the session. Invitations for the members of the Government with the list of questions shall be forwarded thereto no later than five days before the beginning of the work of the session.

603. After the reply of a member of the Government, a deputy who put a written question in advance shall have the possibility to put the member of the Government one oral question for clarification and to speak not more than five minutes on the merits of his/her written question. If a member of the Government has no possibility to be at the sitting of the House of Representatives, he/she shall have the right to give the written reply to the questions, and the deputies of the House of Representatives shall be informed about it by the Chairperson of the House of Representatives or by his/her Deputy. If a deputy of the House of Representatives who put the question is not satisfied with the written answer, he/she shall have the right to raise the question once again to the Government according to the procedure specified by the Rules of Procedure.

604. In this time the deputies of the House of Representatives may also open other issues in written and in oral forms to the members of the Government who take part in the session. Both chambers shall take part in the procedure of impeachment, i.e., removal of the President from the office (Articles 88, Article 97.9, and Article 98.7 of the Constitution).

605. Consideration of decrees, as well as consideration by the Council of the Republic of decrees of the President on the introduction of a state of emergency, martial law, general or partial mobilization and taking on the appropriate decision shall be yet another instrument for carrying out control of the government's activities.

606. Activities of the standing and temporary commissions of the chambers of the Parliament according to the provision thereon (Article 105 of the Constitution) may be also aimed at the realization of the control function. The deputies of the House of Representatives, members of the Council of the Republic shall also have strong means of control. In particular, we must speak here about their right to make requests, appeals and proposals.

Chapter 4. The Executive

§1. The Organs: The Notion of the Government

607. The Government is a collegial, central body of the State power of the Republic of Belarus that shall exercise executive power and leadership of the State bodies and other bodies of the executive subordinated to it under the Constitution. The Government has important place in the system of state bodies. It shall be the basic and the central institution in the administration of state affairs.

608. In the Republic of Belarus the Government has the name of the Council of Ministers.

609. The Government shall have close relations with other state bodies and, first of all, with the President and the Parliament. The influence of the President on government and on its activities is typical for a presidential republic. The President, who formally and legally is a member of none of the branches of power, has, however, a number of constitutional competences in the field of the executive branch of power which signify that he is the real head of this branch of power as in other presidential republics.

610. The modern history of the Republic of Belarus has not borne witness to coalition governments. From the beginning of the nineties their members were more often communists, than former CPSU members. It should be noted that in 1994–1995 ministers were representatives of other parties, however, the Government in that case was formed not on the basis of party affiliation but on the grounds of professional criteria, and the significance of the membership of the Council of Ministers in question was not crucial for the parties which delegated their members to the composition of the Government, but rather for the President, who imposed his will to appoint this or that person to the relevant post in the Government.

611. The Constitution of the Republic of Belarus does not contain an exhaustive list of members of the Government. Article 106.4 of the Basic Law shall only specify that the Government shall consist of the Prime Minister, his Deputies and Ministers. Heads of other central state bodies may also be members of the Government.

612. According to Article 84.7 of the Constitution, the structure of the Government shall be specified by the President. The President shall also appoint and dismiss the Deputy Prime Ministers, Ministers and other members of the Government. The President of the Republic of Belarus shall specify the number of members of the Government, including Deputies of the Prime Minister.

613. The Prime Minister shall manage the activities of the Government. Under Article 106 of the Constitution the Prime Minister shall directly manage the activities of the Government and hold personal responsibility for its activities; sign the acts of the Government; report on the Programme of the Government within two months after his appointment and submit to the Parliament, and in the case of its rejection submit a second report on the Programme of the Government within two months; inform the President on the basic guidelines of activities of the Government and on all the most important decisions; exercise other functions connected with the organization and activities of the Government. Other powers of the Prime Minister shall be stipulated by laws and decrees of the President, as well as resolutions of the Government. The Prime Minister shall settle the most important issues. Apart from management of the activities of the Council of Ministers, the Prime Minister shall also tackle the issues of economic reform, issues of international financial and credit organizations, defence, domestic and foreign affairs, judicature and budget.

614. The Government shall resign before the newly elected President of the Republic of Belarus. Before forming a new composition of the Government, the current composition of the Council of Ministers shall continue to hold office on the request of the President until a new Government shall have been formed. The forming of the Government shall usually be started with the appointment of the Prime Minister by the President. It shall take place with the consent of the House of Representatives. Nobody but the President shall be entitled to nominate the candidate for the Prime Minister. It is inadmissible to have an alternative candidate. Deputies of the House of Representatives shall have only one right – carrying out a discussion of the proposed candidate and agreeing or disagreeing with the proposal of the President.

615. The Constitution shall not specify the time period for the President to submit the proposal of his candidate for the office of the Prime Minister to the House of Representatives. The Basic Law, however, shall fix the time period within which the House of Representatives must take its decision on giving consent to the appointment of the Prime Minister. It should be realized within two weeks after receiving the proposal as regards the candidacy for the office of the Prime Minister.

616. The Rules of Procedure of the House of Representatives shall specify the definite procedure for the consideration of the issue on giving consent to the President for the appointment of the Prime Minister. According to the Rules of Procedure of the House of Representatives, the presentation by the President of the appointment of the Prime Minister shall be considered in the standing commissions of the specified chamber of the Parliament, the opinions of which shall be reported by the standing commission authorized to deal with the issues of the state building before the voting.

617. Deputies of the House of Representatives shall have the right to put questions to the President, to express their opinions with respect to the proposed candidate to the office of the Prime Minister, and to speak for and against this individual.

618. The decision on giving consent to the appointment of the Prime Minister shall be passed by the House of Representatives by secret vote with a paper ballot.

The decision of the House of Representatives on giving consent to the appointment to the post of the Prime Minister must be drawn up by a resolution. In the instance of a discrepancy between the President and the House of Representatives as regards appointment of the Prime Minister, it must be overcome under the procedure enshrined by the Constitution. Thus, under Article 106.5 of the Constitution, if the House of Representatives reject the submitted nomination of the Prime Minister twice, the President shall appoint the acting Prime Minister of his choice, and dissolve the House of Representatives and call new elections.

619. Legislation does not ban the repeated submission of a candidature to the office of the Prime Minister to the Parliament. Therefore, one must not exclude the situation of a repeated refusal of consent for the appointment of the Prime Minister taking place with respect to both the same candidature and other (new) candidature. The Constitution enshrines no special qualifications for the election of the Prime Minister. There are no requirements the individual to be a deputy or other elected official. It is important for the candidate to be a citizen of the Republic of Belarus.

620. The Head of State, who, in principle, is free to make a choice, shall carry out the formation of the Government as a whole. In practice, the Prime Minister shall submit the relevant candidates for the consideration of the President. Deputies of the Prime Minister, Ministers and other members of the Government, as well as chairpersons of state committees which are not in the composition of the Government, and heads of other national state bodies shall be appointed to the office and removed from the office by the President of the Republic of Belarus. Deputy Ministers and heads of state committees shall be appointed to the office and removed from the office by the Council of Ministers with the consent of the President of the Republic of Belarus.

621. Legislation of the Republic of Belarus shall not specify the necessity for the expression of no confidence in the composition of the Government or to its programme in order to take up office. Quite the reverse, the effective Constitution shall grant the Government more guarantees for its peaceful and purposeful work, however, it assumes the possibility for the Parliament to exert influence on the course of the Government. Thus, under point three of part seven of Article 106 of the Constitution the Prime Minister shall submit a report to the Parliament on the Programme of the Government within two months after his appointment, and in the instance of its rejection submit the second report on the Programme of the Government within two months. Under point five of part one of Article 97 of the Constitution, the House of Representatives shall hear the report of the Prime Minister on the policy of the Government and approve or reject it; a second rejection by the chamber of the policy of the Government shall be deemed as an expression of no confidence in the Government. Undoubtedly, in the instance of approval of the policy, the Parliament shall in fact express its confidence in the Programme of the Government, as well as in its policy.

622. Deputies of the House of Representatives shall have the right to put questions to the Prime Minister, to express their opinions on the presented programme of activities of the Government and to campaign for or against it. Decisions on this issue shall be drawn up by resolution of the House of Representatives adopting a majority of votes from the full composition of the House of Representatives. If a decision on the approval of the programme of activities of the Government is not adopted, the programme is considered to have been rejected.

623. In the instance of rejection of the programme of activities of the Government, the House of Representatives shall fix the time period for the hearing of the second programme of activities of the Government in its resolution, but no later than two months after the day of rejection of the programme. The Constitution states that if the programme of activities of the Government has been approved after all, the issue of the liability of the Government may not be discussed in the course of the year after its approval (Article 97.7). In this particular case, to our mind, we shall speak about a certain dependency of the Government on the Parliament and even liability of the Government (but during the specific period of activities).

624. As for the Head of State, proceeding from his constitutional competence, he may also hold the members of the Government liable (this includes dismissal from office) before the expiration of the time period in question.

§2. Legal Status

625. Constitution of the Republic of Belarus shall not definitively specify the terms of powers of the Government. The only specification is that the Government shall resign before the newly elected President. It is possible to come to the conclusion: due to the election of the President, the Government shall also be formed all over again. Therefore, it is possible, with certain objections, to reveal that the term of powers of the Government shall be the same as the term of office of the President. Moreover, one should bear in mind the right of the House of Representatives to a vote of no confidence in the Government, and its right to refuse confidence in the Government with all the ensuing consequences, the right of the President to change the members of the Government (to take resignation and appointment of new members of the Government).

626. As it was emphasized, the Government shall resign before the newly elected President of the Republic of Belarus. However, this must take place not after declaration of results of elections of the President, but after assuming the office by the Head of State, i.e., after taking the Oath (Article 83 of the Constitution).

627. Due to the fact that the formation of the new composition of the Government takes time, the President shall have the right to charge the former composition of the Government to continue its duties until a new Government shall have been formed.

628. The Constitution shall not envisage the obligation of the President to receive the consent of the House of Representatives to the dismissal from office of the Prime Minister by the Head of State. Having this right, the President must simultaneously inform the House of Representatives on the adopted decision.

629. Under Article 106.7 of the Constitution, the Government or any member therein shall be entitled to tender its resignation to the President, if he/she deems it impossible to discharge the duties entrusted with him/her.

630. The Government shall tender its resignation to the President, if the House of Representatives have passed a vote of no confidence in the Government. The Prime Minister may request a vote of à confidence from the House of Representatives with regard to the governmental programme or any other concrete issue. The Prime Minister shall submit the proposal on the consideration of the issue on a vote of confidence in the Government to the Chairperson of the House of Representatives. Preliminary preparation and the procedure of inclusion of the given issue in the agenda of the session shall be carried out according to the procedure specified by the Rules of Procedure. The decision on a vote of confidence in the Government shall be deemed to have been adopted if the majority of the full composition of the House of Representatives casts its votes. If a no confidence vote is passed by the House of Representatives, the President shall be entitled to accept the resignation of the Parliament or to dissolve the House of Representatives within ten days and call for new elections. If the resignation of the Government is rejected, the latter shall continue to discharge its duties. The Constitution shall enshrine both the collective and the individual liability of the Government and its members.

§3. Competences of the Government of the Republic of Belarus

631. The Government, as a central state body, shall have a wide scope of powers that make it possible to successfully affect public relations.

632. The basic powers of the Government are specified in the Constitution of the Republic of Belarus (Articles 106–108). They are revealed in the details in the Law 'On the Council of Ministers of the Republic of Belarus'.

633. Under the Constitution and the laws on the economic sphere, the Government shall put in place a uniform economic policy; regulate activities of all the branches of economy of the Republic of Belarus, take measures on their development; elaborate the forecast, concepts, state programmes of economic and social development of the Republic of Belarus, and ensure their realization; elaborate the basic guidelines of the development of economy as a whole, and of its specific branches; take measures on the acceleration of scientific and technical progress; elaborate the basic guidelines of the domestic and foreign policy, and take measures to its implementation; take measures on securing the most favourable rates of the growth of gross national income and its rational distribution; act on behalf of the State as the owner of state property of the Republic of Belarus, exercise management of the State property; has the right to create, reorganize and liquidate enterprises, organizations, establishments, and associations of which the property is in the sole possession of the Republic of Belarus; improve the integration of economy of the Republic of Belarus and the economy of other states taking into account the interests of the Republic of Belarus, submit the relevant proposals to the President of the Republic of Belarus and to the House of Representatives of the National Assembly of the Republic of Belarus; establish economic liability of the economic entities for the violation of the procedure of carrying out economic activities, if the laws of the Republic of Belarus and the acts of the President of the Republic of Belarus specify no such liability; within the powers granted by the President of the Republic of Belarus, regulate external economic activities, including the specification of measures of tariff and non-tariff regulation of imports and exports of goods and services on the territory of the Republic of Belarus; ensure the attraction of foreign investments; create conditions for free entrepreneurship on the grounds of the equality of all forms of ownership; exercise a uniform state policy in the use and protection of lands, within its powers carry out withdrawal and granting plots of land; coordinate investment activities taking into account the priority of the directions of social and economic development of the State; determine state insurance policy; ensure the exercise of a uniform state policy in the field of the use and saving of energy and materials, take measures on providing the Republic of Belarus with those resources, etc.

634. In the field of budget and finances the Government shall secure the execution of a uniform financial, credit and monetary policy; annually elaborate and submit the draft national budget and the report on its execution to the President of the Republic of Belarus for referral to the National Assembly of the Republic of Belarus; grant governmental guarantees according to the procedure specified by the President of the Republic of Belarus; elaborate and carry out measures on the exercise of a uniform credit and monetary policy, specify measures on securing the balance of monetary income and expenditure of the population, the improvement of financial status of the branches of economy and the use of credit resources, as well as regulate the exchange rate of Belarusian rouble as jointly with the National Bank of the Republic of Belarus; secure the creation, distribution and use of credits which form the external debt of the Republic of Belarus; specify state policy in the field of protection of the rights of consumers; carry out interactions with the National Bank of the Republic of Belarus, and receive statistical and other information on the activities of the banks.

635. In the field of employment the Government shall take measures on the right to work, the right to choose one's profession, occupation and work according to the individual's vocation, capabilities, education, professional skills and taking into account public need, as well as health and safety conditions; elaborate and carry out measures on the rational location of production, putting into effect relevant demographic policies; take measures on forming and improvement of the motivated mechanism of labour activity, strengthen the role of material and moral incentives in enhancing the efficiency and quality of labour; exercise a uniform state policy aimed at securing full and effective employment of the able-bodied population, including improving the branch structure of the national economy and territorial location of the means of production; fixing the minimum wage, as well as specifying the forms, systems and rates of remuneration of the civil servants; finally, the Government shall determine the State migration policy.

636. The Government is called to carry out wide spectrum of arrangements in the social and cultural spheres. It shall secure the exercise of a uniform state policy in the field of science, culture, education, health care, ecology and social security; create conditions for maintaining the stipulated by the legislation of the Republic of Belarus at a secure level; take measures to secure the social protection of citizens, develop the system of social protection; take measures to improve of the system of professional orientation, create conditions for vocational training, acquire new professions, encourage retraining and improvement of workers' skills; take measures on disability prevention and organization of rehabilitation of invalids; specify and carry out the most effective ways of increasing the income of a family through grants, pensions and other social benefits and payments; elaborate and carry out social and economic measures on the improvement of the position of women: strengthen and safeguard the family; ensure control over observance of the rights and guarantees granted the women; take measures on the elaborations and realization of the State youth policy; take measures on the development and strengthening of the network of the State general, vocational and specialized secondary and higher educational institutions; ensure the effectiveness of the State policy in the field of securing the sanitary welfare of the population, and determine the main direction of development and improvement of the system of public care, using new methods of management in this sphere; contribute to the development of physical training and sport; take measures on the improvement of the work of cultural establishments, archives, ensure the protection of historical and cultural heritage, the restoration and conservation of monuments, the accumulation and use of cultural assets, including folk arts, for the spiritual and aesthetic well-being of citizens, enhance their cultural level, as well as contribute to the development of the arts, literature, national book-publishing and periodicals; create conditions for the free development of culture of all the national communities residing in the Republic of Belarus; carry out the State policy directed to the preservation of the Belarusian and Russian languages, creation of proper conditions for the improvement of the status of the languages of other national communities residing on the territory of the Republic of Belarus; take measures on securing the right of citizens of the Republic of Belarus to freedom of religious and political beliefs; finally, ensure a uniform scientific and technical state policy.

637. In the sphere of environment the Government shall determine the State policy in the field of environmental protection, and the procedure of use of natural resources; determine the State policy in the field of meteorological activities; take measures on safeguarding the scientifically sound use of natural resources and the improvement of the environment; determine the State policy in securing technical, nuclear and radiation safety of potentially dangerous objects, in the prevention of disasters and catastrophes; ensure the elaboration and realization of state ecological programmes; approve the list of the natural resources and environmental objects of special value; specify the procedure of counting and keeping state cadastres of natural resources; carry out environmental monitoring; adopt decisions on the creation of nature reserves, national parks, reserves and other natural territories of national significance and elaborate the special regime of their protection, approve the provisions therein and their borders; approve the procedure of working out ecological arrangements; fix the limits of use of natural resources and location of waste; in the instance of necessity declare certain lands of the territory of the Republic of Belarus to be the zones of ecological emergency; organize works on the liquidation of the effects of the Chernobyl Nuclear Power Station (NPS) disaster and take measures on its realization; secure the development of a system of ecological education and upbringing of citizens.

638. In the sphere of legality and law and order the Government shall take measures on securing the rights and freedoms of citizens, and the protection of interests of the State, the safety of ownership and public order, the prevention of crime; secure the State rights and freedoms of citizens, individual protection against any illegal actions, infringements on the life, health, property, honour and dignity, as well as protection of a citizen of the Republic of Belarus both in the territory of the Republic of Belarus and out of its bounds guaranteed by the Constitution of the Republic of Belarus, by laws and by international obligations; determine the main directions of legal policy in the State bodies; carry out activities of national state bodies as regards securing law and order and legality, and the realization of state programmes on the prevention of crime; exercise measures on the prevention of the creation and activities of political parties, public associations and religious organizations which have the aim of forcing change of the constitutional system or which carry out propaganda of war or racial hatred; prevent citizens from performing their state, public, family duties which would cause harm to their health and morals.

639. In the sphere of national security and defence the Government shall take measures on the protection of national security, defence capacity, independence and territorial integrity of the Republic of Belarus, except for those which are carried out by the President of the Republic of Belarus or by other state bodies specified by the President; solve issues of military building, provide the Armed Forces and other military units of the Republic of Belarus with everything required for the sound and reliable armed protection of the republic, as well as the building and location in the territory of the Republic of Belarus of means of defence; exercise control over preparation of citizens for the military service and their recruitment, as well as regulate conscripts and men liable to call-up; carry out the preparation of the national economy of the Republic of Belarus for work under conditions of wartime, as well as mobilized deployment; submit mobilizing plans of the Republic of Belarus to the approval of the President of the Republic of Belarus, as well as plans of accumulation of material values in mobilized reserve; conduct civil defence of the Republic of Belarus according to its competences.

640. In the sphere of foreign policy the Government shall carry out the coordination of activities in the field of relations of the Republic of Belarus with other states and international organizations; take practical measures on the realization and protection of foreign-policy interests of the Republic of Belarus; hold negotiations and conclude international treaties on the issues within its competences; take measures on securing the implementation of international treaties of the Republic of Belarus.

641. The Government shall perform a number of other powers, in particular in the field of personnel. It shall oversee the activities of national state bodies, and local executive and administrative bodies. The Government shall interact actively with the National Assembly, as well as with the local Councils of Deputies as regards the issues in the legislative sphere, execution of the laws.

§4. Organization of Activities of the Government of the Republic of Belarus

642. The work of the Government of the Republic of Belarus shall be organized by the Prime Minister. The Prime Minister shall carry out direct leadership of its activities, shall be at the head of its sittings and is responsible in person for its work.

643. In accordance with the law the sittings shall be held when necessary, but at least once every three months. Sittings of the Council of Ministers of the Republic of Belarus shall be valid if not less than the half of the composition of the Government of the Republic of Belarus takes part in them.

644. The presiding officer at the sitting of the Council of Ministers of the Republic of Belarus shall be the Prime Minister of the Republic of Belarus. In case of the absence of the Prime Minister of the Republic of Belarus, the sittings shall be held by the First Deputy Prime Minister of the Republic of Belarus, and in case of absence of the latter, under the instruction of the Prime Minister of the Republic of Belarus, as well as with the consent of the President of the Republic of Belarus, by one of the Deputies of the Prime Minister of the Republic of Belarus.

645. The President of the Republic of Belarus shall have the right to be the presiding officer at the sittings of the Government of the Republic of Belarus.

646. Decisions of the Council of Ministers of the Republic of Belarus shall be adopted by the majority of the members of the Government of the Republic of Belarus who take part in the sitting. If the votes are equal, the presiding officer shall have the deciding vote.

647. The law shall specify the issues that are subject to the exclusive consideration of the Council of Ministers, and, for that reason, resolutions of the Government may be adopted, but not orders of the Prime Minister. These are the issues of preparation and execution of the national budget, the creation and use of state extra-budgetary funds; projects or programmes of the economic and social development of the Republic of Belarus; the main directions of national and foreign policy of the Republic of Belarus.

648. According to the law, for the operative solution of the issues that are within the competence of the Council of Ministers of the Republic of Belarus there exists the Presidium of the Council of Ministers of the Republic of Belarus with the Prime Minister and Deputies of the Prime Ministers of the Republic of Belarus as its standing body. The President may also include other members of the Government of the Republic of Belarus in the composition of the Presidium.

649. Sittings of the Presidium of the Council of Ministers of the Republic of Belarus shall be held if necessary, but at least once every two weeks with the Prime Minister of the Republic of Belarus as the presiding officer, and in case of his absence, with the Deputy Prime Minister of the Republic of Belarus. In case of the absence of the Deputy Prime Minister of the Republic of Belarus, on the instruction of the Prime Minister of the Republic of Belarus and after coordination with the President of the Republic of Belarus, sittings of the Presidium of the Council of Ministers of the Republic of Belarus shall be held with one of the Deputies of the Prime Minister of the Republic of Belarus as the presiding officer.

650. Sittings of the Presidium of the Council of Ministers of the Republic of Belarus are considered to be valid with the presence of more than half of the full membership of the Presidium. Decisions of the Presidium of the Council of Ministers of the Republic of Belarus shall be adopted by a working majority and shall have the form of resolutions of the Council of Ministers and they must be in line with acts adopted at the sittings of the Council of Ministers of the Republic of Belarus. In case of equality of votes the vote of the presiding officer shall prevail.

651. As for certain urgent issues or as regards the issues that need discussion, the law shall assume the possibility to adopt resolutions of the Council of Ministers of the Republic of Belarus by members of the Presidium of the Council of Ministers of the Republic of Belarus (without consideration at sittings).

§5. Acts of Government

652. Article 108 of the Constitution envisages that the Government shall issue acts that have binding force in the entire territory of the Republic of Belarus. The Prime Minister shall issue orders, which are under his jurisdiction.

653. The Law 'On the Council of Ministers of the Republic of Belarus' contains the list of issues that may be subject to solution by the Government as a collegial body and, therefore, as a result of their consideration the resolutions shall be adopted. The law also specifies the instances when the Prime Minister may issue orders. The orders shall be issued on the issues that are within the competence of the Prime Minister of the Republic of Belarus, as well as with the presence of the Government of the Republic of Belarus on the issues that are within the competence of the Council of Ministers of the Republic of Belarus, but that are not referred to the constitutional authorities of the Council of Ministers of the Republic of

Belarus, if their regulation does not require the adoption of decisions of normative nature.

654. Thus, on the grounds of the law, the Prime Minister may be delegated certain powers following a decision by the Government. Decisions on certain issues may be drawn up as the protocols of the meetings at the office of the Prime Minister of the Republic of Belarus, and their instructions and assignments are obligatory for the execution by the officials of the Apparatus of the Council of Ministers of the Republic of Belarus, and by national state bodies subordinated to the Council of Ministers of the Republic of Belarus. In addition, those instructions and assignments may be of normative nature. All the other instances require the adoption of resolutions of the Government as a collective body or its Presidium.

655. Resolutions of the Council of Ministers of the Republic of Belarus shall be enforced from the date of their adoption, if they do not envisage some other term that may not be previous to the date of adoption of a resolution. Moreover, resolutions related to the rights, freedoms and obligations of citizens shall be subject to enforcement under the law only after their official publication. In the opinion of the author, acts improving the position of citizens may be given retroactivity, and there is no obligation for them to be enforced only after their publication.

656. In case of the publication of the resolution in several official editions in different time periods, the initial publication shall be the term of its enforcement. The publication of resolutions of the Council of Ministers of the Republic of Belarus in the Collection of decrees, edicts of the President and resolutions of the Government of the Republic of Belarus, as well as in the mass media fixed by legislation, shall be considered as official publication.

657. The Council of Ministers of the Republic of Belarus shall secure control over the execution of its resolutions directly or through the State bodies and other bodies of the executive subordinated to it. Resolutions of the Government must be in line with the Constitution, laws, decrees, and edicts of the President of the Republic of Belarus. Analysis of Article 84.25 and Article 116 shall prove this.

658. Resolutions of the Government may be repealed by the edicts of the President, and be found null and void fully or in part by the Constitutional Court in the instance of their submission for its consideration as regards the verification of constitutionality of a resolution. The National Assembly shall not be entitled to repeal the acts of the Government; however, the National Assembly may initiate the proposal to the President or to the Constitutional Court.

Chapter 5. The Judiciary in the Republic of Belarus

§1. Organization of the Judiciary

659. Under Article 6 of the Constitution of the Republic of Belarus the judiciary is one of three branches of power. The principles of its constitutional and legal status shall be enshrined in Chapter 6 of the Constitution, as well as in the Code of the Republic of Belarus on Judicial System and Status of Judges, and in other enforceable enactments.

660. If the legislative power shall be exercised by one body – the Parliament – and in certain specific instances – the President – then judicial power shall be exercised by all the judicial bodies from top to bottom. Each of them is faced with the task to safeguard and protect the rights and freedoms of citizens against infringements on the part of the State bodies, officials and citizens in the name of the Republic of Belarus. The judiciary is the State power exercised by the courts within the procedure specified by the law as regards the consideration of the cases on the constitutionality of enforceable enactments, and the settlement of criminal, civil, administrative and other disputes.

661. Article 109 of the Constitution determines that the courts shall exercise judicial power, meaning that the courts shall be the holders of judicial power. At the same time (with certain observations), we may note that 'judicial' power shall be also occasionally exercised by other state bodies (e.g., the President by issuing the act of pardon or the Parliament by adopting a law on an amnesty). However, the legal nature of decision of the specified bodies is rather different: it shall proceed from the fact of the proof of guilt of persons with respect to whom acts of pardon or amnesty are applying, but who shall be subject to mitigation of the sentence prescribed them by the court.

662. The judiciary, just like any other state power, emanates from the people (Article 3 of the Constitution). Such origins are conditioned not only by the fact that the courts deliver their decisions in the name of the Republic of Belarus, but also by the fact that the judges shall hold their posts due to their appointment by a representative body (the President, the Council of the Republic) which are granted their powers directly or indirectly by the people.

663. The total range of the courts that administer justice shall be the system of the judiciary. The system of the judiciary shall be built on the principle of territory and specialization. The judicial system of the Republic of Belarus shall consist of the Constitutional Court and the courts of general jurisdiction (led by the Supreme Court). In accordance with the decree of the President of the Republic of Belarus of 29 November 2013 No. 6 'On improvement of the judicial system of the Republic of Belarus', the Supreme Economic Court merged with the Supreme Court. The judicial system shall be specified by the law, the Code and the Constitution shall prohibit the formation of special courts.

664. The effects of rulings of the Constitutional Court shall cover all the territory of the Republic of Belarus. The scope of effects of courts of general jurisdiction shall be determined by the territorial level of the courts. The system of courts of general jurisdiction shall consist of the Supreme Court, oblast, the City of Minsk City, and district (city) courts, the economic courts of oblasts and the Economic Court of the City of Minsk (economic courts of cities and regions have not been created yet).

665. Economic courts shall settle economic disputes emerging from civil, administrative and other legal relations. The Economic Code of Procedure of the Republic of Belarus shall specify the subjects which are entitled to appeal to the economic court: (1) legal entities and citizens who carry out entrepreneurial activities without being a legal person and who have the status of the entrepreneur; (2) organizations that are not legal entities (labour collectives included) and citizens who are not individual entrepreneurs in the instances specified by the legislative acts. The same right is granted to the Public Attorney, the State and other bodies in the instances specified by the legislative acts. In all the other instances the disputes on the application of the law shall be examined in the common courts, but, as regards the constitutionality of enforceable enactments, in the Constitutional Court.

666. Thus, outward specialization is fixed in the Constitution and in current legislative acts: the Constitutional Court, courts of general jurisdiction. Each judicial system and each judicial establishment shall have its own (inner) specialization, i.e., compositions of courts, specialization of judges (labour, tax, administrative, criminal, including the categories of crimes, etc.).

667. The judicial system in the Republic of Belarus shall be specified by the Constitution (Article 116), the Code of the Republic of Belarus on Judicial System and Status of Judges.

668. The formation of special courts shall be prohibited. Under all circumstances, even at wartime, due to an emergency situation and martial law, the right to administer justice may not be restricted; justice must be administered under the generally fixed procedures. Therefore, while taking special measures during the period of emergency, the rights stipulated in part two of Article 63 and Article 60 of the Constitution may not be limited.

669. In administering justice, judges shall be independent and subordinated to law alone. Any interference in judges' activities in the administration of justice shall be impermissible and liable to legal action (Article 110 of the Constitution).

670. Article 6 of the Constitution shall fix the principle of separation of powers and that is the grounds for existing of the independent court.

671. First of all, there is a stipulation of the functional independence of the court: in administering justice, judges are independent and subordinated to law alone. This means a certain inadmissibility of putting pressure or other 'influence' upon the positions of judges while administering the function of justice. Undoubtedly, the trial presupposes the expression of various, usually opposite points of view. However, the trial itself shall be carried out according to established procedures. It is the task of the court to maintain their observation. Threats with respect to the court are inadmissible in the building of the court or outside it.

672. Any interference in judges' activities in the administration of justice shall be impermissible and liable to legal action. At this point we are speaking about the subordination of judges to the law. We deem that the term 'law' in this particular case shall be subject to realization in the broad sense, including the Constitution (Article 137, as well as comment to Article 112 of the Constitution).

673. Civil and Criminal procedure shall be based on the norms that exclude unlawful influence on the court. This legislation shall also specify the rights and obligations of the participants of the trial, and the possibility of appealing against the delivered judicial rulings according to the procedure of cassation and supervision.

674. The procedure of substitution and dismissal of a judge (their irrevocability, and the preservation of office within the term of powers), and the inadmissibility of combining the office of judge with performing other work (Article 111 of the Constitution) shall enshrine the independence of the court.

675. The Code of the Republic of Belarus on Judicial System and Status of Judges shall cement the constitutional norms about the independence of judges: functional independence shall be supported by organizational independence. The independence of judges shall be secured by the procedure of their election, appointment and dismissal, immunities of judges, the legal procedure of administering justice, the secrecy of the retiring room while delivering rulings and a ban on the disclosure of how the judge came to his decision, the liability for disrespect to the court or interference in solution of concrete cases, the creation of the necessary organizational and technical conditions for the activities of the courts, as well as the material and social status enjoyed by the judges.

676. According to the law the mass media shall not be entitled to prejudge the results of the proceedings as regards the concrete case or possible influence on the judge or on the court by some other means. The judge must not give any interpretations on the points of fact of the cases examined or which are in the process of consideration, as well as to give this information a person or in the instances and under the procedure specified by the law of procedure (Article 64 of the Law in question).

677. The significant guarantee of the independence of judges shall be their inviolability. Inviolability of the judge shall cover accommodation, official accommodation, transport and means of communication, correspondence, property and documents he/she uses. The judge may not be called to criminal liability without the consent of the body that elected or appointed him/her, taking into account the opinion of a qualified panel of judges. The judge may not be subject to detention or personal examination, and may not be brought to the court. The judge may not be called for any liability for opinions or decisions expressed or made while administering justice, unless his/her guilt in criminal misuse has been found by a valid verdict of the court. The judge detained on suspicion of committing a crime or an administrative offence, or brought to the body of internal affairs or to some other state body, must be released immediately after his/her identification, except for instances of detention concerning a possible crime. Only the Attorney-General of the Republic of Belarus may conduct a criminal case with respect to the judge.

678. Penetration into the accommodation or office accommodation of the judge, inspection of his/her correspondence, tapping of phones, as well as investigations carried out according to the sanction of the Public Attorney may take place if permission is granted by the Attorney-General of the Republic of Belarus or the person acting for him/her, or under judicial ruling and only as regards cases already being judged.

679. In the instance of giving consent for calling a judge to criminal liability or giving consent for imprisonment, a decision on suspension of his/her powers shall be adopted simultaneously. Criminal cases with respect to judges shall be liable for trial only by the Supreme Court of the Republic of Belarus. The material and social status of judges, as well as measures of their legal and social protection shall contribute to their independence. As for the direct independence of the judge, it shall be revealed in the adopted rulings where the main requirement is conformity with the Constitution and the law.

680. At the same time, under Article 111 of the Constitution judges may not engage in business activities or perform any paid work, apart from teaching and scientific research. The grounds for electing judges and their dismissal shall be determined by the law. One may presume that it is also admissible to be engaged in creative activities, if it shall not affect the independence of the court. Judges may not be deputies or members of the Council of the Republic. The procedure for the substitution of offices of the judges shall be specified by the law on the judicial system and the status of judges (special requirements shall be produced for the office of the judge of the Constitutional Court).

681. There are at least three main requirements with respect to the candidate for the office of judge: (1) the relevant education; (2) a certain age limit; (3) relevant moral characteristics. Thus, according to Article 62 of the Code of the Republic of Belarus on Judicial System and Status of Judges in the Republic of Belarus' a judge must be a citizen of the Republic of Belarus aged 25 or above who has a higher legal education (except for the judges of the Judicial Intellectual Property Panel of the Supreme Court of the Republic of Belarus who may have both higher legal education and higher technical or natural scientific education) who have committed no discrediting deeds, who have served as lawyers for not less than three years and who passed the state exam. The candidate for the office of the judge of Intellectual Property Panel who has no legal education must have a length of service in the field of patenting of not less than five years. Moreover, candidates for the office of judges of oblast or Minsk City courts, and the Belarusian Military Court must have a length of service as a judge of not less than three years; judges of the Supreme Court of the Republic of Belarus must have a length of service as a judge of not less than five years.

682. Previously, the judge on administrative cases and executive proceedings must be a citizen of the Republic of Belarus aged 23 or above who has a higher law education and who has committed no illegal deeds. At present, there is the effective rule – the age of 25. The candidates who are appointed as judges or those who are taking new posts must submit their individual information according to the procedure specified by legislation on civil servants in the body dealing with the preparation of the decision in question. The law shall specify the grounds for the termination of powers of a judge. Judges may be deprived of their powers for the intended violation of legality or committing deeds that are not compatible with their high rank according to the decision of the body that elected or appointed the judge, as well as due to the enforcement of a court sentence delivered with respect to them.

683. Judges shall be discharged according to their state of health preventing the continuation of their work; due to election or appointment to another office or due to transferring with his/her consent to another profession; after the expiry of a five-year time period of being in office (for persons appointed for the first time) and refusal of appointment as a judge without a time limit; under the opinion of the qualified panel of judges on the impossibility of further holding of the office of the judge; of their own concord; as a result of loss of nationality of the Republic of Belarus. The decision on the dismissal of the judge shall be adopted by the body which appointed him/her taking into account the opinion of the qualified panel of judges (courts of law) in instances stipulated by the Code of the Republic of Belarus on Judicial System and Status of Judges. The procedure of the withdrawal of powers of judges and their dismissal shall be specified by the legislative acts of the Republic of Belarus.

684. The courts shall administer justice on the grounds of the Constitution and other acts adopted in accordance with it. If, during the hearing of a specific case, a court concludes that an act is contrary to the Constitution, it shall make a ruling in accordance with the Constitution and raise, under the established procedure, the issue of whether the act in question should be deemed unconstitutional. Cases before a court shall be tried collegially, and in the instances specified in law, by judges individually (Article 113 of the Constitution).

685. Criminal and Civil legislation shall specify the instances of consideration of cases before the courts both collegially and by individual judges. The collegial consideration of criminal cases has as its aim to exclude possible legal errors as regards the most complicated cases. According to Article 10 of the Criminal Code of Procedure (hereafter also referred to as CCP) the criminal case in the Court of First Instance shall be subject to consideration collegially, and in instances stipulated by the law by the judge individually. In this particular case the judge shall act on behalf of the court where he/she was appointed. The judge shall consider cases individually in all the courts as in first instance as regards crimes punishable by a deprivation of freedom for a term of up to five years, as well as for a term from five to ten years, if the accused finds himself/herself to be guilty and who agrees to consideration of the case by the judge individually. Collegial consideration of cases in all the courts shall be exercised in the first instance by a judge and two 'People's Assessors' as regards crimes punishable by deprivation of freedom for a term of more than ten years or by the death penalty. Consideration of cases according to the procedure of cassation and supervision shall be exercised by a panel composed of not less than three judges.

686. As for cases that need long-term proceedings, the reserve People's Assessor may be called upon. The reserve People's Assessor may participate in the sitting from the beginning of the given case and to substitute for the People's Assessor in the instance of his/her withdrawal. If the reserve People's Assessor, who acts instead of the removed People's assessor, requires no renewal of the trial, the proceedings shall continue (Article 26 of CCP).

687. The judge may not take part in consideration of the case if he/she is a victim, civil plaintiff, civil defendant, witness, as well as if he/she took part in the case as an expert, specialist, interpreter, inquirer, investigator, Public Attorney, public accuser, legal counsel, lawful representative of the accused person, representative of the victim, civil plaintiff and civil defendant; if he/she has kinship with the victim, civil plaintiff, civil defendant or their representatives, has kinship with the accused or his/her lawful representative, has kinship with the Public Attorney, Public Prosecutor, legal counsel, public defender, investigator or inquirer; if there are other circumstances that make it to think that the judge individually, directly or indirectly, is interested in the given case. Persons who have kinship with each other may not be in the composition of the court that examines the criminal case (Article 27 of CCP).

688. The judge who took part in consideration of the criminal case in the Court of First Instance may not participate in the consideration of this case in the court of cassation or, according to the procedures of supervision, in the Presidium of oblast and Minsk City courts, in the Belarusian Military Court, on the Military Panel of the Presidium of the Supreme Court of the Republic of Belarus. He/she may not participate in any new consideration of the case in the Court of First Instance in the case of a repeal of the sentence or delivery of a ruling on the termination of the case where he/she took part.

689. The judge who took part in consideration of the criminal case in the court of cassation may not participate in the consideration of this case in the Court of First Instance or, according to the procedures of supervision, in the Presidium of oblast and Minsk City courts, in the Belarusian Military Court, on the Military Panel of the Presidium of the Supreme Court of the Republic of Belarus. He/she may not participate in any new consideration of the case in the Court of First Instance in the case of a repeal of the sentence or delivery of a ruling on the termination of the case where he/she took part.

690. The judge who took part in consideration of the case according to the procedure of supervision in the Presidium of oblast or Minsk City courts, the Presidium of the Supreme Court of the Republic of Belarus may not participate in the consideration of the same case in the Court of First Instance or the court of cassation.

691. The judge who took part in consideration of the criminal case as in first instance, according to the procedure of cassation or supervisory procedure may not participate in the consideration of this case in the Presidium or Plenum of the Supreme Court of the Republic of Belarus (Article 28 of CCP). The new Civil Code of Procedure shall regulate the issues of consideration of cases in the first instance according to the procedure of cassation and according to the judicial supervisory procedure.

692. The proceedings in all of the courts shall be open. Secret hearings shall be admissible only in instances specified by the law and with the observance of all the rules of proceedings. The important principle of the trial shall be its open nature. According to Article 13 of CCP the proceedings in all the courts shall be open, except for the instances where it does not meet the interests of protection of state secrecy, as well as in instances specified by the Code. Secret proceedings shall be also admissible under the motivated ruling of the court and by the judge on cases related to the crimes where persons under the age of 16 are involved, cases related to sex crimes, as well as on the other cases for the purposes of prevention of disclosure of information about the private lives of persons who are participants of the case. Secret hearings shall be carried out with the observance of all the rules of proceedings. In the open trial the verdicts shall be pronounced in public. In the secret trial only the motivated part of the verdict shall be pronounced in public. According to Article 17 of the CCP the consideration of the civil cases in all the courts shall be open. Secret proceedings shall be held for the purposes of protection of information containing state or commercial secrets or related to the secrecy of adoption, or other information whose disclosure is prohibited by the law. The court may hear the case as a whole or carry out certain procedural actions in secret for the prevention of disclosure of information concerning the private lives of citizens or information that defames their dignity, honour or business standing. As a result of the request of parties or one party and without the objections of the persons legally interested in the outcome of the case, the court may consider any case in secret. Only the persons interested in the outcome of the case, and in the instances of necessity witnesses, experts, specialists, and interpreters may take part in consideration of the case or in making certain procedural actions. The secret trial shall be held in observance of all the rules of procedure specified by the given Code. The motivated part of the decision of the court shall be pronounced in public. The court shall deliver a ruling as regards the consideration of the case in secret.

693. Justice shall be administered on the basis of competition between the parties in the process. Judicial rulings shall be obligatory for all citizens and officials. Litigants shall have the right to appeal against decisions, sentences and other judicial rulings.

694. The role of the judiciary is to secure the supremacy of law expressed in the universally acknowledged principles of international law, the Constitution, laws, international treaties of the Republic of Belarus, other acts of all-state and other levels as a result of an emerging legal conflict.

695. The outcome of administering justice is the substitution of the rule of violence by the rule of law. Thus, the court, by using the law, shall act on public relations by establishing, changing or terminating legal relations. Rulings of the courts are not always fair and lawful. For securing the supremacy of law, rulings shall be subject to the mechanism of the verification of the constitutionality of delivered decisions. Here the right to make cassation or supervisory complaints, measures which the Public Attorney can use, increase the possibilities for constitutional control.

§2. The Constitutional Court of the Republic of Belarus

696. The legal status of the Constitutional Court shall be specified by the Constitution (Articles 40, 59, 60, 112, 116, 122, etc.), as well as by the Code of the Republic of Belarus on Judicial System and Status of Judges with further alterations and addenda and the law of the Republic of Belarus of 8 January 2014 No. 124-w 'On constitutional proceedings'.

697. The Constitutional Court shall be formed as follows: six judges of the Constitutional Court shall be appointed by the President, and six judges shall be elected by the Council of the Republic (upper chamber of the Parliament). The Chairperson of the Constitutional Court shall be appointed by the President from among the judges with the consent of the Council of the Republic. The term of office of the judges is eleven years. It is admissible to serve repeated terms of office as a Constitutional Judge. Under the Constitution, the Constitutional Court shall be entrusted to supervise the constitutionality of normative acts in the State.

698. The Constitutional Court, on the recommendations of the President of the Republic of Belarus, the House of Representatives, the Council of the Republic, the Council of Ministers, the Supreme Court shall produce rulings on: the conformity of laws, decrees and edicts of the President, international agreements and other obligations of the Republic of Belarus to the Constitution and other instruments of international law ratified by the Republic of Belarus; the conformity of instruments of interstate formations of which the Republic of Belarus is a part, edicts of the President of the Republic of Belarus which are issued to ensure the execution of the law, the Constitution, the laws, decrees and instruments of international law ratified by the Republic of Belarus; the conformity of the ordinances of the Council of Ministers and orders of the Supreme Court, the Supreme Economic Court, Attorney-General to the Constitution, laws and instruments of international law ratified by the Republic of Belarus; the conformity of enactments of any other state body to the Constitution, laws and decrees, as well as to the laws and instruments of international law ratified by the Republic of Belarus. Thus, the Constitutional Court shall give judgments on the constitutionality of acts of both higher state bodies and normative acts of ministries, departments, and local Councils of Deputies and executive and administrative bodies. This, certainly, shall promote a strengthening of constitutional control. The Constitutional Court shall consider the issues of constitutionality of the given acts both as a whole and their particular provisions.

699. According to Article 85 of the Law 'On constitutional proceedings' judgments of the Constitutional Court are final and subject to no appeal or protest.

700. According to the law, the Constitutional Court shall have the right to make proposals to the chambers of the Parliament, the President, the Council of Ministers of the Republic of Belarus and other state bodies on the necessity of the amendment of acts of current legislation, as well as the adoption of new normative acts. Those proposals are subjects to obligatory examination. The Constitutional Court shall also have the right to make other proposals to the State bodies that follow from its competence.

701. The law 'On constitutional proceedings' specifies that laws, decrees and edicts of the President, international treaty and other obligations of the Republic of Belarus, acts of interstate formations where the Republic of Belarus is part, resolutions of the Government, acts of the Supreme Court, the Attorney-General, and acts of other state bodies that were found to be at variance with the Constitution or acts of more higher legal force shall be considered to be null and void as a whole or in part from the moment fixed by the Constitutional Court. Thus, the Court has a certain measure of freedom in its actions and that shall also impose additional responsibility on it. Previously, for example, in case of the Court finding acts that violate human rights and freedoms to be unconstitutional, they were considered to be invalid as a whole and in particular from the moment of adoption of the relevant act. It is easy to imagine the problems that may have appeared when after many years of effect of such an act, this act is found to be unconstitutional.

702. Cases shall be considered by the Court at its plenary sessions by the full composition of the Court under the rules of constitutional proceedings stipulated by the Law 'On the constitutional proceedings'. Sittings of the Court are valid with the presence of not less than eight judges.

703. The final decision must be proclaimed within fifteen days from the moment of finishing the hearing. The presiding officer shall cast the deciding vote. Judges shall vote for and against and have no right to abstentions or to fail to take part in voting. The judgment of the Constitutional Court is considered to have been adopted if the majority of the full composition of judges cast their votes for it. In case of the equality of votes, a decision is considered to have been adopted in favour of the constitutionality of the challenged act.

704. Under the Constitution and the law the Constitutional Court shall have other important powers. Thus, it may give its judgment on instances of systematic or flagrant violation of the Constitution of the Republic of Belarus by the chambers of the Parliament, which may be the grounds for their dismissal.

705. The Constitutional Court shall prepare annual messages to the President and to chambers of the Parliament on constitutional legality in the country. In accordance with the legislation of the Republic of Belarus activities of the Constitutional Court shall be financed by a separate budgetary instrument.

Chapter 6. Independent Non-political Bodies in the Legislative or Executive Branch with an Advisory or Supervisory Task

§1. Advisory Bodies

706. The Constitution (Article 37) and current legislation enshrine the holding of national and local assemblies. The Law of 12 July 2000 'On National and Local Assemblies' specifies the procedure of initiating, calling and holding assembly meetings, as well as the competences of national and local assemblies in the Republic of Belarus. The first All-Belarusian People's Assembly was gathered in Minsk of 19 October 1996 with 5,000 persons in number, including 800 people from the City of Minsk and 650 people from each oblast following Decree of the President of the Republic of Belarus of 29 August 1996 No. 341 'On the Calling of the All-Belarusian People's Assembly' for the purposes of ensuring a fuller participation of wider categories of population in discussion of measures related to overcoming the economic crisis, and the stabilization of the social situation in the society. Theses Assemblies found their regular nature. In 2010 the fourth All-Belarusian People's Assembly took place.

707. According to the law a National Assembly may be called if necessary by the President of the Republic of Belarus for discussing important issues of state and public life and the drafts of the relevant decisions. The norms of representation and the procedure of election of the authorized persons to take part in the National Assembly, as well as the composition of the organizational committee as regards the preparation and holding of the National Assembly shall be fixed by the President of the Republic of Belarus.

708. Participants of the National Assembly shall be elected by labour collectives, by citizens at the meetings according to their place of residence, education or service, by the higher bodies of political parties, trade unions, and religious organizations, and by other public associations that represent all the administrative and territorial units of the Republic of Belarus.

709. The President of the Republic of Belarus, the Prime Minister of the Republic of Belarus, members of the Government of the Republic of Belarus, deputies of the House of Representatives and members of the Council of the Republic of the National Assembly of the Republic of Belarus, the Chairperson of the Constitutional Court of the Republic of Belarus, the Chairperson of the Supreme Court of the Republic of Belarus, the Chairperson of the Central Commission of the Republic of Belarus on elections and holding of national referenda, the Attorney-General of the Republic of Belarus, the Chairperson of the Board of Directors of the National Bank of the Republic of Belarus, representatives of national state bodies, local Councils of Deputies, executive and administrative bodies, other state bodies, associations and organizations subordinated to the Government of the Republic of Belarus, bodies of territorial public self-government, political parties, trade unions, religious organizations and other public associations shall have the right to be the participants of the National Assembly.

710. Officials of diplomatic and consular missions in the Republic of Belarus, representatives of Belarusian Diaspora in other states, and representatives of international organizations and other public associations may be invited to take part in the National Assembly. Officials of diplomatic and consular missions in the Republic of Belarus, representatives of Belarusian Diaspora in other states, and representatives of international organizations and other public associations shall not take part in the adoption of decisions by the assembly.

711. The Chairperson of the organizational committee on the preparation and holding of the National Assembly shall open the National Assembly. The following working bodies shall be elected by the participants for securing the work of the assembly: Presidium; Secretariat; Mandate Commission; Drafting Commission; Accounts Commission. The Presiding Officer elected by the Presidium of the assembly shall be entitled to conduct the National Assembly.

712. Decisions of the National Assembly shall be adopted as resolutions of the assembly as a result of open voting by the majority of the participants and shall be submitted to the President of the Republic of Belarus within three months.

713. The President of the Republic of Belarus shall consider the resolution of the National Assembly and, as regards the issues that are directly within his competence, shall take a decision. As for the issues related to the competences of the relevant state bodies, the Administration of the President of the Republic of Belarus shall transfer the resolution of the National Assembly for its consideration and decision to these bodies.

714. The decision on resolution of the National Assembly must be adopted within three months after the date on which the Administration of the President of the Republic of Belarus received it. The Administration of the President of the Republic of Belarus or the relevant state bodies shall inform the citizens of the Republic of Belarus according to the established procedure.

715. The President of the Republic of Belarus by his Decree of 8 December 2011 No. 573 'On the Council for Legal and Judicial Affairs under the President of the Republic of Belarus' has set up the Council as the consultative body for the discussion of the most important legal problems.

The Council on the legal and judicial activities of the President of the Republic of Belarus is a permanent advisory body to the President of the Republic of Belarus, established to discuss critical issues related to the implementation of the President of the Republic of Belarus in the field of law, and to develop proposals for the improvement of judicial activity.

The main tasks of the Council are:

- preparation of proposals for the formation, implementation and development of the state policy in the field of law in the judicial system and judicial proceedings, analysis of the progress of its implementation and enforcement practice;

- forensic analysis of the activities for the preparation of proposals to improve the organization of courts, including the logistics, staffing courts, enforcement proceedings, raising the professional level of judges and strengthen guarantees of independence;
- development of measures to coordinate the activities of state bodies, other state organizations in the field of law as well as the courts, prosecutors and other law enforcement agencies in the field of administration of justice, the decisions of the President of the Republic of Belarus on legal and judicial activities and monitoring their implementation;
- development of recommendations on improvement of the normative and enforcement activities, coordination of research in the field of law;
- consideration of the operation, development and content of information and legal resources of the global computer network, including the National Legal Internet Portal of the Republic of Belarus, the Children's legal site, and appropriate recommendations;
- prediction based on jurisprudence and practice of public relations, the results (consequences) of application of legislative acts;
- preparation of proposals on improvement of legal work with the population, development of the system of legal education;
- proposal of annual plans for preparation of draft laws;
- study of draft legislation and the preparation of the proposals;
- study of the problems of training of legal personnel, including scientists of the highest qualification and acquisition of state bodies and other organizations, the preparation of recommendations to address these problems.

§2. Organs of State Control

716. In the Republic of Belarus there are two main systems of bodies in the field of carrying out controlling and (according to the specific legal status) supervisory functions: the Committee of State Control and the Public Attorney's Office.

717. Adoption of the acts of legislation presupposes control over their implementation. Previously that was the function of the bodies of the Committee of People's Control (closed as a result of the decision of the Supreme Soviet of the Republic of Belarus), after that the Supervisory Office formed by the Supreme Soviet (prior to 1994). Under the new wording of the Constitution the Committee of State Control is entrusted to carry out state control over the execution of the national budget, use of state property, implementation of the acts of the President, the Parliament, the Government and other state bodies that regulate relations of state assets, as well as economic, financial and tax relations. The distinctive feature of activities of the Committee of State Control: control on its behalf is its role in the field of the economy.

718. The main task of the Committee of State Control shall be the exercise of state control over execution of the national budget, use of state property, implementation of the acts of the President, the Parliament, the Government and other state bodies governing relations of state assets, economic, financial and tax relations.

719. The Law of 1 July 2010 'On the Committee of State Control of the Republic of Belarus and its territorial bodies' shall specify the main directions of activities of the Committee of State Control and its territorial bodies. According to Article 2 of the law the Committee and its territorial bodies shall exercise control over: the execution of the national and local budgets (including state purpose budget funds), budgets of state extra-budget and innovation funds; observance of the legislation in the field of relations of state property, economic, financial and tax relations in the system of local budgets, the State budget and extra-budgetary funds, as well as under the specified procedure carry out verification of execution of the republican budget for the current financial year; use (expenditure) of means of the republican and local budgets for financing activities of the state bodies, other state organizations; taking measures on de-bureaucratization of the state machinery; implementation of the legislation on the issues of rent, privatization and other disposal of objects of state property; observance by the state bodies, other organizations, including residents of free economic zones, and by individual entrepreneurs of the legislation in the field of innovation activities; use (expenditure) by organizations and individual entrepreneurs of budget means, means of state purpose budgets of state extra-budget funds, innovation funds, state property, measures of state support; the legality of use by organizations and individual entrepreneurs of material resources acquired for the state means; observance by state bodies, banks, non-banking credit and financing organizations, other organizations and individual entrepreneurs of legislation regulating the use of credit and currency funds; observance by state bodies, other organizations that carry out revisions, the procedure and exercise of revisions; financial and economic activities of state bodies, including diplomatic representations and consulates of the Republic of Belarus; observance of legislation with rare land metals, precious metals and stones in all types and conditions, including the products made thereof, with products or scrap thereof, including obtaining, collection, dispatch, realization, consumption, accounting, stock-taking, storage, delivery, transference (transportation), processing of rare land metals, precious metals and stones, as well as their collection and registration in the State Fund of Precious Metals and Stones of the Republic of Belarus; observance of the specified procedure of accounting, collection, storage, transportation, use, purchase, processing, delivery and realization of metal production, ferrous and non-ferrous metals and their scrap; implementation of the legislation in the field of state property relations, economic, financial and tax relations in accordance with the laws and decisions of the President of the Republic of Belarus, the National Bank of the Republic of Belarus, other banks, non-banking credit and financial and insurance organizations; observance of the legislation on securities; delivery of goods (works, services) for the State needs; observance by organizations and citizens of legislation that specifies the rules of trade, works, services, the procedure of formation of prices (rates) for goods (works, services), as well as discipline of prices by realizing goods (works, services), requirements to the quality of goods (works, services), their safety for life, health and property of citizens and that regulates protection of consumers' market and the rights of consumers; execution of by the state bodies, other organizations and citizens of the legislation that regulates the foreign trade activities, including lawful use of state means while carrying out foreign trade operations; observance of legislation while making currency operations, including entrance to the Republic of Belarus of export currency receipts, import delivery of goods (works, services, protected information, exclusive rights to the results of intellectual activities), buying and selling, as well as use of currency; activities of organizations and citizens that carry out financing operations as regards observance by them of legislation on prevention of legalization of criminal income and financing of terroristic activities. The Committee of State Control and its territorial bodies within their competence shall: exercise, in accordance with the procedure stipulated by the legislative acts, coordination of the planned inspections that are carried out by controlling (supervising) bodies; take preventive measures of infringements in economic sphere under the Law in question, other laws and resolutions of the President of the Republic of Belarus; take part according to the stipulated procedure in fighting against corruption and organized crime, including in interaction with other state bodies and other organizations; consider according to the legislation applications of citizens and legal entities, organize personal reception of citizens by specialists of the Committee of State Control and its territorial bodies, representatives of legal entities included; exercise control on other issues and perform other functions in accordance with the law and resolutions of the President of the Republic of Belarus. The Committee of State Control shall specify the list of methods and means for exercising inspections by bodies of the Committee of State Control. The Committee of State Control shall adopt within its competence normative legal acts, carry out obligatory agreement of draft legal acts in instances envisaged by legislative acts. Committee of state control of oblasts shall carry out obligatory agreement of draft normative legal acts of relevant bodies of local government and self-government on issues of privatization of state property.

The Committee and its territorial bodies shall exercise control over: the execution of the national budget, observance of the legislation in the field of financial and tax relations in the system of local budgets, the State budget and extra-budgetary funds; spending the means of national and local budgets in the maintenance of state bodies, reservation and disposing of state property; implementation of acts of legislation as regards the issues of renting, as well as privatization and other alienation of objects of the State property; observance by the State bodies and other legal entities (including the residents of free economic zones) of acts of legislation in the field of investments; the legality of use of state resources by legal entities and individual entrepreneurs; observance by state bodies and banks of legislation regulating the use of credit and currency funds; the situation of control and revision work in the State bodies, as well as the inspection of other legal entities and individual entrepreneurs; financial and economic activities of the State bodies, representations and establishments of the Republic of Belarus acting abroad and subject to financing by the national budget; performance of legislation in the field of obtaining, consumption, accounting and storage of precious metals and stones in all types and conditions, as well as collection and registration of their scrap in the State Fund of Precious Metals and Stones of the Republic of Belarus; observance of legislation while using ferrous and non-ferrous metals, adhering to the procedure of collection, accounting, storage, use, and processing of ferrous and non-ferrous metals and their scrap; implementation by the National Bank of the Republic of Belarus and other banks, and by insurance and non-banking financial organizations, of legislation regulating state property, economic, financial and tax affairs; observance by members of the securities market, in conjunction with the National Bank of the Republic of Belarus and by other legal entities carrying out activities related to regulation of the specified market and of legislation while issuing, floating and circulating the securities; shipment of goods for state needs; observance by legal entities and individual entrepreneurs of legislation regulating the rules of trading and servicing the population, the procedure of price formation for goods and the price discipline while selling goods, the quality of manufactured goods, their safety as regards the life, health and property of the consumers and the protection of the rights of the consumer; implementation by state bodies, other legal entities and individual entrepreneurs of legislation regulating the procedure of carrying out external economic activities, as well as the legality of use of state means while carrying out external economic transactions; observance of legislation on carrying out currency transactions in the territory of the Republic of Belarus.

720. The Committee of State Control shall be formed by the President of the Republic of Belarus and the Chairperson of the Committee shall be subordinated directly to the President. The system of the bodies of the Committee of State Control shall be formed of the Committee of State Control and its territorial bodies – committees of state control of oblasts and interregional committees of state control. According to decision of the President of the Republic of Belarus, the territorial bodies of the Committee of State Control may be created in the cities and regions of the Republic of Belarus. The structure and the number of the members of the staff shall be subject to approval by the President of the Republic of Belarus. The Chairperson of the Committee of State Control shall be appointed and dismissed by the President of the Republic of Belarus. The Chairperson of the Committee of State Control shall have personal responsibility for the solution of the tasks vested in the Committee of State Control and its territorial bodies. The First Deputy Chairperson and Deputies of the Chairperson of the Committee of State Control shall be appointed and dismissed by the President of the Republic of Belarus according to the advice of the Chairperson of the Committee of State Control. Chairpersons of territorial bodies of the Committee of State Control, except for the districts and cities, shall be appointed and dismissed by the Chairperson of the Committee of State Control of the Republic of Belarus with the consent of the President of the Republic of Belarus. The procedure of appointment and dismissal of the chairpersons of districts, cities and territorial bodies of the Committee of State Control shall be determined by the President of the Republic of Belarus.

721. The Committee of State Control shall form collegiums with the Chairperson of the Committee of State Control (the presiding officer), his/her First Deputy and Deputies (ex officio) and other officials of the Committee of State Control and its territorial bodies. The number and personal composition of collegiums shall be determined by the President of the Republic of Belarus according to the advice of the Chairperson of the Committee of State Control.

722. The territorial bodies of the Committee of State Control, except for districts, cities, shall form collegiums with the Chairperson of the Committee (the presiding officer), his/her First Deputy and Deputies (ex officio) and other officials of the territorial bodies of the Committee of State Control. The number and personal composition of collegiums shall be determined by the Chairperson of the Committee of State Control according to advice given by the Chairpersons of the relevant territorial bodies of the Committee of State Control.

723. Equally with the Constitution and the specified law, the issues related to the competence, organization and procedure of activities may be also regulated by other laws (e.g., by the Administrative Code), acts of the President (decrees, edicts), other enforceable enactments, as well as in international treaties of the Republic of Belarus.

724. The Law of the Republic of Belarus of 8 November 1994 'On Auditing Activities' with further alterations and addenda shall specify the legal grounds for carrying out auditing activities in the territory of the Republic of Belarus, stipulate the rights and obligations of auditing organizations and auditors, as well as regulate the process of state control of the auditor and the auditing business.

725. Auditing activities (audit) – entrepreneurial activities as regards the independent inspection of accounting, bookkeeping and other documents of organizations, their units, individual entrepreneurs (hereafter referred to as audit persons) and in case of necessity and as a result of the inspection of their activities that shall be reflected in a financial book to express an opinion on the authenticity of financial bookkeeping and the conformity between economic transactions and legislation.

726. Auditing organizations, auditors who carry out activities as individual entrepreneurs shall exercise an audit of: the authenticity of annual bookkeeping; the correctness of transactions on written records; the purpose of use of credit and investments; the financial condition of investors; the financial condition of issuers of securities; other indicators of financial and economic activities of an organization or an individual entrepreneur in instances specified by legislation.

727. As it has been already emphasized, Belarus has a system of bodies known collectively as the Public Attorney's Office that are called to carry out supervision of legality. However, first of all, we must pay attention to the difference of the notions 'control' and 'supervision'. The distinction shall be revealed in those measures that the State bodies may apply with the relevant functions. Supervisory bodies usually do not have the right to annul a legal act, and by way of the relevant reaction shall try to secure legality in practice. As for controlling bodies, on the contrary, they shall be notable not only for the right to annul legal acts, but also for their active interference in unlawful activities. For the controlling bodies it is typical to have the right to make an evaluation of one's activities from the point of view of usefulness. In this respect this resembles the controlling function of the Constitutional Court. Constitutional control shall cover the sphere of norm making from the top to bottom. Moreover, the problem of expediency shall not be of a decisive significance. In addition, the adoption of a less popular decision that finds its realization in an enforceable enactment does not mean its unconstitutionality. Here is the difference of constitutional control from the control carried out by other state bodies, departmental control included.

728. The Attorney-General of the Republic of Belarus and subordinated Public Attorneys shall be entrusted to supervise the strict and unified implementation of the laws, decrees, regulations and other enforceable enactments by ministers and other bodies subordinated to the Council of Ministers, as well as by local representative and executive bodies, enterprises, organizations establishments, public associations, officials and citizens. The Public Attorney's Office shall exercise supervision over the implementation of the laws determining the execution of the verdicts of the courts in civil, criminal and administrative cases in instances determined by the law, and carry out preliminary investigation and support state charges in the courts.

729. Legal literature very often discusses the issue about the legal nature of the bodies of the Public Attorney's Office and their place in the system of the State bodies. To our mind, the Public Attorney's Office is not part of the judiciary or the legislature. The Public Attorney's Office is closer to the executive; in the Republic of Belarus its status has certain peculiarities of formation and subordination. Internationally, very often the bodies of the Public Attorney's Office shall be subordinated to the Ministry of Justice and, therefore, have a specific scope of powers. Proceeding from the experience of the development of our state, and an absence of stable traditions of respect of the law, the specified supervisory body is needed.

Part III. The State and Its Subdivisions

Chapter 1. State Form

§1. Unitary State

730. The Republic of Belarus is a unitary state from the point of view of the State system, being a state that has no other states in its internal structure. There is one effective Constitution, a unique system of legislation and organization of courts, a single citizenship, and a sole legislative body, which is bicameral.

731. Belarus as a unitary state shall have administrative and territorial divisions.

Chapter 2. Component States or Entities

§1. General Description

732. Under the Constitution, the territory of the Republic of Belarus shall be the natural condition of the existence of the Belarusian nation and the spatial limit of the people's self-rule, as well as the basis for the prosperity and the sovereignty of the Republic of Belarus (Article 9). The territory of Belarus shall be unified and inalienable. Moreover, according to the Electoral Code, issues that may infringe upon the territorial integrity of the Republic of Belarus may not be subject to a referendum (Article 112). Article 9 of the Basic Law envisages the division of the territory into regions (oblasts), districts, cities and other administrative-territorial units.

733. A number of normative acts have been issued for the purposes of solution of the issues of administrative and territorial formation, and the further development of constitutional norms on the territorial organization of our state. Among them we should mention the Law of 5 May 1998 'On Administrative and Territorial Division and the Procedure of the Solution of Issues of Administrative and Territorial Formation of the Republic of Belarus', Decree of the President of the Republic of Belarus of 29 September 1998 No. 468 'On the Approval of the Provision on the Procedure of the Solution of Issues Related to Merging Administrative-territorial Units of the Same Name and with a Common Administrative Centre', Resolution of the Council of Ministers of the Republic of Belarus of 5 August 1998 No. 1238 which approved a number of normative acts directed to the realization of the specified law, including the procedure of enumerating and registering administrative-territorial units of the Republic of Belarus, the procedure of naming and renaming enterprises, establishments, organizations, railway stations, airports and other objects located in the territory of the Republic of Belarus, as well as physical and geographical objects, the Provision on Place Names Commission under the Council of Ministers.

734. The administrative and territorial system of the Belarusian State provides for the division of territory of the Republic of Belarus into well-defined parts for the purposes of the effective organization of state government and local self-government, securing legality and law and order, and reinforcing the rights, freedoms and lawful interests of citizens of the Republic of Belarus (Article 13 of the Law). Administrative-territorial units of the Republic of Belarus shall be territories within the spatial limit of which and under the procedure specified by the law local Councils of Deputies, executive and administrative bodies shall be created and given certain powers. Administrative-territorial units in the Republic of Belarus shall be oblasts, regions, village councils, as well as cities and settlements of where local Councils of Deputies, executive and administrative bodies are created. In order to specify the spatial limits of the competences of local Councils of Deputies, executive and administrative bodies the name, borders and administrative centre shall be specified for each administrative-territorial unit. If necessary, the territories of cities shall be divided into districts (which are not independent administrative-territorial units) for an optimal organization of the execution of decisions related to the satisfaction of social, cultural and household needs of citizens, the protection of law and order and the observance of legality. The territory of the Republic of Belarus shall be divided into the capital of the Republic of Belarus and oblasts as administrative-territorial units. The oblast shall be divided into regions and cities of oblast subordination as administrative-territorial units. The region shall be divided into village councils, settlements of city type, cities of region subordination that are administrative-territorial units, as well as settlements of city type, cities of region subordination that are territorial units.

§2. Distribution of Powers

735. The competences of the national state bodies and local Councils of Deputies, executive and administrative bodies within the relevant administrative and territorial units shall be specified by the legislation of the Republic of Belarus.

736. The Law specifies that administrative-territorial and territorial units may be declared as closed territories due to the necessity of the stipulation of a special regime of the State government that is conditioned by requirements of national security, ecological and other demands. The procedure of finding the administrative-territorial and territorial unit to be closed and the peculiarities of its administration and operation shall be specified by the legislation of the Republic of Belarus.

737. The law contains the definition of the populated areas. A populated area is a densely populated part of the territory of the Republic of Belarus, the place of permanent residence of citizens with the necessary dwellings and other premises for the vital functioning of citizens, with its own name and territorial limits fixed under the prescribed procedure. The cities, urban and village localities shall be considered as populated areas. The Republic of Belarus has three categories of cities: the City of Minsk – the Capital of the Republic of Belarus; cities of oblast subordination; cities of region subordination.

738. Populated areas where the local Councils of Deputies are located, executive and administrative bodies shall be the centres of the relevant administrative-territorial and territorial units. There are the criteria for referring the populated localities to the categories. Populated localities of the Republic of Belarus shall be referred to definite categories depending on the size of the population; the level of development and specialization of production infrastructure and social and cultural infrastructure; finally state functions carried out in the relevant territory.

739. The categories of cities shall be: the City of Minsk – the Capital of the Republic of Belarus. The status of the City of Minsk shall be specified by the law. Cities of oblast subordination are populated localities with a population of not less than 50,000 persons which are administrative and large economic and cultural centres with the developed production and social infrastructure; cities of regional subordination are populated localities with a population of more than 6,000 persons which have industrial enterprises, a network of social, cultural and household relations, with perspectives of further development and increase of population.

740. The category of urban localities shall include: populated areas with a population of more than 2,000 persons which have industrial and communal enterprises, social and cultural establishments, trading enterprises, enterprises of public catering, consumer services; health-resort settlements, which are populated areas with a population of not less than 2,000 persons in the territory of which there are sanatoria, rest homes, guest houses, other health institutions, trading enterprises, enterprises of public catering, consumer services; workmen's settlements or populated areas with the population of not less than 500 persons located near industrial enterprises, electric power stations, projects, railway stations and other such objects. All the other populated areas (villages, settlements and other) shall be referred to in the category of village populated areas.

741. Alongside administrative-territorial units, the creation of territorial units of the Republic of Belarus shall be envisaged. Territorial units of the Republic of Belarus shall be populated areas where there are no local Councils of Deputies, no executive and administrative bodies, as well as territories of special regime of use (nature reserves, national parks, territories of historical and natural monuments, territories of defence purpose and other). The procedure of formation, reorganization, liquidation, use and registration of territorial units shall be specified by the Law of 5 May 1998 and other acts of legislation of the Republic of Belarus. In the Republic of Belarus there is an obligatory registration of territorial units. The law shall specify the competences of the State bodies in solving the issues of administrative-territorial system.

742. The main and the most important issues in that field shall be settled by the Head of State. Thus, according to Article 8 of the Law the President of the Republic of Belarus, as a result of the representation of the Council of Ministers of the Republic of Belarus and taking into account the opinions of local Councils of Deputies, shall: create and close oblasts and regions, specify and transfer their administrative centres, fix and change the borders of the City of Minsk, oblasts and regions; rename oblasts, regions, cities of oblast subordination and their regions, as well as the districts of the City of Minsk; take decisions as regards the disputes among the oblast Councils of Deputies related to the issues of the administrative and territorial system; refer the populated areas to the categories of the cities of oblast subordination, fix and change their borders, create, change and annual the districts in the cities; take decisions on the transfer of urban villages and urban localities to the administrative subordination of the city Councils of Deputies, executive and administrative bodies of the City of Minsk and cities of oblast subordination; combine, taking into account the opinion of the population and with the consent of local Councils of Deputies, the administrative-territorial units of the same name which have a common administrative centre into one unit. The procedure of liquidation of local Councils of Deputies, executive and administrative bodies of the relevant administrative-territorial units shall be determined by the President of the Republic of Belarus (Article 8).

743. The Law shall specify the powers of the Government and other bodies in the field of administrative-territorial system.

Chapter 3. Decentralized Authorities

744. In modern countries the centralized management of state affairs shall be combined with local government and self-government.

745. According to Article 2 of the Law 'On Local Government and Self-government in the Republic of Belarus' local self-government in the Republic of Belarus shall be in the form of the organization and activities of citizens for independent solutions directly or through the local bodies of social, political, and cultural issues elected by them and proceeding from the interests of population and peculiarities of the development of administrative-territorial units on the grounds of their own material and financial resources and attracted funds.

746. The Constitution, the Law on local government and self-government and certain other normative acts shall specify the system of local government and self-government. Under Article 117 of the Constitution local government and self-government shall be exercised by the citizens through local Councils of Deputies, executive and administrative bodies, bodies of public territorial self-government, local referenda, assemblies and other forms of direct participation in state and public affairs.

747. Local self-government shall be exercised within the borders of administrative-territorial units: village council, settlement, city, region, and oblast.

748. The main level of local self-government shall be local Councils of Deputies – representative bodies of state power in the territory of the relevant administrative-territorial units. Local Councils are called to secure the coordinated activities of the bodies of public territorial self-government.

749. The unique system of local Councils of Deputies in the Republic of Belarus shall consist of Councils of Deputies of settlements, villages, cities, regions, oblasts. The unity of the system of local Councils shall be ensured by the community of legal bases, principles of formation and activities, as well as the tasks they are called to solve in the interests of population, social and economic development of the relevant territory.

750. In our Republic there are three territorial levels of local Councils: the most powerful is the oblast. Classification of the Councils by groups shall make it possible to specify the powers of the Councils of different names more precisely in the legislation. The primary territorial level shall be Councils of villages, settlements, cities (cities of regional subordination); the next level shall be Councils of cities (cities of oblast subordination) and regions; the oblasts level shall be the Councils of oblasts and Minsk City Council shall have the rights of the Councils of based and oblasts level.

751. Under Article 118 of the Constitution local Councils of Deputies shall be elected by the citizens of the relevant administrative-territorial units for a four-year term.

752. Local self-government may not come only to the election and activities of the representative's bodies – local Councils of Deputies. It is more large-scale and must include local referenda, assemblies, work of the bodies of territorial public self-government and other forms of direct participation in state and public affairs.

753. The Councils shall create their bodies independently; specify their structure and competences, set up expenses for their maintenance according to the law and other acts of the legislation of the Republic of Belarus. The Councils of oblasts (Minsk City Council), regional and city Councils, (city of oblast subordination) shall set up presidiums. The Chairperson of the relevant Council shall organize the work of the City Council (city of regional subordination), Councils of settlement and village. Presidium of the Council shall consist of the Chairperson of the Council, his/her Deputy (Deputies), and chairpersons of standing committees of the Council. According to decision of the Council other deputies may join the composition of presidium. Chairpersons of standing commissions who are the members of the presidium shall perform their duties without breaking off their main official or production activities. The main form of activities of presidium of the Council shall be the meeting. Meetings of the Presidium of the Council shall be carried out if necessary, but at least once a quarter. Meetings of presidium of the Council shall be called and conducted by the chairperson of the Council or his/her Deputy in the instance of the absence of the chairperson. Decisions of the Presidium of the Council shall be adopted by the majority of its composition. Meetings of Presidium of the Council shall be judged valid with the composition of not less than two-thirds of its composition. The presidium of the Council shall: organize work as regards the calling of sessions of the Council, inform the deputies and the population about the date and place of session, as well as the issues submitted for consideration of the Council and decisions thereupon; exercise leadership of preparation of sessions, as well as issues submitted for the consideration of sessions; coordinate activities of standing and temporary commissions and groups of deputies, submit the proposals for the Council on the creation of standing commissions of the Council; organize control over implementation of decisions of the Council; inform the Council about its activities; render assistance to the deputies in the use of their powers and provide them with the necessary information; help the deputies in receiving visiting citizens, preparation of reports before the electorate, labour collectives; solve other issues stipulated by the legislation.

754. The Chairperson of the Council shall be elected from among the deputies at the session of the relevant Council by way of secret ballot and perform his/her duties before the opening the first session of the Council of new calling. The Chairperson of Councils of villages, settlements and cities (city of regional subordination) shall be, at the same time, the Chairperson of the relevant Executive Committee. Candidates for the office of Chairpersons of oblast (Minsk City) Councils shall be proposed by the deputies of the relevant Councils and the Chairpersons of the relevant higher Councils. The same procedure is for the proposals on dismissal of the Chairpersons of the Councils. Chairperson of the Council is considered to be elected; if more than half of the elected deputies of the relevant Council cast their votes for him/her. Chairperson of the Council in his/her activities is subordinated to the Council that elected him/her and may be dismissed only by the Council. The procedure of dismissal or retirement of the Chairperson of the Council shall be specified by the Rules of Procedure of the Council.

755. It is inadmissible to combine the office of the Chairperson of the Council with any other office, to carry out work for remuneration, except for work related to teaching, science or the creative industry, unless otherwise stipulated by the Law or other acts of the legislation of the Republic of Belarus. The Chairperson of the Council shall: represent the Council in relations with other state bodies, bodies of territorial public self-government, enterprises, organizations, establishments, associations and citizens; propose the candidature for the office of the Deputy Chairperson of the relevant Council for election at the session of the Council from among the deputies; be at the head of Presidium of the Council; report the Council about the state of affairs in the territory under the jurisdiction of the Council, as well as about the other issues related to his/her competence, present the report before the session of the Council and before the population if necessary, but at least once a year, about his/her activities, and the activities of the Presidium of the Council, and more generally to inform the citizens about the state of affairs in the territory under the jurisdiction of the Council; forward draft decisions of the Council for the opinion of the relevant standing committees, charge the Chairpersons of the standing committees with a certain affair or case; call sessions of the Council, organize the work concerning preparation of sessions of the Council, meetings of its Presidiums, conduct the meetings, secure its control over the execution of the adopted decisions; solve other issues according to legislation.

756. During the work of sessions from among the deputies of the Councils standing committees shall be elected for the preliminary examination and preparation of the issues related to the authority of the Councils, as well as organization and control over the execution of decisions of the Councils and higher state bodies. As for the Councils of villages, standing committees may not be created except for credentials committees. The procedure of election and activities of the standing committees shall be specified by the Rules of Procedure of the Council. Advisers and experts with the right to be heard may be engaged in the work of the committees under the procedure specified by the Rules of Procedure of the Council.

757. Recommendations of the standing committees shall be subject to obligatory consideration by the relevant state bodies, enterprises, organizations, establishments, associations and bodies of territorial public self-government. The committee shall be informed within a month about the results of the consideration of recommendations.

758. The system of local bodies of government shall consist of the territory of oblast, region, city, settlement, and village executive and administrative bodies. The

Executive Committee with an independent legal entity is the executive and administrative body in oblasts, regions, cities, settlements, and villages. According to Article 9 of the law on local government and self-government the Executive Committees of primary, intermediary and oblast levels shall be within the system of the bodies of the executive and are the bodies of the local government. The Executive Committee shall consist, apart from its Chairperson, of the Deputies of the Chairperson of the Executive Committee, an executive officer (secretary (in a village, a settlement, city (cities of regional subordination))), and members of the Executive Committee.

759. The distinctive feature of organization of local government power shall be the absence of parallel structures (representatives of the central power and local bodies of government).

760. Two branches of power shall take part in forming the Executive Committees. Thus, the Chairperson of oblast Executive Committee shall be appointed by the President of the Republic of Belarus and shall be approved by the oblast Council (Article 10 of the law on local government and self-government). The candidature for this office is considered to be approved if the majority of the elected deputies cast their votes for him/her. For instance, where the Councils of Deputies failed to approve a candidacy, the President of the Republic of Belarus would propose another candidature under the same procedure. In case of the repeated refusal of oblast and Minsk City Councils of Deputies to approve the candidature appointed to the office of the Chairperson of the Executive Committee, the decision of the President of the Republic of Belarus adopted with respect to this or that candidature shall be final. Legislation envisages the grounds for dismissal of the Chairperson of the executive commission.

761. Appointment and dismissal of the Chairperson of the Executive Committee shall be drawn up by Decree of the President of the Republic of Belarus. Candidatures of Deputy Chairpersons of the Executive Committee, the executive officer and the staff composition of the Executive Committee shall be agreed with the President, and after that the Chairperson shall have the right to make the relevant appointments. Appointment and dismissal of the Chairpersons of regional Executive Committees and proposals of their candidatures for the approval of regional Councils of Deputies shall be made by the Chairperson of the oblast Executive Committee. The Chairperson of the oblast Executive Committee shall also take the final decision on the appointment of the Chairpersons of regional (city) Executive Committees in case of any repeated refusal of the relevant Councils of Deputies to approve the proposed candidatures.

762. The Executive Committee within its powers shall take decisions. Decisions of the Executive Committee shall by adopted by a majority of votes of the fixed composition of the Executive Committee, shall be signed by the Chairperson of the Executive Committee and by the executive officer (secretary) of the Executive Committee. Meetings of the Executive Committee shall be called by the Chairperson of the Executive Committee whenever necessary but at least once a month and shall be deemed to be lawful if not less than two-thirds of the fixed composition of members shall take part in it.

763. The Executive Committee shall report to the Council on its activities, and shall inform the citizens at the meetings of labour collectives and according to the place of residence whenever necessary but at least once a month. The Executive Committee shall: elaborate and submit the plan of management of the local economy and communal property, and proposals on the organization of the protection of law and order and protection of the rights of citizens to the Council for its approval; elaborate and submit the draft programmes of economic and social development and the local budget to the Council for approval, and take measures on the implementation of programmes and execution of the local budget, presenting reports on the execution of the budget. The Executive Committees in the process of execution of the local budget shall have the right to submit its proposals to the relevant Council as regards any alteration on revenue and expenditure of this budget.

764. Oblast and Minsk City Executive Committees shall submit the consolidated budgets for the fiscal year and reports on the execution of the budget for the previous fiscal year to the national state body handling the field of finances according to the procedure and within the terms fixed by this body; secure the observance of the Constitution of the Republic of Belarus, laws of the Republic of Belarus, acts of the President of the Republic of Belarus, the execution of decisions of the Council and the decisions of higher state bodies concerning the relevant territory; organize returns of the local budget and their use, take decisions on the issue of securities and the holding of auctions; dispose of communal property of an administrative-territorial unit according to the procedure specified by the Council; take decisions on the creation, reorganization and liquidation of enterprises, organizations, establishments and associations of communal property; approve the working conditions of those enterprises, organizations, establishments and associations, as well as coordinate the working conditions of other enterprises, organizations, establishments and associations irrespective of the forms of ownership located in the territory subordinated to it, unless otherwise stipulated by the legislation of the Republic of Belarus; give consent for location of the enterprises, organizations, establishments and associations that are not in the communal property of the relevant administrative-territorial unit in the subordinated territory; conclude treaties with legal and natural persons; cooperate with enterprises, organizations, establishments and associations and organize their interest in the social and economic development of the territory; exercise control in the subordinated territory over the use of the communal property according to the procedure specified by the legislation of the Republic of Belarus; cancel decisions within its competence of heads of other bodies of local government adopted in violation of the legislation of the Republic of Belarus or that are at variance with decisions of the Council and the Executive Committee; form commissions on the issues of its activities and determine their powers and carry out their activities; take measures on securing and protecting interests on the territory, encouraging local economy through the courts, as well as through higher bodies of state government and other state bodies; solve other issues in accordance with legislation.

765. The executive and administrative body in the territory of a district in the city shall be considered as the local administration with the right to a legal entity. Local administrations shall be considered part of the executive and are the bodies of local government. The composition of the local administration shall consist of the head of local administration, his/her deputies and members of local administration.

766. The head of local administration shall be appointed and dismissed by the President of the Republic of Belarus according to the relevant procedure. Deputy (Deputies) of the head of local administration shall be appointed and dismissed by the Chairperson of a city Executive Committee. Other members of local administration, as well as officials of local administration, shall be appointed and dismissed by the head of the local administration.

767. Meetings of the local administration shall be held by its head whenever necessary but at least once a month and shall be deemed to be lawful if not less than two-thirds of members of the stipulated composition of the local administration take part in their work. Decisions of the local administration shall be adopted by a working majority of the stipulated composition of the local administration.

768. The structure and number of personnel of the local administration shall be approved by the city Executive Committee. Local administration shall: secure the observation of the Constitution of the Republic of Belarus, of the laws of the Republic of Belarus, acts of the President of the Republic of Belarus, execution of decisions of higher Executive Committees and Councils adopted within their competence in the relevant territory; elaborate and submit the management plan for the territory and its development, proposals on the structure and number of personnel of the local administration for consideration to the city Executive Committee; dispose of communal property of the city within the powers granted by the relevant city Council; organize receipts and other budget returns and exercise control over their use; cooperate with the owners of enterprises, organizations, establishments and associations and organize their interest in the social and economic development of the territory; submit proposals on issues of local significance and take part in their examination for the consideration of the Councils and their bodies, Executive Committees; shall organize control over the conservation of atmospheric air, water mineral wealth, forests, the vegetable kingdom and the animal world according to the procedure specified by the legislation of the Republic of Belarus, as well as the use of communal property; organize the work of the bodies of public territorial self-government, call meetings, including meetings of the authorized representatives of citizens of the relevant territory (hereafter is also referred to as meeting of authorized persons), secure implementation of their decisions; consider the complaints of citizens; solve other issues in accordance with the legislation.

769. Forms of direct democracy such as local referenda shall have a special significance in the development of local self-government. Local referenda may resolve the most important issues involving the interests of population. Participation in referenda shall be based on the principles of electoral law: they must be held by way of universal, free, equal and secret ballot. A local referendum may raise the issues that are within the jurisdiction of the relevant local Councils of Deputies. The procedure of holding of local referenda shall be determined by the Electoral Code of the Republic of Belarus.

770. Unfortunately, since the moment of adoption in June 1991 of the Law on plebiscites, there have been no local referenda in the republic. At the same time, we have specific practice of holding of meetings (gatherings) of citizens in their localities. They are devoted to discussion of state and local issues.

771. According to the Law of 12 July 2000 'On National and Local Meetings' citizens of the Republic of Belarus of the age of 18 and who live permanently in the relevant territory of the Republic of Belarus may take part in national and local meetings according to the procedure specified by the present Law and other legislative acts of the Republic of Belarus. Local referenda may not be attended by persons found by the court to be legally incompetent as a result of mental disorder (mental disease, imbecility), persons imprisoned under the verdict of the court, persons who are in places of forced medical treatment awaiting the verdict of the court, as well as persons with respect to whom, according to the criminal legislation of procedure, taking into custody was prescribed as a preventive punishment.

772. Local meetings shall be legitimate, if no less than 25% of citizens of the age of 18 and who live permanently in the relevant territories take part in the local meeting, or no less than two-thirds of the persons invited take part in the local meeting.

773. Participants of the meeting shall be entitled to discuss issues of national and local significance, to make proposals or to create recommendations on the issues of state and social life according to the legislative acts of the Republic of Belarus.

774. Local meetings shall have the right to make proposals to the President of the Republic of Belarus, to the National Assembly of the Republic of Belarus, to the Council of Ministers of the Republic of Belarus, to other state bodies, as well as to public associations and other organizations. Local meetings may be held in the territory of administrative-territorial unit or within its part (micro-districts, dwelling complexes, streets, yards, settlements, villages, etc.). Local meetings shall be called if necessary by local Councils of Deputies, executive and administrative bodies or bodies of territorial public self-government. Local meetings may be also called on the initiative of no fewer than 10% of citizens who live permanently in the relevant territory. For the preparation of the holding of a local meeting the local Councils of Deputies, executive and administrative bodies, bodies of territorial public self-government or citizens may create initiative groups or organizational committees.

775. Norms of representation and procedures for elections of the persons authorized for the participation in the local meeting, as well as of the Chairperson of the organizational committee (initiative group) shall be set up by the initiator of the meeting.

776. The decision on the calling of a local meeting, on the norms of representation and procedure for elections of the persons authorized for the participation in the local meeting shall be drawn up by the record of the session of the organizational committee or the initiative group and shall be brought to the attention of all citizens residing in the relevant territory fifteen days before the local meeting at the latest with indication of the time, place of its holding and the issues put for discussion.

777. Participants of the local meeting shall be citizens of the Republic of Belarus aged at least 18 and who live permanently in the Republic of Belarus in the relevant territory or authorized to take part in the local meeting, elected according to the procedure specified by the initiator of the meeting. Representatives of the State bodies, enterprises, organizations and establishments may take part in the meeting with the right of a deliberative vote.

778. The local meeting shall be opened and conducted by the chairperson of the organizational committee (initiative group) who is the Chairperson of the meeting. The secretary of the meeting, as well as the counting commission shall be elected for holding the record of the meeting. Agenda and the rules of procedure of the work shall be approved by the local meeting.

779. Decisions of the local meeting shall be adopted by the working majority of its participants. The procedure of voting shall be established by the meeting, and the meeting may be open or secret. Decisions of the local meeting shall be drawn up by the record. The record shall be signed by the Chairperson and by the secretary of the meeting. The list of its participants shall be attached to the record of the meeting.

780. The meeting shall be entitled to make appeals to the State bodies, enterprises, organizations, establishments and associations which are bound under the prescribed procedure to consider the demands of the meeting's participants and inform the citizens who live in the relevant territory about the adopted decisions. The competence of the local meeting shall be: consideration of the issues referred to the authority of the bodies of local government and self-government, making proposals thereupon, as regards setting the local taxes and dues included; discussion of draft decisions of local Councils of Deputies, executive and administrative bodies as regards local issues in economic, social and cultural spheres; the evaluation of the activities of the bodies of local government and self-government; submission of proposals on the agenda of sessions of local Councils of Deputies, and meetings of local executive and administrative bodies; consideration of proposals on giving names and renaming of the populated areas and their constituents and giving recommendations to that effect; discussion of measures as regards the protection of public order; the consideration of draft plans of development of the relevant territories, the rational use of natural resources; the adoption of decisions on the creation and closing of the bodies of territorial public self-government, the election of members and approval of the statutes of these bodies; election of the authorized persons to take part in the national meeting; discussion of other issues, including those of national importance which involve the interests of citizens of the relevant territory.

781. On the basis of the voluntary will of the citizens, other bodies of territorial public self-government may be created that carry out their activities in close connection with local Councils, executive and administrative bodies, deputies, labour collectives and public associations.

782. Territorial public self-government is the self-organization of citizens directly by the population or through its bodies of territorial public self-government (individual or in the forms of Councils, committees and other forms) in a part of the territory of an administrative-territorial unit (territories of micro-districts, dwelling complexes, streets, yards, settlements, villages, etc.) for the independent exercise of initiatives related to issues of local significance.

783. Only one body of territorial public self-government may be created in the relevant part of an administrative-territorial unit. The body of territorial public self-government may be granted the status of a legal entity as non-commercial organization, and its activities shall be subordinated to the meeting that founded or elected it, or to the relevant Council. Persons at the age of 18 and who live permanently in the given territory shall be elected to the bodies of territorial public self-government. Candidates for the bodies of territorial public self-government may be proposed by the residents of the relevant territory, as well as by the representative and executive bodies of the given administrative-territorial unit.

784. Creation of the body of territorial public self-government and the vote on its members' approval of its statutes shall be carried out at the meeting. The procedure of election and work of individual bodies of territorial public self-government (starosta, elder, etc.) shall be specified by the provision approved by the Council of the relevant administrative-territorial unit. Members of the body of territorial public self-government shall be elected by open or secret ballot.

785. The statute of the body of territorial public self-government shall specify the name, aims, tasks and the subject of activities of the body of territorial public self-government, the territory of its activities, the forms and procedures of participation of inhabitants in the work of the body of territorial public self-government and the procedure of forming of its bodies and the term of powers of the body of territorial public self-government that must not exceed the term of powers of the Council of the relevant administrative-territorial unit, the procedure of forming of the ownership of the body of territorial public self-government, the procedure of disposal of its property, as well as other information specified by the legislation of the Republic of Belarus.

786. A body of territorial public self-government shall be subject to registration in the relevant Executive Committee (local administration). The following documents shall be forwarded to the relevant body for registration of the body of territorial public self-government within a month after the date of its creation: the application drawn up according to the prescribed procedure; the statutes; the decision of the initiative group or the organizational committee on the holding of the meeting concerning the creation of a body of territorial public self-government; records of the meeting; a general list of participants of the meeting with specification of the first name, second name and patronymic name, the date of birth, residence and citizenship; other documents stipulated by the legislation of the Republic of Belarus.

787. A body of territorial public self-government shall be entitled: to submit its proposals on all local issues for the consideration of the Council and its bodies, Executive Committees and local administrations; to participate in the State bodies when these institutions are dealing with local issues; to call meetings in the relevant territory for the discussion of local issues; to accumulate financial means, voluntary contributions and donations of citizens and legal entities and transfer them for the development of social infrastructure of the territory according to the procedure specified by the legislation of the Republic of Belarus; carrying out cultural and educational, as well as sanitary, arrangements; to take the possession and disposal of buildings, premises, playgrounds and playing fields, clubs, other social and cultural objects, and elements of local historical and cultural heritage from the Councils, executive and administrative bodies and other legal entities; to submit proposals on the issues of the organization of activities and location of enterprises of trading, public catering, consumer service, establishments of health care, education, culture, physical training and sport, other social objects, as well as specification of their working conditions for consideration of the Council, Executive Committee and local administration.

788. The Council may delegate the body of territorial public self-government certain powers on carrying out self-government in the relevant territory except for powers referred to the exclusive competence of the Council.

789. The liquidation of the body of territorial public self-government shall take place as a result of expiry of the time period for which it was created, as well as in other instances specified by the legislation of the Republic of Belarus. In case of flagrant violation of the legislation of the Republic of Belarus by the body of territorial public self-government, the Council, the Executive Committee and local administration may suspend its activities. A decision on early termination of powers of the body of territorial public self-government shall be adopted by the Council of the relevant administrative-territorial unit or by a meeting of citizens.

790. The integral feature of local self-government and government shall be the stipulation by the legislation of independent powers of the bodies of local government and self-government.

791. The main powers of the bodies of local self-government and government are enshrined in the Constitution and the law of the Republic of Belarus on local government and self-government. They have a wide scale of rights and obligations in the field of economics, social relations, budget, finances, protection of public order, etc.

792. The most important power of the bodies of local self-government (local Councils of Deputies in this particular case) shall be the approval of programmes of economic and social development (Article 121 of the Constitution). Taking into account the peculiarities of the competence of local Councils of different levels (primary, intermediary, oblast) they shall be also entitled to approve programmes of housing construction, provision of facilities, highway engineering, social and cultural services for the population, and environmental protection (Articles 16, 17 and 18 of the law on local government and self-government). They shall be also charged with organization, control and approval of reports on the implementation of those programmes.

793. In the field of the budget and finances the local Councils of Deputies shall approve and execute budgets, approve reports on their execution; set local taxes and dues in accordance with the law.

794. Local Councils of Deputies shall specify, within the limits of power specified by law, the procedure governing the management and disposal of municipal property. They shall specify the legal regime of property that is in the communal ownership of the relevant administrative-territorial entity. The competence of the Councils of Deputies of the based territorial level shall be giving consent for the location and development in the territory of the Council of enterprises, economic organizations and establishments that are not in communal property of the relevant administrative-territorial entity; considering the plans and programmes of location, development and specialization of enterprises (associations), as well as social and cultural establishments of different forms of ownership, giving the relevant opinions and in the instances of necessity submission of proposals to the relevant state bodies.

795. In the field of land relations and use of natural resources the local Councils of Deputies shall exercise control over the use of lands, mineral wealth, waters, forests, fishing, and other natural resources that are within the authority of the Councils. The right to dispose of land and of other natural resources shall be exercised by the local Councils by way of transferring them according to the law to the possession and in use of enterprises and citizens.

796. Local Councils of Deputies shall carry out management of establishments of public health care, education, culture, social securing, as well as of other organizations that are within their authority. Local Councils of Deputies shall also have other powers. The Constitution, laws, acts of the President shall also stipulate the powers of executive and administrative bodies, bodies of territorial public self-government.

797. The important guarantee of normal functioning of local government and self-government shall be the regulation of relations with other state bodies.

798. Local Councils of Deputies, executive and administrative bodies shall take binding decisions in the relevant territory on the grounds of the current legislation. The Constitution and the law on local government and self-government shall envisage a procedure of annulment of decisions of local government and self-government. Higher representative bodies shall be entitled to annul decisions of local Councils of Deputies that are not in line with the legislation. Decisions of local executive and administrative bodies that are not in line with legislation shall be subject to cancellation by the relevant Councils of Deputies, higher executive and administrative bodies, as well as by the President of the Republic of Belarus. Decisions of local Councils of Deputies or executive bodies that restrict or violate the rights, freedoms and lawful interests of citizens, as well as in other instances specified by the legislation may be subject to appeal to the court.

799. One shall bear in mind here that the acts of the bodies of local government and self-government of the normative nature may be verified by the Constitutional Court as for their conformity with the Constitution, with acts of higher legal force. Citizens and economic entities may appeal to a court of common law or to an economic court only against acts of law applying nature that violate or restrict the rights, liberties and lawful interests of citizens.

Part IV. Citizenship and Administration of Justice

Chapter 1. Rules concerning Nationality and Relevance of Nationality

§1. Citizenship of the Republic of Belarus

800. Citizenship shall express the political and legal relationship of an individual with the State regardless of the nationality of the individual in question. This relationship is not limited by the space of the State. Under Article 10 of the Constitution, a citizen of the Republic of Belarus shall be guaranteed the protection and patronage of the State both in the territory of Belarus and beyond.

801. Relations in the field of citizenship shall be regulated by a number of legal acts. Among them we must specify the Constitution of the Republic of Belarus (Articles 10, 84, etc.), the Law 'On citizenship of the Republic of Belarus' of 1 August 2002, the Provision on the procedure of consideration of issues related to citizenship of the Republic of Belarus approved by the Decree of the President of the Republic of Belarus of 17 November 1994 (with *further* alterations and addenda), Treaty on creation of Union State (Articles 14–16) concluded on 8 December 1999, or Agreements of the Republic of Belarus with Kazakhstan and Ukraine on simplified procedure of acquisition of citizenship.

802. For instance, if there are no diplomatic and consular missions of the Republic of Belarus in the country where a citizen of the Republic of Belarus is residing or visiting, the protection of the rights and lawful interests of citizens of the Republic of Belarus according to the international treaties of the Republic of Belarus may be carried out by the relevant bodies of other states. In accordance with the Treaty on Creation of Union State between the Republic of Belarus and the Russian Federation (ratified by the law of 24 December 1999), every citizen of the Member State shall have the right to protection in the territory of the third state where there is no mission of his/her Member State on behalf of diplomatic or consular missions of another Member State under the same conditions as the citizen of the Member State in question (Article 15 of the Treaty).

803. Citizenship of the Republic of Belarus shall be acquired: due to birth; as a result of admission to the citizenship of the Republic of Belarus; according to the procedure of registration; under other grounds specified by the law and international treaties.

804. The main grounds for acquiring citizenship shall be birth. In an instance of acquisition of citizenship due to birth, both the principle of *jus sanguinis* (citizenship of parents shall be taken into account) and the principle of jus soli (the place of birth shall be taken into account) shall be effective.

805. Belarusian law on citizenship is directed to resolve the issues of acquisition of citizenship of the Republic of Belarus in favour of the birth. All these situations shall be taken into account: both parents are citizens of the Republic of Belarus; only one parent has citizenship of the Republic of Belarus; or neither parent is a citizen of the Republic of Belarus. Thus, according to Article 13 of the law, a child, where if only one of his/her parents is a citizen of the Republic of Belarus at the moment of his/her birth shall be the citizen of the Republic of Belarus regardless of his/her place of birth.

806. The child shall also acquire the citizenship of the Republic of Belarus due to birth, if at the date of birth the parents (only parent) of the child residing in the territory of the Republic of Belarus are stateless persons under condition that the child was born in the territory of the Republic of Belarus; the parents (only parent) of the child residing in the territory of the Republic of Belarus are foreign citizens under condition that the child was born in the territory of the Republic of Belarus, and the States of the parents (subjects thereof) grant him/her no citizenship.

807. The child in the territory of the Republic of Belarus whose parents are unknown shall become a citizen of the Republic of Belarus. Naturalization shall presuppose conformity to certain requirements of the person in question.

808. General requirements (conditions) for admission to the citizenship of the Republic of Belarus are stipulated in Article 14 of the law on citizenship of the Republic of Belarus. Thus, a person may be given citizenship, if he/she shall: undertake the obligation to adhere and to respect the Constitution and other acts of the legislation of the Republic of Belarus; have knowledge of one of the languages of the Republic of Belarus within the limits necessary for communications; reside in the territory of the Republic of Belarus after admission for permanent living in the Republic of Belarus during last seven years continuously, except for certain instances where more short periods for living are fixed; have a legitimate livelihood that secure living wage for himself/herself and for disabled members of his/her family who are dependants; have no citizenship of another state or forsake the citizenship of a foreign state through acquisition of the citizenship of the Republic of Belarus or appeal to the competent body of a foreign state on termination from citizenship of the given state, except for the instances where termination of citizenship is impossible for reasons beyond his/her control.

809. There are specific conditions for certain persons for their admission to the citizenship. They shall be fixed for the following persons: Belarusians, as well as persons who identify themselves as Belarusian and their descendants (next of kin of right line: children, grandchildren, great-grandchildren) born beyond the present territory of the Republic of Belarus; persons who have performed outstanding public services to the Republic of Belarus, high progress in the field of science, technology, culture and sport or who have profession or qualifications that are of state interest for the Republic of Belarus; individuals who have citizenship of the Republic of Belarus or the right to citizenship of the Republic of Belarus, whose parents (persons who adopted them) had preferred them other citizenship in accordance with Article 23.1, Article 26 and Article 27.4 of the Law of 1 August 2002; persons who are foreign citizens or stateless persons who previously were nationals of the Republic of Belarus.

810. For those persons the seven-year period of time for residing may be reduced or is subject to no application at all.

811. The right to acquire citizenship under the procedure of registration shall be specially emphasized. This right shall have only certain categories of persons (Article 15 of the Law). Citizenship of the Republic of Belarus shall be terminated due to seceding from the citizenship of the Republic of Belarus and as a result of loss of citizenship of the Republic of Belarus. Seceding from the citizenship of the Republic of Belarus shall not be admissible if a person who applies for seceding is an accused or convicted person; has tax liabilities and other active debts before the Republic of Belarus, its legal and natural persons; has no other nationality or guarantees for its acquisition. Citizenship of the Republic of Belarus shall be lost owing to a person entering into military service, police, security bodies, bodies of justice and other state bodies of a foreign state, with the absence on the grounds for refusal in close of the citizenship of the Republic of Belarus. If the citizenship of the Republic of Belarus was acquired or closed as a result of giving false evidence or counterfeit documents, the previously adopted decision shall be subject to repeal (Articles 21–22 of the Law).

812. There are special instances of changing, preservation or loss of citizenship. In case of changing citizenship, the parents (a single parent) may change the citizenship of the child, if he/she is under the age of 14. According to the will of parents, in case of changing the citizenship to that of the Republic of Belarus, the Belarusian nationality of the child who is before the age of 16 may be preserved. Changing of the nationality of children at the age from 14 to 18 in case of changing the citizenship by their parents, as well as changing of the nationality with respect to the adopted children shall be admissible only with the consent of the children expressed in written notarized form.

813. If the parents or one of the parents of the child who reside(s) in the territory of the Republic of Belarus and who is subject to guardianship on behalf of the citizens of the Republic of Belarus are seceding from the citizenship of the Republic of Belarus or lose it and, moreover, takes no part in upbringing the child, the child shall preserve the citizenship of the Republic of Belarus.

814. If the citizenship of the Republic of Belarus is acquired by one of the parents, and another one remains a citizen of another state or a stateless person, the citizen may acquire the citizenship of the Republic of Belarus under the joint request of the parents or a parent who is acquiring the citizenship of the Republic of Belarus, when the location of another parent is unknown. If the citizenship of the Republic of Belarus is acquired by one of the parents, and another one remains a stateless person, the child residing in the territory of the Republic of Belarus shall become a citizen of the Republic of Belarus; otherwise he/she would become a stateless person. If one of the parents is seceding from or loses citizenship, and another one is remaining a citizen of the Republic of Belarus, the child shall preserve the citizenship of the Republic of Belarus. According to the joint request of the parents, this child may be permitted to secede from the citizenship of the Republic of Belarus.

815. The law shall also specify the issues of citizenship of the child in case of his/her adoption. A child who is a foreign citizen or a stateless person in case of his/her adoption by a citizen of the Republic of Belarus or by spouses who are citizens of the Republic of Belarus or by spouses where one of them is a citizen of the Republic of Belarus and another one is a stateless person, shall become a citizen of the Republic of Belarus from the date of adoption. The child who is a foreign citizen or a stateless person in case of his/her adoption by the citizen of the Republic of Belarus or by spouses where one of them is the citizen of the Republic of Belarus and another one is a foreign citizen, may acquire the citizenship of the Republic of Belarus under the joint request of the persons adopting him/her.

816. The child who is a citizen of the Republic of Belarus shall preserve the citizenship of the Republic of Belarus in case of his/her adoption by: spouses who are foreign citizens or a foreign citizen; spouses who are stateless persons or a stateless person; spouses where one of them is the citizen of the Republic of Belarus and another one is a foreign citizen or a stateless person. For the child adopted by the spouses who are foreign citizens or a foreign citizen the citizenship of the Republic of Belarus may be closed off to him after reaching the age of 16 according to the procedure of seceding from the citizenship on the grounds of the request of persons having adopted the child.

817. The decree of the President of 17 November 1994 No. 209 (with further alterations and addenda) had approved the Provision on procedure of consideration of issues related to the citizenship of the Republic of Belarus and created a Commission on the issues of citizenship under the President of the Republic of Belarus. According to the Provision the President shall take a decision on admission to the citizenship, seceding from citizenship, or loss of the citizenship of the Republic of Belarus.

818. Applications on the issues of citizenship shall be addressed to the President with specification of the date of its drawing up. The applicants shall enclose the form in two copies; five photos; autobiography in two copies; copy of birth certificate of the applicant, and if necessary of other persons; documents of payment of the State tax or notice of exemption from its payment; document of seceding from foreign citizenship, proof of no citizenship of another country; reference from the place of residence with indication of the structure of the family. Other relevant documents may be attached to the application. Applications on issues related to citizenship shall be submitted to interior bodies according to the place of residence of the applicant, and the persons who live permanently abroad shall refer their applications to diplomatic and to consular missions. The time limit for examination of applications in local interior bodies, the Ministry of Internal Affairs, diplomatic and consular missions, the Ministry of Foreign Affairs, the Committee of State Security (KGB) and the Council of Ministers of the Republic of Belarus shall not be more than one month. According to the law the time limit for examination of applications on admission to the citizenship of the Republic of Belarus shall not be more than one year. The time limit for examination of applications for seceding from the citizenship of the Republic of Belarus shall not be more than six months, and the time limit for examination of applications on admission to the citizenship of the Republic of Belarus according to the procedure of registration shall not be more than two months (Article 34).

819. In case of absence of legitimate grounds for drawing up the materials on the issues of citizenship, as well as in the presence of obstacles (failure to present a document on seceding from a foreign citizenship; serving by the applicant of a sentence in custody, etc.), the body of interior, a diplomatic, consular mission of the Republic of Belarus shall refuse the applicant to take the application on the issues of citizenship and shall inform this in written form. This refusal may be subject to appeal by the applicant to a higher body according to the subordination, which is bound within one month period of time to examine it and to give the applicant a sound answer in written form. In case of a disagreement with decision of the higher body or failure to receive a sound reply from this body within a month, the applicant shall have the right to lodge the complaint to the court.

820. Ending citizenship may take place due to seceding from the citizenship of the Republic of Belarus or its loss, as well as under other grounds specified by the law. The Provision stipulates that the petition on seceding from the citizenship of the Republic of Belarus shall be attached to the application form in two copies; four photos; autobiography in two copies; certificate from the place of residence about the structure of the family; certificate from the place of work or study, and as for those who are unable to work – from the place of residence, present or previous (for persons who live permanently abroad) with specification of the fact whether a person has commitments before the State, or property obligations related to essential interests of citizens or state organizations, cooperative and public associations; a certificate from the military commissariat on the release of a person of draft age from obligatory military service in the Armed Forces of the Republic of Belarus; document on payment of the national tax or exemption from its payment. If an applicant has a spouse, as well as dependents, the applicant must present notarized written applications for those persons on the absence of material and other claims. If necessary, the copies of the documents of divorce, death of one of the parents, adoption, deprivation of parental rights, or alimony shall be presented.

821. According to the *above specified* Provision, there is a clear determination of what being a citizen of the Republic of Belarus means that shall be carried out in all instances where there are doubts as regards the justification of the citizenship of the Republic of Belarus. In addition, the relevant bodies shall receive the application, two photos, and documents proving the circumstances where the legislation makes requirements for citizenship of the Republic of Belarus. It must be emphasized, that in instances of necessity the determination of the rightful citizenship of the Republic of Belarus may take place as a result of a court ruling, which shall determine the compatibility of the current and past living situation with the law in place at the time when the individual first arrived on Belarusian soil.

Chapter 2. Fundamental Rights and Freedoms

§1. General

822. The current Constitution of the Republic of Belarus (contrasting to previous four Constitutions) enshrines human rights and freedoms as the key element of the whole document: if earlier we could find them at the end of the text of the Constitution, now they are placed directly after the first section dedicated to the bases of the constitutional system. Moreover, the character of interrelations between the individual and the State has been changed. From a paternalistic type of relations we passed on to the individual, his/her rights and freedoms, and guarantees of their protection as the supreme value inspiring society and the State. The State shall bear responsibility towards a citizen for the creation of conditions for free and dignified development of his/her identity. A citizen bears a responsibility towards the State to discharge unwaveringly the duties imposed thereupon by the Constitution.

823. Thus, the norms on diversity of the forms of ownership, political pluralism, the nature of the relations between the individual, society and the State specified by the Constitution shall make it possible to confirm the presence of legal conditions that allow us to confirm that the Republic of Belarus is a democratic welfare state under the rule of law.

824. The Constitution used many of the norms in the Universal Declaration of Human Rights, the International Covenant on Civil and Political Rights, the International Covenant on Economic, Social and Cultural Rights, as well as the European Convention for the Protection of Human Rights and Fundamental Freedoms, however, the latter, unlike the first two Covenants, is not legally binding for Belarus. The comparable analysis of the provisions of the *above mentioned* international instruments and the provisions of the Constitution of the Republic of Belarus shall make it possible to come to the conclusion that, if not full duplication, there is an extreme closeness of wordings of many of their common provisions.

825. Under Article 8 of the Constitution, the Republic of Belarus shall recognize the supremacy of the universally acknowledged principles of international law and ensure that its laws comply with such principles. The conclusion of international treaties that are contrary to the Constitution shall not be permitted. This fundamental norm shall signify the aspiration of the law maker to build an independent state on democratic legal principles. There are several aspects here. Basing oneself on universally acknowledged principles of international law means that these texts are the vector for the development of the whole legal system. If one understands this, one understands the phrase ‘ensure that its laws comply with such principles’. The universally acknowledged principles of international law were taken into account while elaborating the constitutional norms, and in their interpretation.

826. Our legal tradition of integration of the international treaty by way of the relevant procedure (ratification, joining, and approval) shall predetermine the place of the international treaty depending on the place of the laws on ratification of treaties.

827. Under part three of Article 8 and Article 116.4 of the Constitution they have sub-constitutional but super-national nature, including codes and programme laws (there are two of them), meaning that they shall also have, with respect to the latter, a higher legal force. In addition, in the instance of a discrepancy between the norms of international treaties and new laws, the universally acknowledged rule that the new law shall repeal the old one shall not be applied, i.e., in case of discrepancy of the specified acts; priority shall be given to the norms of international treaties. In essence, the principle of *lex specialis* shall be effective here. The principle in question shall be observed even where the new law shall directly specify its supremacy with respect to the international treaty. Exclusion, as it has been already emphasized, is possible in case of stipulation in the law of greater scope of guarantees.

§2. Civil and Political Rights

828. Right to life. The right to life shall be the basic right of everyone. Under Article 24 of the Constitution every person shall have the right to life. The State shall protect the life of the individual against any illegal infringement. Until its abolition, the death penalty may be applied in accordance with the law as an exceptional penalty for especially grave crimes and only in accordance with the verdict of the court of law.

829. The right to life neither shall be appreciated in the narrow sense as inadmissibility of infringement of the human life, nor as the impossibility of existence of the death penalty in the State. This is a broader notion. It shall include the right to a sound environment; presuppose the obligation of the State not to allow ecological disasters and to take measures on their elimination or reducing their aftermath. This problem is closely connected with the problem of abortions, death by lethal injections, living standard, etc.

830. The Constitution shall not prohibit the death penalty. First, it is possible only according to the law for especially grave crimes; second, it has an exclusive character, i.e., before the forming of all the conditions for its abolition by the society the forced nature of its application is consequently emphasized; third, the death penalty is assumed only under the verdict of the court of law. The Criminal Code of the Republic of Belarus stipulates that the death penalty (by firing squad) as an exclusive punishment until its full abolition may be applied for certain grave crimes involving the deliberate taking of human life under aggravating circumstances. The death penalty cannot be imposed on: persons who have committed a crime under the age of eighteen; women; men who reached the age of sixty-five by the day of the sentencing (Article 59 of the Criminal Code).

Since the 1990s the legislator – following international trends – started to narrow the sphere of application for capital punishment, excluding it from Criminal Code clauses describing responsibility for crimes that are not connected to wilful human life infringement (practically the law was adjusted in accordance with practice trends).

The narrowing of capital punishment was realized alongside increasing the groups of people who cannot be sentenced to death. In particular, according to the Criminal Code of 1960, before the acceptance of the Law dated 1 March 1994, these were minors, women pregnant while committing a crime or by the time of passing or applying sentence. According to Clause 22 of the Criminal Law mentioned above, capital punishment was not applied to women at all.

In the Criminal Law of the Republic of Belarus dated 9 July 1999 and implemented on 1 January 2001, the sphere of capital punishment application has been decreased half as much. It is applied only to grave crimes connected with wilful homicide under aggravating circumstances.

At the same time the group of people who cannot be sentenced to death now included men aged 65 by the day of passing the sentence.

In other words, the development of criminal legislation in the Republic of Belarus regulating the application of capital punishment shows that there is a tendency to reduce capital punishment, which shows a perspective of a negative attitude to such a penalty.

The same trend is evidenced by judicial practice. First, for decades the death penalty has been used only for intentional murder with aggravating circumstances. Second, prior to and including the year of 1999, there were dozens sentenced to death each year (e.g., in 1995, 1996, 1997, 1998, 1999; 37, 29, 46, 47, 13 people were sentenced to death respectively). Then, beginning from 2000, this number fell: in 2000, 2001, 2002, 2003, 2004, 2005, 2006, 2007, 2008, 2009, 2010, 2011; 4, 7, 4, 4, 2, 2, 9, 4, 2, 2, 2, and 3 people, respectively, were sentenced to death. As a percentage of the total number of convictions, these figures are 1/1000. In 2012, no one was sentenced to death.

Also of note is that the average annual number of persons convicted of aggravated murder is about 360. However, most of them are not condemned to life imprisonment as an alternative measure for the death penalty, but to imprisonment for various terms, including a period of twenty-five years (a life sentence in the Criminal Code imposed only by the end of 1997, for example, resulting between 1998 and 2006 in 3, 29, 18, 11, 15, 12, 12, 8 and 7 life sentences respectively). Both exceptional punishments are insignificant in the application of penalties for the most serious crimes committed in aggravating circumstances. For example, between 2002 and 2011, 117 people have been convicted of the death penalty and life imprisonment, which is 3.2% of the total number of those convicted of crimes for which the law provides the possibility of applying these exceptional punishments.

Thus, court practice itself shows the desire to have a moratorium on the death penalty, treating such cases rather cautiously and tending to pass life imprisonment instead.

Characteristically, the choice of exceptional punishment affected the positive dynamics of the crimes for which the former are prescribed by law and therefore of persons convicted. For example, since 2007, there has been a reduced number of murders, including those committed under aggravating circumstances. Accordingly, there has been sharply reduced number of persons convicted under Part 2 of Article 139 of the Criminal Code. Over 2007, 2008, 2009, 2010 and 2011, there were 392, 270, 241, 209 and 164 convicted, respectively. In these years, the death penalty was imposed on 4, 2, 2, 2, and 3 people respectively.

The process of evolution of government attitude to the death penalty as the European one demonstrates not only legislative development and practice in Belarus. The issue was brought to a Republican Referendum in November 1996. Belarus also holds international conferences and seminars on this issue and follows public opinion by means of mass media.

A serious step was to conduct parliamentary discussions on this issue in May 2002 arranged by the House of Representatives of the National Assembly of the Republic of Belarus, after which a number of recommendations were accepted.

It is necessary to stress that the fact of such discussions draw lawyers' and public attention to this problem which is still being discussed in the press and other mass media.

A great impact in identifying approaches to the death penalty was its discussion in the Constitutional Court of the Republic of Belarus. The House of Representatives of the National Assembly initiated the case applying to the Constitutional Court to check the constitutionality of Criminal Code clauses dealing with application of capital punishment.

The Constitutional Court in its Conclusion issued on 11 March 2004 stressed the comparison of Constitutional clauses of the Republic of Belarus and international acts ratified by the government to Criminal Code norms. In that Conclusion, the Constitutional Court paid special attention to such important documents of the Council of Europe as the European Convention on Human Rights of 1950 and its Protocols No. 6 of 28 April 1983 and No. 13 of 3 May 2002 which determined the 'fate' of capital punishment in Europe.

At present the overwhelming majority of Member States of the Council of Europe have abolished capital punishment. The tendency to decrease its usage is observed all over the world. Currently about 100 states do not apply capital punishment.

The Constitutional Court of the Republic of Belarus, treating positively this trend, has studied legal ways of solving the capital punishment issue in its own country. To answer this question we need to look at Clause 24 of the Constitution.

831. The death penalty may be considered in different aspects, including as a measure of punishment of the person who committed an especially grave crime and as a measure of deterrence, as a preventive measure against future cases of the relevant criminal deeds being committed. A person who takes human lives intentionally as a result of a criminal deed may find himself/herself excluded from the situation where he/she is guaranteed the right to life. The death penalty can be substituted by life imprisonment as a measure of pardon (Article 59 of the Criminal Code).

832. For the purposes of securing the right to life, a person shall have the right both to assistance and protection on behalf of the State that is also obliged to take all measures for the creation of domestic and international law and order necessary for the full exercise of the constitutional rights and freedoms of the citizens of the Republic of Belarus.

833. Moreover, everyone shall have the right to self-defence. According to Article 34 of the Criminal Code everyone has the right to defence against socially dangerous infringements. This right belongs to any person, regardless of the possibility to avoid an infringement or to turn for help to other persons or authorities.

834. An act shall not constitute a crime if it is has been committed in a state of self-defence, that is, in defending one's life, health, the rights of the defending person or another person, interests of the society or of the State against a socially dangerous infringement by inflicting harm to the culprit, if in such a case the limits of unnecessary defence were not exceeded. Exceeding the limits of necessary defence shall be deemed to be a disparity, obvious to the defending person, between the defence and the character and danger of the infringement, where the guilty party unnecessarily and intentionally inflicts death or a severe bodily injury.

835. Our legislation prescribes a lighter penalty for murder committed when exceeding the limits of necessary defence. It shall be punishable by correctional labour for the term of up to two years, restriction of liberty for the term of up to three years or deprivation of liberty for the same time period.

836. The peoples' vote of 24 November 1996 on the issue of the conservation of the death penalty was of no legally binding significance; therefore, the law maker has no obstacles for a gradual alteration of the grounds for application of death penalty for especially grave crimes and for further refusal of this type of punishment. It may be possible to declare a moratorium on executions and after expiry of the definite time period to make analysis of the criminal situation. At the same time, prescription of life imprisonment as an alternative criminal punishment shall mean 'transference' of liability burden for application of the death penalty from the law maker to the courts.

837. Personal liberty, inviolability and dignity. Under Article 25 of the Constitution the State shall safeguard personal liberty, inviolability and dignity. The restriction and denial of personal liberty is possible in the instances and under the procedure specified in law. A person who has been taken into custody shall be entitled to a judicial investigation into the legality of his/her detention or arrest. No one shall be subjected to torture or cruel, inhuman or undignified treatment or punishment, or be subjected to medical or other experiments without one's consent. The Constitution shall enshrine the right of everyone to liberty and inviolability. Only the law may specify exemptions. First of all, these are the Administrative Code and the Criminal Code of Procedure.

838. Right to private life. Under Article 28 of the Constitution everyone shall be entitled to protection against unlawful interference with one's private life, including encroachments on the privacy of one's correspondence and telephone and other communications, and on one's honour and dignity. The Article in question fixes the inviolability of individual (private) life. Legal literature shall speak about private life as physical and spiritual inner spheres controlled by the individual himself/herself. This right shall include separate elements: the right to personal and family secrecy, freedom of communications, freedom to dispose of oneself, inadmissibility of tapping and recording of conversations, review of correspondence, right to secret voting, or the right to protection of personality.

839. An individual shall dispose of his/her private life independently. A person is free in choice of the range of contacts in informal atmosphere. Marriage (divorce), procreation (adoption), disposal of property, use of family budget, secrecy of deposits, information about the state of health, freedom of religion shall be referred to the sphere of private life. That is why the right to personal life shall presuppose inadmissibility of tapping his/her phone calls, his/her surveillance, violation of his/her rights to confidentiality of mail and other contacts, violation of secrecy of bank deposits, medical, advocate secrecy, violation of secrecy of religious confession, etc.

840. The right to inviolability of private life shall belong to a person from birth, it shall not be granted by the State. At the same time, taking into account the requirements specified in Article 23 of the Constitution, the intrusion upon private life for the purposes of the prevention of crimes; due to epidemics or natural calamities and liquidation of their effects; under conditions of war and emergency is admissible.

841. Safety of housing. The right of the people to be secure in their dwellings and other legitimate effects shall be guaranteed. No person shall have the right, save in due course of law to enter the premises or other legal property of a citizen against one's will (Article 29 of the Constitution). Citizens shall be guaranteed the safety of housing. No one shall have the right to enter the premises against the will of those persons who live therein without the legitimate grounds. Safety of housing is the guarantee of an individual right to a personal life. Private life of citizens, secrecy of correspondence, telephone conversations and telegraphic messages shall be protected by the law.

842. Search, seizure, arrest of mail and telegraphic correspondence, as well as other messages, tapping and recording of conversations may take place only on the grounds and under the procedure prescribed by criminal legislation. Thus, according to Article 208 of the CCP an investigator with availability of sufficient data to assume that in some room or another place or with some person there may be instruments of crime, objects, documents and values that may have bearing on the case as well as for detection of persons and corpses being searched for. The search shall be performed on the grounds of a sound ruling of the investigator and only under the sanction of the Public Attorney or his/her deputy. In exclusive urgent cases the search may be performed without a sanction of the Public Attorney followed by a message on the search performed to be sent to him within twenty-four hours (Article 210 of CCP).

843. According to Article 209 of CCP, in case of necessity to perform seizure of definite objects and documents having a bearing on the case, the investigator shall perform the seizure if it is known for sure where and with whom they are present. Seizure of documents containing a state or another secret protected by law must be performed under the sanction of the Public Attorney or his/her deputy in accordance with the procedure agreed with the head of the relevant establishment. Seizure shall be performed on the grounds of the sound ruling of the investigator.

844. The Criminal Code of Procedure (Article 210) stipulates that search and seizure shall be performed with the participation of witnesses at the site of the official search or seizure. During search and seizure it is necessary to assure the presence of the person who is subject to search and seizure or the members of his/her family of legal age. If their presence is impossible, then representatives of the housing organization or local administration shall be invited. Search and seizure of rooms of enterprises, institutions and organizations shall be performed in the presence of the representatives of the administration whereas in places of storage of material values – in the presence of the person who bears material responsibility. Persons who are subject to search or seizure, witnesses, representatives must be explained their right to participate in all actions of the investigator and to make the statements thereon that must be entered in the records. CCP shall regulate in details the performance of other procedural actions.

845. Freedom of movement and choice of the place of residence. Citizens of the Republic of Belarus shall have the right to move freely and choose their place of residence within the Republic of Belarus, to live in it and to return to it without hindrance (Article 30 of the Constitution). There is no individual freedom without the freedom of movement. The Constitution enshrines the right of citizens to move freely and choose their place of residence within the Republic of Belarus, to live in it and to return to it without hindrance. In this particular case we are speaking about the freedom of movement of citizens of Belarus; foreign citizens and stateless persons shall be restricted in the right to immigrate in Belarus.

846. According to Article 12 of the International Covenant on Civil and Political Rights ratified by the Republic of Belarus, everyone lawfully within the territory of a state shall, within that territory, have the right to liberty of movement and freedom to choose his/her residence. Everyone shall be free to leave any country, including his/her own. The aforementioned rights shall not be subject to any restrictions except for those that are provided by law, that are necessary to protect national security, public order (*ordre public*), public health or morals or the rights and freedoms of others, and are consistent with other rights recognized in the present Covenant. No one shall be arbitrarily deprived of the right to enter his/her own country.

847. The right to freedom of movement shall presuppose the right to move freely inside the State and to choose the place of residence, as well as the right to live in the country and to return to it. Certain acts of the USSR that stipulated the so-called institute of propiska were effective recently. Decree of the President of the

Republic of Belarus of 7 September 2007 'On improvement of system of registration of citizens on place of staying' has abolished the system of propiska. Registration of citizens on place of living within the Republic of Belarus is envisaged. For registration on place of living a citizen shall be obliged within one month from the moment of arrival for a new place of living to apply to the person who is responsible for registration, and in case of his/her absence, to the body of registration. There is no need to make an appeal to the person who is responsible for registration or to the body of registration for crossing off the register on former place of residence. For registration on place of living a citizen shall be obliged to produce an application on registration on place of residence, identity card and certain other documents.

848. On the grounds of constitutional guarantees for the freedom of movement and choice of the place of residence within the Republic of Belarus, the right of ownership and the right of citizens to housing, as well as the norms of international treaties, the Constitutional Court has liberalized the previous limits in their realization by its Decision of 25 March 1997. The Court emphasized that the citizens of the Republic of Belarus, including those of them who live permanently out of it, shall have the right to purchase flats or houses under contracts of purchase and sale in any locality of the Republic of Belarus regardless of their place of residence. The foreign nationals and stateless persons who reside in the territory of the Republic of Belarus and who have lawful source of income shall also use this right. The peculiarities of the purchase and sale of flats (houses) may be specified in the City of Minsk, the Capital of our Republic, the status of which shall be stipulated in the law. As for foreign citizens who do not reside in the territory of our Republic, the right to purchase and sell flats (houses) may be realized in accordance with international treaties and according to the procedure of realization of those treaties.

849. As it was already noted, Article 30 of the Constitution stipulates the right of citizens of Belarus to live in their country, to leave it and to return to it without hindrance. This constitutional norm found its development in a number of other normative acts and, in particular, in the Law of 20 September 2009 'On Procedure of Leaving the Republic of Belarus and Entering the Republic of Belarus of Citizens of the Republic of Belarus'. According to the Law, a citizen of the Republic of Belarus may not be deprived of the right to leave the Republic of Belarus. According to the Law this right shall be subject only to temporary restriction.

850. Thus, citizens are obliged to perform the obligations faced by all other citizens who are under the jurisdiction of the Republic of Belarus before moving to live abroad. They shall have the right to preserve in the territory of the Republic of Belarus their dwelling and other belonging to them property except for the land.

851. At the same time, moving abroad for a citizen, on the grounds of Article 7 of the specified Law, may be restricted temporarily: if he/she knows information that is a state secret – until the end of circumstances preventing them from leaving; a criminal case was brought against him/her – until the end of the trial; he/she was convicted for the crime – until the end of the sentence or release from punishment;

preventive supervision is instituted thereover – until its termination; he/she avoids performing of property and other obligations imposed by the court – until the meeting of the obligations; he/she is prosecuted (civil action) – until the end of the trial; he/she is a debtor on case on economic insolvency or bankruptcy – for the time period fixed by the court but not more than until the ending of case on economic insolvency or bankruptcy; he/she is deviated from active military service – until the end of service or the release from it in accordance with the law.

852. According to the Law 'On the procedure of leaving the Republic of Belarus and entering the Republic of Belarus of citizens of the Republic of Belarus' the persons who are under the age of 18 may leave the Republic of Belarus according to the notarized application of lawful representatives or accompanying by them. In instance of absence of the agreement of one of the parents, a person under age may ask the court for specification of the procedure of leaving. Citizens found by the court to be incapable shall have the right to leave abroad only when accompanied by their lawful representatives.

853. If any country faces an emergency preventing the safe living conditions for the citizens of the Republic of Belarus, the law shall specify that the Council of Ministers of the Republic of Belarus may take decisions related to the restriction to travel to the country in question. Those decisions and information about their recall shall be subject to publication. The indicated restrictions shall be effective until the end of the circumstances preventing the individual from leaving.

854. Legislative fixation of the time period for the consideration of applications of citizens, as well as a specification of the procedure for appealing the circumstances preventing from them from moving abroad, shall be the guarantees for the realization by the citizens of the right to move abroad. Restriction of the freedom of movement may be conditioned by the purposes stipulated in Article 23 of the Constitution, for example, prevention of disorder, epidemics, protection of the neglect of teenagers and prevention of criminal deeds.

855. Freedom of movement shall be lawfully restricted in case of prescription under the law of a criminal sentence related to deprivation of liberty or specification of other measures of punishment (measures of liability) preventing free movement and military service. These are instances where we are dealing with both sanctions for crimes committed and the necessity of performing the constitutional obligation to serve in the military.

856. The right to determine the attitude towards religion. Everyone shall have the right to determine one's own attitude towards religion, to profess any religion individually or jointly with others, or to profess none at all, to express and spread beliefs connected with one's attitude towards religion, and to participate in the performance of acts of worship and religious rituals and rites, which are not prohibited by the law (Article 31 of the Constitution). Every person shall have the right to adopt a religion or beliefs at one's choice; to have religion or beliefs; to profess religion both individually and jointly in public and in private; perform acts of worship and religious rituals and rites; to secure a religious and moral upbringing of one's children in accordance with one's faith.

857. Under Article 16 of the Constitution religions and faiths shall be equal before the law. Relations between the State and religious organizations shall be regulated by the law with regard to their influence on the formation of the spiritual, cultural and state traditions of the Belarusian people. The activities of confessional organizations directed against the sovereignty of the Republic of Belarus, its constitutional system and civic harmony, or involving a violation of civil rights and family duties by its citizens or detrimental to their health and morality, shall be prohibited.

858. Freedom of thought, conscience and religion shall be the most important fundamental human right. Its essence shall be revealed in a number of international instruments. Thus, under Article 18 of the International Covenant on Civil and Political Rights this right shall include freedom to have or to adopt a religion or belief of his/her choice, and freedom, either individually or in community with others and in public or private, to manifest his/her religion or belief in worship, observance, practice and teaching. Freedom to manifest one's religion or beliefs shall exclude any restrictions that may be put on an individual due to his/her attitude towards religion. As regards a demonstration of this freedom, the legislative regulation shall be admissible here.

859. Besides the Constitution, relations in the field of freedom of confession shall be regulated by the Law 'On Freedom of Religion and Religious Organizations' adopted on 17 December 1992 in the wording of 31 October 2002.

860. Freedom of thoughts and beliefs. Everyone is guaranteed freedom of thoughts and beliefs and their free expression. No one shall be forced to express one's beliefs or to deny them. No monopolization of the mass media by the State, public associations or individual citizens and no censorship shall be permitted (Article 33 of the Constitution).

861. The specified Article of the Constitution shall fix both freedom of speech and freedom of the press, which is a tool for expression of the freedom of speech. It is impossible to abuse the freedom of speech; it may not be used to the detriment of the rights and freedoms of other persons. Therefore, the Constitution and international legal documents shall assume its restriction. One of the methods of realization of the freedom of opinions, beliefs and their free expression shall be use of the mass media, participation in meetings and in other public arrangements, participation in discussion of draft laws and other issues of state and social life, or participation in pre-election campaigns. According to the law on the press and other mass media the citizens shall be guaranteed freedom of press and other mass media. Citizens of the Republic of Belarus shall have the right without hindrance to search, receive, use and disseminate information with the help of the press and other mass media, to freely express their thoughts, views and beliefs by their own means.

862. The State shall consider the system of the mass media as the grounds for the realization of the constitutional right of citizens of the Republic of Belarus to freedom of speech and information, as an important component of national culture and shall specify the measures directed to securing economic support of the mass media (Article 3 of the Law).

863. Censorship of the mass media shall mean a requirement for the editorship to make preliminary coordination of information, as well as the requirement to recall this or that information from airwaves or press on behalf of the State bodies, organizations, establishments, public associations, their officials. It is inadmissible to create and finance organizations, establishments, bodies or officials whose tasks and functions are to censor mass information (Article 4 of the Law).

864. The law on the press and other mass media shall specify that the founder (co-founder) of an organ of the mass media may be a citizen, group of citizens, political party and other public association, enterprise, establishment, organization, the state body.

865. The right to national affiliation, use of native language. Under Article 50 of the Constitution everyone shall have the right to preserve one's ethnic affiliation, and equally no one may be compelled to define or indicate one's ethnic affiliation. Insults to ethnic dignity shall be prosecuted by the law. Everyone shall have the right to use one's native language and to choose the language of communication. In accordance with the law, the State shall guarantee the freedom to choose the language of education and teaching.

866. Nationality shall be the affiliation of a person to any nation or ethnic national group. The right to preserve one's ethnic affiliation both the citizens of the Republic of Belarus and foreign nationals and stateless persons have.

867. Against the background of ethnic national contradictions, Belarus on the whole seems to do quite well. The Constitution shall prohibit any discrimination, national discrimination included. Article 50 of the Constitution enshrines the guarantees of the right of everyone to preserve one's ethnic affiliation, and the inadmissibility of compelling a person to define or indicate one's ethnic affiliation. Moreover, insults to ethnic dignity shall be prosecuted by the law.

868. There is a constitutional ban on the creation and activities of political and other public associations that conduct propaganda of hatred (Article 5 of the Constitution). The State shall undertake the obligation to regulate relations among the national and other communities on the grounds of the principle of equality before the law and respect for their rights and interests (Article 4 of the Constitution). There is also the constitutional obligation of everyone to preserve historical, cultural and spiritual heritage and other national treasures (Article 54 of the Constitution).

869. In elaboration of the constitutional norms there have been adopted the legislative acts and other normative acts. Among them the Law of 1993 'On National

Minorities in the Republic of Belarus' shall make the legal ground in the sphere of international relations of the Republic of Belarus, shall guarantee free development of national minorities in the Republic of Belarus, shall be based on the principles of international law in the field of human rights and national minorities.

870. There are 130 nationalities that live in the territory of the Republic of Belarus. According to the census of 2009 Belarus from among 9.5 million has the following nationalities: Belarusian – 83.7% of the whole population, Russian – 8.3%, Poles – 3.1%, Ukrainians – 1.7%, Jews – 0.1%, Armenians – 0.1%, Lithuanians – 0.1%, Tatars – 0.1%, all the other nationalities – 2.8%. Thus, we can see Belarus as a poly ethnic state.

871. The Constitution shall fix the Belarusian and Russian languages as the official languages of the Republic of Belarus (Article 17).

872. Moreover, everyone shall have the right to use one's native language and to choose the language of communication. In accordance with the law, the State shall guarantee the freedom to choose the language of one's education and teaching (Article 50).

873. The Law 'On Languages in the Republic of Belarus' shall fix the provision on free development and use of the national languages that the population of the Republic uses (Article 21); there is the proclamation of protection of languages (Article 6); the right to use one's native language in upbringing and education (Article 21).that is confirmed in the Law of the Republic of Belarus 'On Education in the Republic of Belarus' (Article 6) – upbringing and education is possible in the language of the national minority.

874. Right to judicial protection. Under part one of Article 60 of the Constitution, everyone shall be guaranteed protection of his/her rights and liberties by a competent independent and impartial court of law within time periods specified by law. The competence of the court shall be revealed, first of all, in the professionalism of judges, their capability to examine everything objectively and to deliver the ruling based on the law. Independence of the court shall mean that the judges (jury) while administering justice shall be subordinated to the law only. Any interference in the activities of the judges (jury) while administering justice is inadmissible. The independence of judges shall be secured by the procedure of their election, appointment and discharge, the immunity of judges, the legal procedure of administering justice, the secrecy of deliberation of judges while delivering decisions and the prohibition to require disclosure, liability for disrespect to the court or interference in handling concrete cases, creation of necessary organizational and technical conditions for the activities of the court, material, social securing of the court, etc.

875. Impartiality of the court shall be revealed in justifiable evaluation of the facts, ban on discrimination. For securing the impartiality of the court, legislation shall specify special guarantees, for example, challenging a judge.

876. Article 60.1 shall specify the possibility of protection of the rights and freedoms within the time period specified in law. Therefore, the time period within which the court is obliged to take the case for its consideration on points of fact is fixed. Thus, according to Article 197 of the Civil Code of the Republic of Belarus, the general time limitation of actions shall be three years. Special terms of time limitation of actions may be fixed by the legislative acts for certain types of claims.

877. Right to legal assistance. The right to legal assistance shall be one of the main elements of the legal status of any individual. This right shall be guaranteed both by the Constitution and by a number of international documents.

878. The Bar is called to carry out professional legal assistance. According to the law on the Bar the legal counsel may be a citizen of the Republic of Belarus with higher law education, professional length of service of not less than three years or, without such a length of service, a probation period from six months to one year at the Bar, who passed the qualifying exam and obtained the license for the right to deal with lawyer activities. Lawyers and probationers may not be civil servants, may not work for public and other organizations, except for the persons involved in scientific and pedagogical activities.

879. Lawyers shall render the following types of legal assistance: give advice and explanations on law issues, oral and written information on legislation; draw up applications, complaints and other legal documents; carry out representation in the courts and in other bodies and organizations on civil and administrative cases; participate in preliminary investigations and in the court on criminal cases as a defence counsel, and representatives of victims, civil plaintiffs and civil defendants. Lawyers shall also render other legal assistance to natural and legal persons.

880. Free legal aid shall be provided by collegiums of the bars at their own expenses with respect to the plaintiffs in the Courts of First Instance while conducting cases related to labour relations, collection of alimony, recovery of damages caused as a result of severe injury or other damages for health related to work, as well as invalids of I and II groups by giving advice that needs no familiarization with the files, to natural persons exempted from payments for legal aid according to the procedure specified in the effective legislation.

881. A legal counsel in his/her activities is independent and shall be subordinated to the law only. It is prohibited to interfere in the professional activities of the lawyer, to require any information from him/her that falls under attorney-client secrecy laws, as well as to require him to provide similar information to the officials and technical workers of the bodies of local government and pressure groups. The subject of attorney-client secrecy shall be the issues that were put forward by the person asking for help and assistance, but also the explanations this person obtained from the lawyer. Information that is secret may not be obtained from the lawyer and used as evidence in civil, administrative and civil trials. All the bodies and officials of the Republic of Belarus while performing their professional duties shall acknowledge and keep legal advice secret.

882. The right to protection of international organizations. Under Article 61 of the Constitution, everyone shall have the right in accordance with the international instruments ratified by the Republic of Belarus to appeal to international organizations to defend their rights and liberties, provided all available interstate means of legal defence have been exhausted.

883. To exhaust all available interstate means of legal defence shall mean the use by a citizen of all legitimate national means for the protection of one's rights and freedoms. Those means shall be the examination of disputes in the courts or in administrative bodies.

884. Application to the international treaties for the protection of the rights and freedoms under Article 61 of the Constitution shall be carried out in accordance with the international treaties ratified by the Republic of Belarus. These States are in the Council of Europe, under the aegis of it the European Court of Human Rights, which operates in accordance with the European Convention for the Protection of Human Rights and Fundamental Freedoms. Admission of the Republic of Belarus to the Council of Europe will promote the protection of the rights and freedoms of citizens of our state by using international instruments.

885. One should bear in mind that the Supreme Soviet of the Republic of Belarus in its Resolution of 10 January 1992 has ratified the Optional Protocol to the International Covenant on Civil and Political Rights of 16 December 1966 on the acknowledgement of the competences of the Committee on Human Rights in accordance with Article 41 of the specified Covenant (Vedamastsi Vyarkhovnaga Saveta Respubliki Belarus, 1992, No. 5, Article 84). According to the given Resolution the Republic of Belarus stated that 'it shall recognize the competence of the Committee on Human Rights in accordance with Article 41 of the International Covenant on Civil and Political Rights to receive and to consider the information that any State Party to the International Covenant on Civil and Political Rights asserts that another State Party does not meet its obligations within the present Covenant'.

886. The right to participate in the management of state affairs. The Constitution shall contain the norms specifying the right of a citizen to participate in the management of state affairs. Citizens of the Republic of Belarus shall have the right to take part in solution of state affairs directly or through the freely elected representatives.

887. Direct participation of citizens in the management of the society and state affairs shall be secured by holding referenda, discussion of draft laws and national and local issues, by other means specified in law. According to the procedure specified by the legislation, the citizens of the Republic of Belarus shall take part in discussion of the issues of state and public life at national and local meetings.

888. The main forms by which citizens may exercise state powers shall be referenda (plebiscites), discussion of draft laws and national and local issues, countrywide gatherings, as well as meetings of citizens Holding of referenda and national discussions shall be regulated by the Electoral Code of the Republic of Belarus and the Law of 12 July 2000 'On National and Local Assemblies'. If the plebiscite may be attended by the persons who have the right to vote, i.e., at the age of 18, the national discussion is for every citizen. The legislation may envisage the holding of national and local assemblies.

889. The right to vote and to be elected. Article 38 of the Constitution enshrines the right of citizens of the Republic of Belarus to vote freely and to be elected to state bodies on the basis of universal, equal, direct or indirect suffrage by secret ballot. The given Article fixes the basic principles of electoral law. They are developed further in the Electoral Code.

890. Elections are universal: the citizens of the Republic of Belarus shall have the right to elect their representatives at the age of 18. The Constitution and national legislation may specify an additional electoral qualification, i.e., the conditions for obtaining and exercising the electoral law. For example, age qualification (Article 80, Article 92, and Article 92.2 of the Constitution), residence qualification (Article 80 and Article 92.2 of the Constitution), education qualification (Article 116.2 of the Constitution), official service qualification (Article 92.4 of the Constitution). Citizens who are deemed incapable by a court of law or kept in places of confinement under the verdict of the court shall not take part in elections. Persons in respect to whom preventive punishment such as detention is being administered shall not take part in voting. Any direct or indirect restrictions on citizen's rights in other instances shall be impossible and punishable by the law (Article 64.2 of the Constitution).

891. Elections shall be free: the voter decides himself/herself to take part in elections or not and for whom to cast his/her vote. Several countries stipulate the obligation of citizens to participate in voting. Free participation shall mean, first of all, the absence of an impact on a citizen which would force him/her to participate or not participate in elections, which would be construed in Belarus as an influence on free will.

892. Elections shall be equal: voters shall have an equal number of votes, and the candidates for the State posts shall take part in elections on equal grounds. That shall be secured by the fact that the voter may not be included in more than one list of voters, there shall be formed the equal in number electoral districts, etc.

893. Elections may be both direct and indirect (multistage). The President, deputies of the House of Representatives of the National Assembly of the Republic, and deputies of local Councils of Deputies shall be elected by way of direct elections. The Council of the Republic of the National Assembly shall be elected by way of indirect elections (Article 91 of the Constitution). Voting during elections shall be secret: control over the will of the electorate in the process of voting shall be prohibited. In order to exclude this control over the freedom of choice which the voters possess, they shall be given the possibility to use polling booths. The ballot-paper shall be taken out by the voter personally, and he/she shall pull it into the polling-box. The right to vote and to be elected shall be referred to as political rights. Therefore, only the citizens of the Republic of Belarus may have these rights in full. In accordance with the Electoral Code, the citizens of the Russian Federation who reside on the territory of the Republic of Belarus shall have the right to take part in elections of deputies of local Councils of Deputies according to the international treaties of the Republic of Belarus.

894. The right to address the State bodies. Under Article 40 of the Constitution everyone shall have the right to address personal or collective appeals to state bodies. State bodies, as well as officials thereof, shall consider any appeal and furnish a reply within the period of time specified in the law. Any refusal to consider an appeal that has been submitted shall be justified in writing. The right to address the State bodies shall be the most important constitutional right existing in Belarus, and may be considered as one of the displays of direct democracy. The obligation of the state bodies and officials to examine the application and to give a reply within the fixed time period shall correspond to the right in question. This is the way of securing the interaction of the power and a citizen. Any person irrespective of age shall have the right to make an address. The procedure of making addresses with proposals, applications and complaints to officials of both the state bodies and public associations, organizations and enterprises regardless of the form of ownership, as well as the procedure of examination of proposals, applications and complaints shall be specified in the Law of 18 July 2011 'On complaints of citizens and legal entities' with further alterations and addenda.

895. Taking into account the fact that Article 40 of the Constitution enshrines the right to make addresses for any person, and not only the citizens of the Republic of Belarus, this right also provides guarantees to foreign citizens, as well as to stateless persons. The Law shall cover proposals, applications and complaints of citizens, except for complaints that are subject to examination under the procedure of constitutional, criminal, civil, economic and administrative proceedings.

896. The new wording of the Law shall strengthen guarantees of the rights of citizens while considering their applications. This right shall be realized voluntarily, it must not violate the rights, freedoms and lawful interests of other persons, any discrimination is prohibited, meaning that there can be no restriction of the rights of citizens or granting of any privileges depending on sex, race, nationality, language, religion, beliefs or social origin. The Law shall stipulate a ban on interference in the rights and freedoms, as well as the lawful interests of citizens and members of their families due to their appealing to the state bodies, other organizations, officials. Thereby, we deal here with the State policy of securing the right to appeal freely.

897. The Law shall qualify the types of appeals and reveal their content. The appeals may be individual or collective proposals, applications, and citizen complaints to the state body, to other official organizations in oral or in written form.

898. A proposal shall be a recommendation as regards the improvement of the activities of the state bodies, other organizations or officials, the improvement of legal regulation of relations in state and public life, the solution of issues in the economic, political, social and other spheres of the activities of the State and society.

899. An application is a motion on the realization of the rights, freedoms and lawful interests of a citizen that are not related to their violation.

900. Complaints shall be claims on restoration of the rights, freedoms and lawful interests of a citizen violated by actions or negligence of officials working for the state bodies, other organizations or citizens.

901. Written application must contain the signature with specification of the first name, second name, patronymic name, data about the place of residence or work (study), the substance of the proposal, application or complaint. Complaints without such information shall be found to be anonymous and subject to no consideration, except for those that contain the information about the offence. Applications shall be addressed to the officials of the bodies, establishments, organizations and enterprises that are competent to solve the issues raised in the applications. Applications forwarded to officials of bodies, establishments, organizations and enterprises that are not competent to solve the issues raised, shall be referred within five days to the officials of the relevant bodies, establishments, organizations and enterprises with notification of the citizens. Anonymous applications shall not be subject to consideration, except for the applications with the information about the imminent crime, the crime in progress or completed crime. Applications of citizens shall be subject to registration and obligatory examination.

902. Officials of the bodies, the relevant bodies, establishments, organizations and enterprises within their competence shall be obliged to examine thoroughly and in full the application, to take the necessary measures for its objective solution and to notify the citizens about the results.

903. Appeals, proposals and complaints must be forwarded by the citizens to the instances that are competent to solve them. According to Article 10 of the Law written complaints to the instance that is not competent to solve the given issue shall be referred to the relevant state bodies and other organizations with the notification of citizens or within five days period of time they shall be given the reply with explanation to which state body or organization they must refer. Thus, the legislator shall allow the subject that receives the application to take the relevant decision thereupon, to transfer this application to the competent body or give the relevant explanation as regards the further appropriate instance for making the application.

904. The total annual number of applications, proposals and complaints in the Republic is about two million. It shall be noted that this is the indication of both problems in the field of application of our legislation and the open nature of our society and active position of our citizens. Of course, one shall do one's best to decrease the conflict situations. It is necessary to develop administrative justice.

905. It is prohibited to refer complaints of citizens to the officials of the bodies, establishments, organizations and enterprises which are being criticized or accused of wrongdoing. The decision on the points of fact of the application or the refusal of its consideration should be motivated in written form.

906. An application must be considered on or before one month from the date of its registration, and the application that needs no additional injury or revision – on or before fifteen days, unless another time period is specified by the legislative acts. If it is necessary to carry out a special review, request of additional materials, the head of the relevant body, establishment, organization and enterprise that deals with the application, may prolong the fixed term, but for not more than one month with immediate notification of the applicant. The time limit for consideration of the application in case of the necessity of forwarding the request to a foreign state and or to the international organizations may be subject to prolongation for up to six months by the head of the organization that received the application with notification of the applicant.

907. According to the Law, the repeated applications that contain no new arguments or newly disclosed circumstances shall be considered. They are subject to no examination, if there are already relevant results of their exhaustive revisions and the citizens were given a reply. In addition, the applicant who made an application shall be informed in written form that the repeated applications are groundless and the correspondence on the issue with him/her shall be finished. The Law shall also stipulate that the complaints may be forwarded by the citizens to the state bodies, other organizations or officials up to three years from the day of violation of the rights, freedoms and lawful interests of citizens or from the date when the violations became known to them (the time period for forwarding the proposals and applications shall not be restricted). Officials shall have the right to refuse consideration of the complaint in case of missing the term. If the three years time period was missed due to a reasonable excuse (serious illness, disablement, long-term business trip, etc.) and that is secured by the document, the term in question shall be returned under decision of the head of the state body or the person he/she authorized.

908. The fixation of three years time period for forwarding the complaint will, on the one hand, inject a little common sense into litigation (one should not harbour a grudge for ever), and on other hand shall impose liability on the officials for their proper, lawful consideration. The decision adopted as a result of the application may be subject to appeal to a higher body, establishment, organization or the court under the procedure specified by the legislation of the Republic of Belarus. On the grounds of Article 40, Article 122.4 Article 116.4 of the Constitution of the Republic of Belarus, the Constitutional Court shall be entitled to deliver its decision owing to the application of a citizen.

909. Freedom of association. Freedom of association is one of the most important freedoms. The Constitution shall grant everyone the freedom of association. However, judges, employees of the Public Attorney's Office, the staff of bodies of internal affairs, the Committee of State Control and security bodies, as well as servicemen may not be members of political parties or other public associations that pursue political goals (Article 36 of the Constitution).

910. There are various types of public associations. Political parties and trade unions have a special place among them. According to the Law 'On Public Associations' of 4 October 1994 with further alterations and addenda the public association shall be comprised of citizens that formed an official grouping on the grounds of a community of shared interests for the joint realization of civil, economic, social and cultural goals (Article 1).

911. The Constitution and legislation shall determine the restrictions for the creation of public associations. It is prohibited to create public associations that have the aim to change the constitutional system by force or which carry out propaganda of social, national, religious and racial hatred (Article 5 of the Constitution). The Law on public associations shall also stipulate the inadmissibility of the creation of public associations aimed at the overthrow of the constitutional system, the violation of the integrity and the security of the State, and the propagation of violence. However, in spite of those variant readings, we deem that the norms of the law in question are within the constitutional wordings.

912. It is admissible to create international, national and local public associations. They shall be created on the initiative of not less than ten citizens of the Republic of Belarus aged at least 18. Citizens at the age of 16 may create youth and children's public associations. As for the membership in public associations, their members may be citizens at the age of 16. In the instances specified by statutes of public associations, their members may be persons under the fixed age under the condition that they have the relevant written permission of their lawful representatives.

913. Procedure of creation and activities of political organizations shall be determined by the special Law 'On Political Parties' of 5 October 1994 with further alterations and addenda. A political party shall be an independent association of citizens formed on the grounds of individual voluntary membership acts within the framework of the Constitution and the laws of the Republic of Belarus, as well as contributing to revealing the political will of citizens. A party, above all, takes part in elections (Article 1). According to Article 10 of the Law 'On political parties' the creation of a political party needs no less than 1,000 members from the majority of oblasts of the Republic of Belarus and the City of Minsk. If both citizens of the Republic of Belarus and foreign citizens may be members of public associations, the right to associate in a political party is limited only to citizens of the Republic of Belarus.

914. Affiliation or non-affiliation of a citizen to a political party may not be the grounds for restriction of his/her rights or for inadmissibility to perform duties specified in law. Exemptions from this rule shall affect certain categories of citizens. Thus, the President of the Republic of Belarus must suspend his membership of any political parties for the whole term. Judges, employees of the Public Attorney's Office, the staff of bodies of internal affairs, the Committee of State Control and security bodies, as well as servicemen may not be members of political parties for the whole period of their terms of office. Those persons must specify their membership in a political party in the official documents. The founders of political parties may be citizens of the Republic of Belarus at the age of 18 who have the right to vote, who are not restricted in their active capacities by the court and who are not in places of confinement.

915. Political parties shall have a fixed number of members. In contradiction to public associations, the law draws no distinction as regards the age depending on foundation (creation) and membership in a political party. One may deem that the right to be both the founder and in future a member may be obtained by reaching the age of 18. Citizens shall have the right to be associated in trade unions.

916. The freedom to hold assemblies, rallies, street marches, demonstrations and pickets. The freedom to hold assemblies, rallies, street marches, demonstrations and pickets that do not disturb law and order or violate the rights of other citizens of the Republic of Belarus shall be guaranteed by the State. The procedure for conducting the *above* events shall be determined by the law (Article 35 of the Constitution). Analysis of this Article shall signify that the Constitution, having proclaimed the right to freedom of public expressions of dissent, shall envisage the legislative regulation of the procedure of their holding. At present, the procedure of organization and holding of assemblies, rallies, street marches, demonstrations and pickets is determined by the Law 'On Mass Arrangements' of 30 December 1997 with further alterations and addenda. The Law shall specify the procedure of permission (not the procedure of notification) for holding of mass measures. However, the freedom to hold them guaranteed by the Constitution may be restricted in instances specified in law, in the interest of national security, public order, the protection of morals and the health of population, as well as the rights and liberties of other persons (Article 23.1 of the Constitution).

917. The Law shall give a definition of public measures: assembly – joint attendance of a group of citizens in a previously specified place in the open air at a fixed time for a collective discussion and solutions to questions involving their interests; meeting – mass assembly of citizens for public discussion and expression of their attitude towards the actions of persons and organizations, events of social public life, as well as solutions to issues involving their interests; street procession – organized mass movement of citizens by the footpath or along the carriageway (avenue, square) in order to attract attention to any problems or expression their social and public views, their religious mood or their reasons for protesting in public; picket – public expression by a citizen or a group of citizens of a social or political group, personal and other interests or just to protest (without procession), including by means of hunger strike, as regards any problem with or without use of placards, transparencies and other devices.

918. According to the law the organizers of the assembly, meeting, street procession, demonstration and picket may be citizens of the Republic of Belarus who reside in its territory at the age of 18 and who have the right to vote. Application on holding of a measure shall be made in written form on or before fifteen days prior to the fixed date of holding of assembly, meeting, street procession, demonstration or picket.

919. Head of a local executive and administrative body or his/her deputy shall be obliged to consider the application and on or before give days prior to the date of the holding of a measure to inform the organizer in written form about the decision taken. The decision of the head of a local executive and administrative body or his/her deputy about the prohibition of the assembly, meeting, street procession, demonstration and picket shall be subject to appeal to the court. Assemblies, meetings, street processions, demonstrations and pickets may be held in any suitable places, except for the places where it is illegal to protest, decided by local executive and administrative bodies. Assemblies, meetings, street processions, demonstrations and pickets not far from the building of the residence of the President of the Republic of Belarus, the National Assembly of the Republic of Belarus, the Councils of Ministers of the Republic of Belarus, television and radio centre, pedestrian subways, metro stations may be held no less than 200 metres away, and no less than 50 metres away from buildings of the national state bodies, local executive and administrative bodies, diplomatic and consular missions, courts, the Public Attorney's Offices, territories of organizations that secure defence potential and national safety, as well as vital functions of the population (public transport, water-supply, energy and thermal energy supply, as well as provision of other types of powers, hospitals, pre-school children establishments, polyclinics). Assemblies, meetings, street processions, demonstrations and pickets may be held from 8:00 a.m. to 10:00 p.m. Local executive and administrative bodies may specify the regular places for holding of assemblies, meetings, street processions, demonstrations and pickets, as well as places where their holding shall be inadmissible.

920. Freedom of press and information. The Constitution shall guarantee the citizens of the Republic of Belarus to receive, store and disseminate complete, reliable and timely information of the activities of state bodies and public associations, on the political, economic, cultural and international life, and on the state of the environment. State bodies, public associations and officials shall afford a citizen of the Republic of Belarus the opportunity to familiarize themselves with material that affects their rights and legitimate interests. The use of information may be restricted by legislation with the purpose to safeguard the honour, dignity, personal and family life of the citizens and the full implementation of their rights (Article 34 of the Constitution). Due to the requirements of this Article, the activities of state bodies and public associations must be open. They are obliged, within their competence, to give complete, reliable and timely information on political, economic, cultural and international life, and on the state of the environment. For these purposes the Constitution, as well as other acts shall stipulate various rights and obligations of the subjects of power. Thus, according to Article 84 of the Constitution, the President, as the Head of State, shall deliver annual messages to the people of the Republic of

Belarus on the state of the nation and on the guidelines of domestic and foreign policy; he shall deliver annual messages to the Parliament and express his evaluation of the state of affairs in the country and in society, as well as perspectives of further development. The state bodies shall give regular information to the citizens about the meetings of the state bodies through television, radio, and other mass media.

921. The requirement of the Constitution (Article 7) and of the acts of current legislation to publish and to promulgate the enforceable enactments of the state bodies shall be principally significant from the point of view of giving information about the activities of the state bodies, as well as from the position of the realization by the citizens of their rights and obligations. It is current practice, for example, for our citizens to request information on the state of the environment. This obligation shall be imposed both on the bodies of general and special competence, in particular, the Ministry on Emergencies, the Ministry on Public Health Protection, etc.

922. Materials that may involve the rights and lawful interests of a citizen may be decisions related to depriving him/her of any privileges; materials of examinations of the bodies of inquiry, investigation, prosecution and other; criminal, civil and other cases about calling to liability or where under consideration are other issues on the initiative of the citizen in question (e.g., he/she acts as a plaintiff). A citizen shall have the right to familiarize them self with the process of settling his/her application to the state body or to the officials. Specific materials and information thereon may have restricted access; for example, as regards state or commercial secrets (in particular, the law on state secrets shall specify the information that may be referred to the State secrets).

923. Right to equal access to any post in the state bodies. Citizens of the Republic of Belarus, in accordance with their capabilities and vocational training, shall be entitled to equal access to any post in the state bodies (Article 39 of the Constitution).

924. Under Article 39 of the Basic Law citizens of the Republic of Belarus shall be guaranteed without any discrimination equal access to any post in the state bodies. Moreover, there shall be no distinction of any kind, such as race, colour, sex, language, religion, political and other opinion, national or social origin, property, birth or other status (Articles 2.25 of the International Covenant on Civil and political Rights). The only criteria when performing civil service shall be capabilities and professional training of an application. In certain instances there are age limitations, for example, for the judge office one shall be at the age of 25, as for the judges on administrative and execution procedures – 23, for the Presidency – 35. The Law on civil service shall regulate the procedure of civil service.

925. Under Article 11 of the Constitution, foreign citizens and stateless persons in the territory of the Republic of Belarus shall enjoy the rights and liberties and execute duties on equal terms with the citizens of the Republic of Belarus, unless otherwise specified in the Constitution, the laws and international treaties. According to Article 17 of the Law 'On the Legal Status of Foreign Citizens and Stateless Persons in the Republic of Belarus' foreign citizens and stateless persons may not hold posts where the appointment in accordance with the legislation is related to the affiliation to the citizenship of the Republic of Belarus. By the fact that the aim of Article 39 of the Constitution is to fix the equality of citizens of the Republic of Belarus, we consider this to be constitutional and correspond to the norms of the law and the international treaty specifying the peculiarities of taking for certain state offices (first of all, as regards non-political posts) of international citizens or stateless persons.

§3. Economic, Social and Cultural Rights

926. Right to work. Under Article 41 of the Constitution citizens of the Republic of Belarus shall be guaranteed the right to work as the worthiest means of an individual's self-assertion, that is the right to choose one's profession, type of occupation and work in accordance with one's vocation, capabilities, education and vocational training, and having regard to social needs, and the right to healthy and safe working conditions. The State shall create conditions necessary for full employment of the population. Where a person is unemployed for reasons that are beyond one's control, he/she shall be guaranteed training in new specializations and an upgrade of his/her qualifications with regard to social needs, and to unemployment benefit in accordance with the law.

927. Under Article 41.3 of the Constitution, citizens shall have the right to protect their economic and social interests, including the right to form trade unions and conduct collective contracts (agreements), and the right to strike. The Basic Law shall prohibit forced labour, other than work or service specified in the verdict of a court of law or in accordance with the law on a state of emergency or martial law. Article 41 of the Constitution shall proclaim the right to work as the worthiest means of an individual's self-assertion. This wording in combination with other norms of the Constitution shall also imply the right not to be engaged in labour activities: unemployment may not be the ground for calling a person to any legal liability (administrative, criminal, and other).

928. The Constitutional right to work shall include the right to choose one's profession, type of occupation and work in accordance with one's vocation, capabilities, education and vocational training, and having regard to social needs. Such a wording shall mean that, first of all, individuals may realize their capabilities to work through the procedure of recruitment (e.g., by way of concluding the labour contracts), but also as an entrepreneur, farmer, etc.; second, these capabilities may be realized taking into account social needs, their absence result in the fact that there will be unemployed persons in localities or in the State as a whole due to satisfaction of the job market by the relevant specialists included.

929. In accordance with the labour legislation, the conclusion of a labour contract shall be admissible with persons of the age of 16. With the written consent of one of the parents (tutor, trustee) the labour contract may be concluded with a person of the age of 14 for simple work that causes no damage to the health and that does not impinge on their course of study. A list of simple jobs for persons of the age from 14 to 16 shall be subject to approval by the Government of the Republic of Belarus or by the body it authorized. Hard work and work under harmful and dangerous conditions, underground and mining work is prohibited before the age of 18. Members of a cooperative may be persons of the age of 16. Citizens (not only those who are employed at the present time) may protect their economic and social interests by different ways. The most common one is application to the commission on labour disputes, the court of law, professional association, conclusion of collective contracts (agreements), and termination of work (strike).

930. According to the Law of 22 April 1992 'On Trade Unions' with further alterations and addenda the right to associate in trade unions is without any distinction, including persons who are studying at higher, specialized secondary and vocational training schools. All trade unions shall enjoy equal rights. Affiliation or non-affiliation to the trade unions shall not entail any restrictions of labour, social economic, political, individual rights and freedoms of citizens guaranteed by the legislation. It is prohibited to condition employment, promotion, as well as dismissal by affiliation to the particular trade union, joining or withdrawal from it (Article 4 of the Law on Trade Unions).

931. Trade unions shall be empowered by a wide scope of rights on the protection of labour and other rights of workers. Decree of the President of the Republic of Belarus of 6 May 2010 'On exercise public control by trade unions' public control shall be exercised by trade unions in the form of inspections over observance of legislation on labour, labour protection, execution of collective agreement.

932. Right to a just share of remuneration for the economic results of the labour. Employees shall be guaranteed a just share of remuneration for the economic results of their labour in accordance with the quantity, quality and social significance of such work, but it shall not be less than the level that shall ensure them and their families a life of independence and dignity. Women and men, adults and minors shall be entitled to equal remuneration for work of equal value (Article 42 of the Constitution). The Constitution shall enshrine the guarantees of employees to remuneration that must be just and may not be less than the level that shall ensure them and their families a life of independence and dignity.

933. Totality of remunerations calculated in monetary units that the employer shall be obliged to pay the worker for his/her work, as well as for the periods including the working hours, shall be the wage. Proceeding from the minimum consumer budget, the Government shall fix the rate of the minimum wage. Collective treaties (agreements, except for those where a party is an organization with state budget and governmental subsidies) may stipulate a higher rate of the minimum wage. The

Labour Code shall specify the forms, systems and the size of work. Women and men and shall be entitled to equal remuneration for work of equal value.

934. Minors shall be subject to special protection. The wages for workers under the age of 18 with shortened working days shall be paid at the same rate as for the relevant categories of full time workers. Work of minors who perform piece-work shall be subject to remuneration according to the piece-rates fixed for adults with extra payments according to the tariff rate for the time period for which their working hours are lessened in comparison with the working hours of adults. Remuneration of the work of students of general education, vocational and secondary special education establishments who are working in their spare time shall be made in proportion to the time worked off or depending on productivity. Employers may grant extra benefits for students.

935. The Labour Code shall fix directly that the wages shall be paid in monetary units of the Republic of Belarus. Substitution of monetary remuneration fully or partially for the remuneration in kind (mixed form of remuneration) shall be possible only with the consent of the worker. In addition, remuneration in kind must be reasonable and suitable for personal consumption, as well as expedient for the worker and his/her family. Remuneration in kind shall be made by goods, the list of which shall be approved by the Government of the Republic of Belarus. Remuneration shall be made as a rule at the working places. If a worker at the date of paying the wage executed the order of the employer out of the working place (in the organization of the client, in business trip, at the extension courses, etc.), then at the request of the worker the employer must send him/her the wage at their own expenses. At the will of the worker the wage in full or in part shall be transferred to a bank account.

936. In case of dismissal of the worker, all due payments from the employer shall be paid at the date of dismissal. If the worker was off work on the date of dismissal, the relevant payments must be paid on or before the next date after the date required to make final payment.

937. In case of a dispute on the size of payments that are due to the worker in the instance of his/her dismissal, the employer shall be obliged within the time period fixed in the labour legislation to pay a certain indisputable sum.

938. A wage that was not obtained at the date of the death of the worker shall be paid to the members of his/her family who are dependants of the dead person at the date of his/her death.

939. If, through the fault of the employer, the due sums were not paid, the worker shall have the right to recover from the employer the average earnings for each day of delay.

940. Right to holidays. The right to holidays shall be enshrined as one of the constitutional rights of working people. For employees this right shall be safeguarded by the establishment of a working week of no more than forty hours, shorter working hours at night and the provision of an annual paid leave and weekly rest days (Article 43 of the Constitution).

941. The Labour Code of the Republic of Belarus shall regulate in detail the provision for workers of rest days. Thus, according to Article 134, workers shall be provided break time during the working hours for rest and for catering of not less than twenty minutes and not more than two hours that shall be used by the worker at his/her own discretion and shall not be included in the working hours.

942. For certain types of work, equally with break time for rest and for catering, there shall be provided additional special breaks during the working hours that shall be included in the working hours (breaks for nursing (breast-feeding), breaks to warm-up, breaks for rest from loading and unloading work, etc.). Types of those works, length and procedure for provision of such breaks shall be determined by the office labour regulations. All workers shall be provided days of rest (weekly regular holidays). In case of a working week of five days, there shall be provided two days of rest each calendar week, except for those weeks when for one of the Saturdays the timetable specifies recompense for the arrears of work up to a weekly standard of working hours. One day of rest shall be provided in such a week. In case of a working week of six days, there shall be provided one day of rest. The common day of rest shall be Sunday. In exceptional cases Sunday may be declared as a working day by the President of the Republic of Belarus. The second day off in case of the working week of five days shall be determined by the labour office regulations or by the schedule of works (shift works), unless otherwise specified by the agreement of the parties. Both days off shall be provided, as a rule, running together.

943. According to Article 138 of the Labour Code the length of weekly regular rest must be not less than forty-two hours. Workers shall have the right to labour and social leave under the grounds stipulated by the Labour Code.

944. Right of property. Under Article 44 of the Constitution the State shall guarantee everyone the right of property and shall contribute to its acquisition. A proprietor shall have the right to possess, enjoy or dispose of assets either individually or jointly with others. The inviolability of property and the right to inherit property shall be protected by law. Property acquired in accordance with the law shall be safeguarded by the State. The State shall encourage and protect the savings of citizens and guarantee conditions for the return of deposits.

945. It is very important, especially taking our history into account, that the compulsory alienation of assets shall be permitted only by reason of public need, under the conditions and procedure specified by the law, with timely and full compensation for the value of the alienated assets, and in accordance with a ruling of a court of law. The exercise of the right of property shall not be contrary to social benefit and security, or be harmful to the environment or historical and cultural treasures, or infringe upon the rights and legally protected interests of others (Article 44 of the Constitution).

946. The basic acts regulating relations related to the property shall be the Constitution and the Civil Code. Property may be state and private. Subjects of the right to state property shall be the Republic of Belarus and administrative and territorial units. Subjects of the right to private property shall be the natural and non-governmental legal persons. Citizens and legal persons may be owners of any assets, except for the certain types of property that, in accordance with the law, may not be the property of citizens and legal persons. The quantity and the value of the property owned by citizens shall not be limited, except for the instances where these limits are specified by the law in order to protect national security, pubic order, public health or morals or the rights and freedoms of others. As for the legal persons, those limitations may be stipulated by the legislative acts.

947. The proprietor shall have the right to possess, use and dispose of one's assets. The property owner shall be entitled at his/her discretion to make any transactions with his/her assets that are not contrary to legislation, social benefit and social security, that are not harmful to the environment, historical and cultural values, as well as that do not infringe upon the rights and lawful interests of other persons, including to alienate his/her property, to transfer them, remaining the owner, the right to possess, use and dispose of one's assets, and to dispose of the assets by some other means.

948. Possession, use and disposal of land and of other natural resources to the extent that their turnover is admissible by legislation, shall be carried out freely by their owner, as long as this exploitation is not harmful to the environment, and does not infringe upon the rights and lawful interests of other persons. The proprietor may transfer his/her assets to another person for their managing by proxy. Turning over the assets to the manager by proxy shall not entail the vesting of the right of property to the manager by proxy in the interests of the owner or the third person he/she specified.

949. Under Article 44 of the Constitution, the inviolability of property and the right to inherit property shall be protected by the law. Inheritance shall be regulated by the Civil Code and by other acts of legislation adopted in accordance with the Civil Code.

950. Right to housing. Citizens of the Republic of Belarus shall be entitled to housing. This right shall be safeguarded by the development of state, and private housing and assistance for citizens in the acquisition of housing. The State and local self-government shall grant housing free of charge or at available prices in accordance with the law to citizens who are in need of social protection (Article 48 of the Constitution). The constitutional right to a dignified standard of living shall include the right to housing. The right to housing may be realized by different ways, and the support on behalf of the State shall be presumed here.

951. Citizens of the Republic of Belarus, in the field of housing, shall have the right: to obtain a dwelling for its use under the conditions and according to the procedure specified by the Housing Code; to obtain a plot of land for individual house-building; to carry out individual or collective house-building; to grant, according to the procedure specified by the legislation of the Republic of Belarus, soft credits, subsidies and other forms of state support for building or acquisition of a living accommodation; to obtain, according to the procedure specified by the legislation of the Republic of Belarus, grants for payment of the use of accommodation and of public services; to acquire a place to live under the grounds stipulated by the laws of the Republic of Belarus; use of an abode under a lease contract or under other grounds specified by the Code in question; to possess, use and dispose of living accommodations owned by the individual in question at his/her discretion, except for the instances determined by the Housing Code and other laws of the Republic of Belarus; to independently choose the forms and the ways to improve one's housing conditions, repairs and operation of an accommodation.

952. The right to have an accommodation may have originated under the lease or sub-lease system. Housing legislation shall stipulate the procedure of taking into account those citizens who are in need of improvement of their housing conditions in order to grant them further funding or priority on the housing list. Articles 43 and 44 of the Housing Code shall specify the grounds for finding citizens to be needy of improvement of their housing conditions and registration of those citizens that is carrying out both according to the places of residence by the local executive and administrative bodies and at the working places.

953. Citizens shall acquire the right of ownership to a living accommodation under the grounds of: building of a house, or part of the dwelling; a flat; privatization of occupied living accommodation of the State housing stock; inheritance of a living accommodation; drawing up the right of ownership to a living accommodation by a member of the organization of citizens having built; transfer of a living accommodation into their ownership instead of a torn down dwelling as a result of withdrawal of the plot of land for the State's needs; transfer of an accommodation into their ownership instead of being lost as a result of heavy repairs or reconstruction of the dwelling; civil law transaction; under other grounds specified by the legislation of the Republic of Belarus.

954. Right to health care. Citizens of the Republic of Belarus shall be guaranteed the right to health care, including free treatment at state health care establishments. The State shall make health care facilities accessible to all of its citizens. The right of citizens of the Republic of Belarus to health care shall also be secured by the development of physical training and sport, measures to improve the environment, and the opportunity to use fitness establishments and improvements in occupational safety (Article 45 of the Constitution).

955. According to the law of the Republic of Belarus on public health, the right to health care shall be secured by free medical aid at state health care establishments, except for the types of treatment that must be specified by the Council of Ministers of the Republic of Belarus; strengthening the material and technical basis of the health care establishments; training the medical and pharmaceutical personnel; creation of a favourable habitat for a human being; possibility to use medical, preventive and fitness establishments; creation of conditions for physical training and sport.

956. Each citizen shall have the right to medical check-ups and to get medical and sanitary assistance in any establishment of public health care, taking into account the type and capacity of the establishment. In order to prevent diseases and for continued observation of sick persons in clinics, the bodies of public health care shall assign the citizens at their will to the establishment of public health care, taking into account the type and capacity of the establishment, and the heads of establishments of public health care shall assign them to the doctors respectively.

957. Each citizen shall have the right to receive complete and reliable information about his/her state of health. This kind of information, as it is specified in Article 7 of the Law, may be incomplete or restricted, if, in the opinion of the medical and pharmaceutical officials, the complete and reliable information will make the state of health of the sick person worse. Health security shall consist of wide complex of measures, including a healthy environment, occupational safety, etc.

958. Right to a healthy environment. Everyone shall be entitled to a healthy environment and to compensation for loss or damage caused by the violation of this right. The State shall supervise the rational utilization of natural resources to protect and to improve living conditions, and to preserve and restore the environment (Article 46 of the Constitution).

959. Environmental protection and rational utilization of natural resources and the security of the ecological safety of the human being shall be the most important conditions for the stable economic and social development of the State.

960. According to the Law on environmental protection, the state bodies, legal and natural persons, by planning and exercising activities affecting the environment, shall be obliged, in particular, to proceed from the priority of protection of human health and life as compared with other purposes of nature tenure and use; securing the rights of persons to conducive surroundings for life, work and rest; a scientifically grounded combination of ecological and economic interests of the society; a regional use of natural resources with the possibilities of the surroundings taken into account; the necessity of reproduction of natural resources and inadmissibility of irreversible consequences for the environment and for the human health.

961. Guided by these principles, both the types of natural resources that are involved in everyday economic turnover and the types of natural resources that are not used directly at a definite period of time shall be subject to protection. These are climate resources, atmosphere, including the ozone layer, land, mineral wealth and the bowels of the earth, waters, the vegetable and animal kingdom, as well as other natural objects.

962. Rational utilization of natural resources shall be stipulated by other legislative acts, including the Codes on (Land, Mineral Wealth, Water, Forests), as well as the Law on drinking water supply, the Law on natural territories and objects with special conditions of security, etc.

963. Right to education. One of the historical successes of our state has been to have secured a high level of education. Article 49 of the Constitution enshrines the right of everyone to education. Accessible and free general, secondary and vocation-technical education shall be guaranteed. Secondary specialized and higher education shall be accessible to all in accordance with the capabilities of each individual. Everyone may, on a competitive basis, obtain the appropriate education at state educational establishments free of charge.

964. Right to equal possibilities to access to a national system of education shall be applicable to all the persons who reside in the Republic of Belarus (including foreign citizens and stateless persons who reside in the territory of the Republic). This right, according to Article 5 of the Law on education, shall be secured by the creation of conditions for general, secondary and vocation-technical education, taking national traditions, individual needs and capabilities into account; development of the State and other educational institutions of various types and forms of study; free education in state, as well as other in other non-governmental, educational institutions for those who get through the entrance examination and who successfully fulfil the requirements of the necessary educational level or those who have the privileges in accordance with the legislation of the Republic of Belarus.

965. All state and non-governmental educational and educative institutions in the territory of the Republic of Belarus shall belong to the national system of education of the Republic that shall include: pre-school education; general secondary education; out-of-school education, vocation-technical education; secondary specialized education, higher education, training of scientific, as well as scientific and pedagogical personnel; raising the level of professional skills and retraining of the personnel; self-education of citizens.

966. Unity and continuity in the system of education shall be ensured by the consistency of plans and programmes, the succession of the levels and forms of education, and the creation of educational establishments that unite various types of education. The law shall specify the rights and duties of students, other categories of the students, as well as the rights and duties of the parents and persons in *loco parentis*.

967. Students from other towns shall have the right to have a room in the student hostel or to state grants in case of renting the unit under the procedure specified by the Government of the Republic of Belarus. Students of higher and secondary specialized educational institutions who successfully study part-time shall have the right to additional paid leave at their place of work, a shorter working week and other privileges specified by the legislation. Students of higher, secondary specialized and vocation-technical educational institutions of who are studying successfully under the part-time form shall have the right to a guaranteed grant. Those students who study with good and excellent marks shall be paid larger grants. Students of vocation-technical and secondary specialized educational institutions, audience of preparatory courses, students who are studying successfully under the out-of-service form shall be given deferment of military service for the whole term of study. Students of higher, secondary specialized and vocation-technical educational institutions shall have the right to conclude contracts with enterprises and organizations according to the procedure specified by the Government of the Republic of Belarus. The contracts may stipulate full or partial payment for training, payments of grants, increasing grants included, provision of credits, working places, housing, as well as other conditions and duties of the students.

968. Pupils from villages shall be provided with free hostels and free transport to their place of study in accordance with the procedure specified by local Councils of Deputies.

969. Children who are orphans, children who are without the guardianship of parents, children from families of moderate means, children who reside in zones of medical and sanitary control (or those who were settled out of these zones), children who are invalids and who have defects of development shall have privileges in accordance with the legislation of the Republic of Belarus.

970. Rights of other categories of students shall be specified by provisions on educational establishments (statutes), by the relevant legislative and normative acts with the indicated norms of social security taken into account.

971. Students of secondary and higher educational establishments and other categories of students shall be bound to respect the teachers and lecturers, to master sound knowledge and practical skills according to the established requirements, to follow office regulations, as well as to fulfil other requirements determined by the legislation of the Republic of Belarus and the statute of an educational institution.

972. Parents and persons in *loco parentis* shall be entitled to: choose their child's pre-school establishment; the choice of a primary school must take into account the will, individual bents and peculiarities of a child, and require from the administration of the school to create proper conditions for care and catering of children in primary and secondary establishments, full value of teaching and upbringing in accordance with the individual peculiarities and capabilities of children, respectful treatment to the individuality of a child; take part in discussion of the issues of education and upbringing, in out-of-school educational work. Parents and persons in *loco parentis* shall be responsible for the education of the children. They shall be obliged to respect the dignity of a child; promote his/her progress of full value; to secure a decent primary education for the child, to create necessary conditions for study and rest, and to strengthen the health of the child.

973. Part two of the Article of the Constitution under description shall enshrine the accessibility and free nature of education of only general secondary and vocation-technical education.

974. Right to social security. Citizens of the Republic of Belarus shall be guaranteed the right to social security in old age, in the event of illness, disability, loss of fitness for work and loss of a bread-winner and in other instances specified in the law. The State shall display particular concern for veterans of war and labour, as well as for those who lost their health in the defence of national and public interests (Article 47 of the Constitution).

975. Effective legislation shall envisage different types of pensions (labour (old age) pensions, disablement pensions, survivors' pensions, long service pensions, pensions for special services to the republic, social pensions). The law on pension security shall set up the norms and the procedure of pension security of citizens of the Republic of Belarus depending on the type of pensions.

976. Thus, disabled members of the family of the deceased bread-winner who were his/her dependants shall have the right to a survivors' pension. In addition, for the children, as well as for certain persons, the pensions shall be awarded regardless of the status of their dependants. At the request of the members of the family, they may be awarded more than one pension in common.

977. For the purposes of value care and upbringing of children in the family, the State shall provide payment of birth grants until a certain age of the child, shall pay other benefits, guarantee the right to use, if necessary, a pre-school establishment, as well as shall grant privileges in accordance with the legislation of the Republic of Belarus.

978. The Law 'On State Benefits for the Families Who Bring up Children' of 29 December 2012 with further alterations and addenda has specified the level of support guaranteed by the State of families who have minors, meaning the system of minimum social guarantees and contributing allowances to allow the citizens the necessary conditions for the birth and the raising of children. According to the law in question a maternity benefit shall be awarded; a birth benefit; a benefit for a women who were registered before the twelfth week of pregnancy; benefits for the care of the child till the age of three: at the age from three and more; for care of the child who is ill up until 14; for care of the child up until three and the child who is an invalid up to 18 years old in case the mother or another person, who in fact is looking after the child, is ill; for care of the child who is an invalid at the age 18; in case of using facilities for the medical treatment of children who are invalids in sanatoria and health resorts before the age of 18; for children before the age of 18 who are infected with immunodeficiency or AIDS. Certain categories under the law are subject to bonus granting and paying.

979. The benefits, except for the beneficial payments for the single mothers, who are raising the child until the age of one year and a half, shall be added by the following allowances: for the children of the single mothers, divorced women and men, if one of the parents does not pay alimony or in other instances specified by the legislation, where the recovery of alimony is impossible; for children of single mothers, children who are orphans and children who are without the guardianship of the parents who formerly were brought up in a Children's Home (boarding schools); for the children who are invalids before the age of 18 and who are raising by their family; for the children of fixed term military personnel.

980. Awarding and payment of benefits, as well as allowances, shall be carried out, as a rule, at the place of work or study of the mother of the child; if the mother is unemployed and is not studying, then at the place of work or study of the father of the child (a person who adopted a child, a tutor) or another relative who has the right to the benefits necessary for the upbringing or care of the child on the grounds of the application and on the basis of all the necessary documents.

981. Right to participation in national cultural activities. Article 51 of the Constitution shall enshrine the right of everyone to take part in the cultural life of Belarus. This right shall be secured by universal accessibility to the treasures of domestic and world culture that are held in state and public collections and by the development of a network of cultural and educational establishments.

982. Citizens of the Republic of Belarus shall have the right to freedom of artistic, scientific and technical creativity and teaching shall be guaranteed. They may be also engage in any type of cultural activities, except for those prohibited by the law (Article 4 of the law on culture in the Republic of Belarus).

983. For the purposes of the realization of this right by the citizens, the State bodies shall be charged with certain obligations: they are bound to improve the system of social, organizational and legal, as well as economic guarantees for the development of art and culture, to create the necessary conditions for giving the citizens access to national and world cultural heritage; to form a system of enterprises and establishments of art and culture; to allot the necessary material and financial means; to secure scientific researches and elaboration of scientific drafts in the field of culture, training of the qualified personnel; to create the guarantees and impetus for arts creation by preserving the traditional culture (folklore, popular industry, trade and handicraft), use of cultural achievements; protection of the interests of people of the Republic of Belarus in the field of culture.

984. The important guarantee against discrimination shall be the provision of the law (Article 10) that the persons of any nationality or ethnic group who reside in the territory of the Republic of Belarus shall be guaranteed the right to develop one's culture and to perfect one's language, to set up national schools, enterprises and establishments (theatres, museums, publishing houses, etc.). Citizens of the Republic of Belarus of any nationality shall have the right to set up cultural associations, cultural and educational partnerships and societies, national cultural centres.

Chapter 3. Legal Protection of Aliens

985. Foreign nationals in the Republic of Belarus are individuals who are not citizens of the Republic of Belarus with evidence of citizenship of another state. It shall be noted that in the Republic of Belarus aliens who have two or more citizenships are considered to be citizens of the State under the documents of which they entered the territory of the Republic of Belarus. In the Republic of Belarus stateless persons are individuals who are not citizens of the Republic of Belarus and who have no evidence of citizenship of another state.

986. The legal status of aliens and stateless persons is specified in the Constitution, by the Law of 4 January 2010 'On the Legal Status of Aliens and Stateless Persons in the Republic of Belarus' and by other legislative acts. The legal status of aliens in the Republic of Belarus may be defined on the basis of international treaties of the Republic of Belarus.

987. Aliens and stateless persons in the Republic of Belarus have the same rights, liberties and obligations as the citizens of the Republic of Belarus, unless otherwise specified by the Constitution of the Republic of Belarus, the *aforementioned* law or other legal acts of the Republic of Belarus. The restriction of the rights and liberties of aliens and stateless persons should be imposed only to protect the rights and fundamental liberties of the citizens of the Republic of Belarus, to ensure state security, maintenance of public order and health of the population. Aliens and stateless persons in the Republic of Belarus are equal before the law irrespective of origin, social and property status, race and nationality, sex, education, language, religion or occupation. Realization of rights and liberties in the Republic of Belarus by aliens and stateless persons should not violate the interests of the Republic of Belarus, rights and legal interests of citizens of the Republic of Belarus and other individuals.

988. Provisions of the Law of 4 January 2010 specify the rights and liberties of these individuals applicable on the mutual base. If another state restricts or violates the universally acknowledged rules of legal regulations of aliens towards citizens of the Republic of Belarus, the Republic of Belarus may impose retaliatory restrictions on the rights and freedoms of the citizens of this state.

989. Under the Constitution of the Republic of Belarus and laws of the Republic of Belarus aliens in the Republic of Belarus are guaranteed personal immunity and inviolability of property, as well as other rights and liberties.

990. Arrested aliens should be immediately informed in a language they can understand of the reasons of their arrest or detention and about the rights they have in accordance with legislation of the Republic of Belarus. The body that detained or arrested the alien should notify the Foreign Ministry about this within three days after the day of arrest or detention so that the diplomatic or consular agency representing the aforementioned foreign tourist or immigrant can be informed.

991. Aliens are permitted free movement in the Republic of Belarus except for the places that require special permission of internal security organs or authorized organizations, and places that require special permission of the administrative body of these places to enter them and for staying there. Aliens may join trade unions and other public unions of the Republic of Belarus, if it is stipulated in their statutes. Aliens may not be members of political parties of the Republic of Belarus and other public unions of the Republic of Belarus that pursue political aims. Aliens, who are living permanently in the Republic of Belarus and are engaged in lawful labour or entrepreneurial activities, shall have the same social and economic rights as citizens of the Republic of Belarus, including the right to social security.

992. Social and economic rights of aliens who are living temporary in the Republic of Belarus and are engaged in lawful labour or entrepreneurial activities in the territory of the Republic of Belarus shall be stipulated in laws and international treaties of the Republic of Belarus.

993. In the Republic of Belarus aliens have the right to use their labour skills, to choose their occupation and profession, as well as the right to use their skills and property in labour and entrepreneurial activities in accordance with the legislation of the Republic of Belarus. Aliens who are staying and living temporarily in the Republic of Belarus shall have the right to be engaged in labour, entrepreneur and other activities under special permissions issued in accordance with the procedure determined by the Council of Ministers of the Republic of Belarus. In the Republic of Belarus aliens may have property, inherit or legate it, use other property and non-property rights in accordance with the legislation of the Republic of Belarus, including the international treaties of the Republic of Belarus.

994. Aliens who are living permanently in the Republic of Belarus shall have rights to health protection equal to the citizens of the Republic of Belarus, unless otherwise specified by the laws and international treaties of the Republic of Belarus. As for the aliens who are staying and living temporary in the Republic of Belarus, they are normally supposed to be privately insured, unless otherwise specified by the legislation of the Republic of Belarus and international treaties of the Republic of Belarus.

995. The procedure and conditions for compulsory medical insurance of aliens who are entering the Republic of Belarus for a temporary stay shall be fixed in the legislative acts of the Republic of Belarus. Aliens who are living permanently in the Republic of Belarus shall have equal rights with the citizens of the Republic of Belarus to education, unless otherwise specified by the laws and international treaties of the Republic of Belarus. Aliens who are temporarily staying and temporarily living in the Republic of Belarus shall have the right to education in the Republic of Belarus in accordance with international treaties of the Republic of Belarus or under educational agreements concluded with educational establishments or scientific organizations of the Republic of Belarus, including international treaties of the Republic of Belarus. Aliens in the Republic of Belarus shall have the right to preserve and improve their national language and culture, and to follow national traditions and customs in accordance with the legislation of the Republic of Belarus.

996. Abuse of the national dignity of aliens shall entail liability in accordance with the legislation of the Republic of Belarus. Aliens shall have no right to vote and to be elected in the state bodies of the Republic of Belarus and to participate in referenda. Aliens may not hold posts that require Belarusian citizenship in accordance with the legislation of the Republic of Belarus. Aliens in the territory of the Republic of Belarus shall not perform military duties. Aliens should leave the Republic of Belarus before the expiration of the time period of their temporary stay in the Republic of Belarus. Aliens who failed to fulfil obligations on leaving the Republic of Belarus shall bear responsibility under the legislative acts of the Republic of Belarus. An alien may enter the Republic of Belarus and leave it on the grounds of a valid passport or other substitute document for going abroad and that is issued by the relevant body of the state of national affiliation or of regular place of residence of an alien or by the international organization with the presence of a visa, unless otherwise specified by international treaties of the Republic of Belarus. Aliens may temporarily stay and permanently reside in the Republic of Belarus.

997. Under Article 43 of the law, the period of a temporary stay of an alien in the Republic of Belarus shall depend on the period of visa validity and should not exceed ninety days per year from the day of entering the Republic of Belarus. The time period of the temporary stay of an alien who enters the Republic of Belarus under the procedure without any visa should not exceed ninety days a year from the day of entering the Republic of Belarus. An alien who is staying temporarily in the Republic of Belarus should leave the Republic of Belarus upon the expiration of the visa period or the time period stipulated in Parts One and Two of the Article in question, if at the moment of expiration of the fixed periods he/she had not prolonged the term of the temporary stay or the permission for temporary or permanent residence had been not obtained. The term of the temporary stay of an alien in the Republic of Belarus may be extended or reduced in case of changes or loss of reasons on the basis of which an alien was permitted to enter the Republic of Belarus.

998. Permission for the temporary living shall be given to aliens who enter the Republic of Belarus, for a period exceeding ninety days a year: if to study in educational establishments of the Republic of Belarus, then for a period of education not more than one year; if to a spouse, near relations who are citizens of the Republic of Belarus and who live permanently in the Republic of Belarus, then for a period of not more than one year; if to be engaged in labour and entrepreneurial activities in the Republic of Belarus under the procedure stipulated by the legislation of the Republic of Belarus, then for not more than one year; if they, in accordance with the legislation of the Republic of Belarus, filed for refugee status or asylum in the Republic of Belarus or applied to get permission for permanent living, then for the period of consideration of the motion or application; if they have property in the Republic of Belarus as their ownership, then for a period of not more than 180 days a year; under other circumstances stipulated by the legislation of the Republic of Belarus, including international treaties of the Republic of Belarus. The procedure of issuing permission for temporary living shall be approved by the Council of Ministry of the Republic of Belarus.

999. An alien who lives temporarily in the Republic of Belarus should leave the Republic of Belarus upon the expiration of the period of temporary living permission, if at the moment of expiration of the mentioned period he/she failed to obtain new permission on temporary or permanent living. Residence permits should be given to aliens who: are spouses, close relatives of citizens of the Republic of Belarus who are living permanently in the Republic of Belarus; are married with aliens who are living permanently in the Republic of Belarus; were found to be refugees or are the individuals who were granted asylum in the Republic of Belarus; have the right to reunite with the family; lived legally in the Republic of Belarus for the last seven or more years; have sufficient reasons for acquisition of the citizenship of the Republic of Belarus under the procedure of registration; are employees and specialists whom the Republic of Belarus requires; have unique abilities and talent or rendered great services to the Republic of Belarus, considerable achievements in science, technology, culture and sport; have invested not less than 150,000 Euros in the economy of the Republic of Belarus or in realization of concrete state programmes of the Republic of Belarus.

1000. Residence permits may be given to other aliens who are not specified in part one of the given Article on the grounds of a decision of the Council of Ministers of the Republic of Belarus and in coordination with the President of the Republic of Belarus. The procedure for issue of the residence permit shall be approved by the Council of Ministers of the Republic of Belarus. To control the state regulation of the process of aliens entering to reside in the Republic of Belarus, the Council of Ministers of the Republic of Belarus may fix an immigration quota for each particular state. Aliens who have the right to reunite with the family shall enter the Republic of Belarus to reside and to live together and to manage a household outside of the fixed immigration quota. The President of the Republic of Belarus may take a decision to let aliens to reside in the Republic of Belarus in excess of the immigration quota.

1001. Aliens who have obtained permission to live permanently shall be given the residential permit. Aliens should pay national charges or consular dues at the rate of tariff set by the legislation of the Republic of Belarus for the issuing of visas, registration, for prolongation of the period of temporary residence, as well as for the issue of permission for temporary residence, permission for permanent residence, for the travel document and the residential permit. Aliens may be subject to deportation in accordance with the legislative acts of the Republic of Belarus.

Part V. Specific Problems

Chapter 1. War, Treaty and Foreign Affairs Powers

1002. Under Article 18 of the Constitution in its foreign policy the Republic of Belarus shall proceed from the principles of the equality of states, the non-use of force or the threat of force, the inviolability of frontiers, the peaceful settlement of disputes, non-interference in internal affairs of states and other universally acknowledged principles and standards of international law. The Republic of Belarus pledges itself to make its territory a neutral and nuclear-free state.

1003. Foreign policy of the Republic of Belarus is directed towards peaceful settlement of all the disputes. Its territory is nuclear free. The strategic target is to make our state neutral.

1004. The character of the Belarusian State and of its people was formed under the pressure of historic development. For instance, during the period of World War II Belarusian people lost more than three million of a population of ten million fighting fascism. Belarusian people were fighting at the front, as partisans and in the underground.

1005. The Law of 3 January 2002 in wording of the Law of 12 December 2013 approved the Military Doctrine of the Republic of Belarus. By proclaiming a Military Doctrine that is of particular defensive origin, the Republic of Belarus proceeds from the fact that at present there is no single state that is a potential adversary for it and its military security sees in protecting national interests in the course of possible transformation of military dangers into military threats for the State. The legal basis of the Military Doctrine is in the Constitution of the Republic of Belarus, the concept of national security of the Republic of Belarus, international treaties on military security and other legislative acts of the Republic of Belarus.

1006. The basic aims of the military policy of the Republic of Belarus are to maintain world peace and security, to prevent the threat of war and to guarantee the national security of the Republic of Belarus against potential military threat. The Republic of Belarus forms its relations with other countries on the principles of equality, mutual respect and non-interference in domestic policy, as well as the other major principles and rules of international law.

1007. While carrying out its independent military policy in accordance with the national interests, the Republic of Belarus shall: observe the principle of inviolability of the state border of the Republic of Belarus; make no territorial claims to other countries and accept no such claims on behalf of other countries; respect the political independence and national sovereignty of other countries and acknowledge their right to solve issues on national security in accordance with their interests without causing a threat to the security of other states; consider that all international disputes should be resolved by way of negotiations on mutually admissible grounds; help encourage a balanced reduction of arms on the European continent within the framework of obligations specified by international treaties and agreements; exclude one-sided reductions of arms to the detriment of military security of the State, but assuming this reduction only after taking into account the economic possibilities and objective expediency for securing the necessary level of national defence capability of the Republic of Belarus.

1008. The Republic of Belarus is for the establishment of a system of European security directed towards an active role of international institutions of security on the global and local level, taking into account the interests of all the States concerned on the basis of the principles of confidence and mutual understanding.

Chapter 2. Taxing and Spending Powers

1009. According to Article 56 of the Constitution citizens of the Republic of Belarus shall contribute towards the funding of public expenditure through the payment of state taxes, dues and other payments. A citizen may be compelled to discharge his/her duties, including in the field of taxation, if they are stipulated by the Constitution of the Republic of Belarus and its laws (Article 58 of the Constitution).

1010. Taxes and dues paid to the budget of the Republic of Belarus are compulsory payments from tax-payers at rates set up by legislation. Local Councils of Deputies, within the rights granted them by legislation, may set up local taxes, fees and dues paid in their territory. National taxes and dues, in particular, shall be: value-added tax; excise taxes; profit and income tax; ecological tax; real-estate tax; land tax; fuel tax; transit tax; national fees and dues and income tax from citizens.

1011. The Tax Code specifies the system of taxes and fees collected into the budget of the Republic of Belarus; the main principles of taxation in the Republic of Belarus, it regulates relations of powers related to setting, imposing, altering, and termination of the effect of taxes and fees and relations originating in the process of tax obligation fulfilment; tax control appeals against decisions of the tax bodies, actions of their authorities, and specifies the rights and obligations of tax-payers, tax-collecting bodies and other participants of relations regulated by the tax legislation.

1012. Legal and natural persons that in their interest carry out legal actions and receive legally effective documents shall pay fees to the relevant authorized bodies. These are collected, in particular, from the claims and applications to the courts of law, for notarial actions, for registration of the acts of civil status, for the issue of documents on exit abroad and invitation to the Republic of Belarus of persons from other countries, for hunting permits, and so on.

The President of the Republic of Belarus issued on 2 April 2015 Decree No. 3 'On prevention of social dependency.' According to the Decree, citizens of the Republic of Belarus, foreign citizens, and stateless persons who have received a permanent residence permit in the Republic of Belarus (hereinafter 'citizens'), in case of their non-participation in the financing of public spending or of participating in such financing less than 183 days in the fiscal period considered payers collection to finance government expenditure (hereinafter – the collection) The Nalogovym collection period is a calendar year.

The fee for the tax period is twenty basic units on the basis of the size of the base rate, set at 1 January of the tax period, unless otherwise provided by this Decree. Payment of the fee for the relevant tax period exempts nationals who in the tax period:

– were persons below 18 years of age or have reached the age of 18;
– were persons of retirement age (women – 55 years, men – 60 years);

- have been recognized as, or are, disabled (regardless of the group, reason, and date of the period of disability);
- have been recognized as, or are, incapacitated;
- have arrived in the Republic of Belarus for permanent residence after 31 March or diminution of the Republic of Belarus for permanent residence outside of the Republic of Belarus;
- actually within the territory of the Republic of Belarus for at least 183 calendar days;
- have worked for a full season in seasonal jobs on the list approved by the Council of Ministers of the Republic of Belarus.

For the relevant tax period, income tax on individuals, the single tax from individual entrepreneurs and other natural persons, the tax under the simplified system of taxation in the amount of not less than twenty basic units on the basis of the size of the base value set at 1 January of the tax period.

In the year following the tax period have recognized:

- disabled (regardless of the group, the causes, the date of onset and duration of disability in this year);
- incapacitated.

1013. One of the elements of a financial credit system is the budget system that includes national and local budgets. The budget system of the Republic of Belarus includes national and local budgets. Budget revenue shall be formed from taxes set by the law and from other compulsory payments and receipts. National expenses shall be realized by the national budget in accordance with its expenditure. Extra-budget funds may be created in the Republic of Belarus according to the law. Subventions, subsidies and loan proceeds may form the budget. Revenues that enter the local budgets shall be allocated among local, regional, municipal budgets, budgets of urban settlements and village councils depending on territorial level of local Councils of Deputies in accordance with the legislation of the Republic of Belarus.

1014. Composition and rates of a part of national taxes and other compulsory dues paid into the local budgets and into the budget of the City of Minsk shall be specified annually in the Law on the budget of the Republic of Belarus for the following financial (budget) year.

1015. Allocation of part of national taxes and other compulsory dues between oblast budgets and budgets of regions and towns of oblast subordination shall be carried out by local Councils of Deputies. Allocation of part of national taxes and other compulsory dues between regional budgets, budgets of towns of regional subordination, urban settlements and village councils shall be carried out by local Councils of Deputies.

1016. The law on budget for the following year shall specify the types of local taxes and dues that local Councils of Deputies of oblast and intermediary levels shall set in the current year. The national budget shall finance: capital investments in objects of national property; environmental protection measures carried out in accordance with national programmes; measures on the liquidation of effects of the Chernobyl NPS disaster; national programmes on the social protection of citizens; other national programmes; expenses on foreign economic activity; state institutions of education, personnel training, science, culture, health, physical culture, social security organizations; expenses on allocation and renewal of state reserves; expenses on state bodies, including courts, law enforcement bodies and security bodies; national defence, frontier troops, customs bodies; repayment of bank credits given for meeting budgetary expenditures, national debt and payments of interest; foreign debt repayment and payment of interest on credits obtained from foreign countries and banks, international financial organizations; creation of reserved and state purpose extra funds; granting of loans, subsidies, subsidies for legal and natural persons, oblast budgets and the budget of the City of Minsk; other expenses stipulated in national budget for the relevant financial (budget) year.

1017. Local Councils of Deputies shall determine independently, within their powers, directions for the use of funds of the local budgets, except for the financial resources transferred them from the higher budget. Reserved budget funds, the rate of which shall be fixed by the relevant local Councils of Deputies, shall be formed in the composition of local budgets. Local executive and administrative bodies may put provisional spare money resources into economic activities, securities, other investment activities, including granting of loans to legal persons in accordance with the procedure specified in the legislation of the Republic of Belarus.

1018. Budget creation shall be an exclusive competence of the Government of the Republic of Belarus and the relevant local executive and administrative bodies. Direct drawing up of the budget shall be carried out by the Ministry of Finance and by local financial bodies (relevant executive and administrative bodies).

1019. The law on the budget of the Republic of Belarus for the regular financial year and decisions of local Councils of Deputies as regards the approval of the relevant budgets must be adopted in accordance with the prescribed legal procedure by 1 January of the regular financial year. Approval of local budgets shall be carried out after the approval of the relevant higher budgets.

1020. In case of failure to approve the national and (or) local budgets before the beginning of the financial year, the Government of the Republic of Belarus and local executive and administrative bodies are entitled to use funds every month before the approval of the relevant budgets in accordance with the prescribed legal procedure at the rate of one-third of planned assignations of the fourth quarter of the previous year within the framework of incoming returns.

1021. The Government of the Republic of Belarus and local executive and administrative bodies shall secure the implementation of the relevant budgets. Within the financial year revenue and expenditure of the budget may be subject to amendment by a law, by acts of the President of the Republic of Belarus, the Government of the Republic of Belarus, or by decisions of local Councils of Deputies within the framework of the approved budget and the granted rights. Increase and reduction of the size of revenue and expenditure of the national budget shall be carried out by the Parliament of the Republic of Belarus or with its authority by the President of the Republic of Belarus, and as for the local budgets – by the relevant local Councils of Deputies.

1022. The report on execution of the national budget shall be presented for consideration by the Parliament no later than five months after the day of the end of the accounting year. The report on execution of the national and local budgets shall be subject to publication. The report on the execution of the national budget shall be subject to approval by the law of the Republic of Belarus. The report on the execution of the local budget for the previous financial year shall be subject to approval together with the draft local budget for the regular financial (budget) year. The report on execution of the local budget with the indicators adopted while approving the budget shall be subject to publication.

Chapter 3. Emergency Laws

1023. The President as the Head of State shall play the main role in ensuring national security and, owing to that, the President is the Commander-in-Chief of the Armed Forces of the Republic of Belarus; the Parliament plays the role of the state body that adopts laws, military doctrine included; the Government, as well as the Constitutional Court of the Republic of Belarus that is empowered to verify the constitutionality of normative acts.

1024. Thus, under Article 84.22 of the Constitution, in the event of a natural disaster, a catastrophe, or unrest involving violence or the threat of violence on the part of a group of persons or organizations that endangers people's lives and health or jeopardizes the territorial integrity and existence of the State, the President of the Republic of Belarus can declare a state of emergency in the territory of the country or in specific areas thereof and submit the decision to the Council of the Republic within three days.

1025. A state of emergency is a temporary measure and it may be declared with the aim to normalize a situation and renew legality and law and order. The Constitution and the Law of 24 June 2002 'On a State of Emergency' regulates the most important issues on the establishment and effects of the emergency option. Any decision of the President on the declaration of a state of emergency shall be submitted within a three days period of time for the approval of the Council of the Republic. The issue on the approval of the decision of the President of the Republic of Belarus of the declaration of a state of emergency shall be subject to consideration within three days from the moment of the President's presentation of the relevant decision.

1026. If, as a result of the circumstances of an emergency, the members of the Council of the Republic cannot arrive without delay, and the session of the Council may not be held in the building, another place for the session should be chosen and the members of the Council of the Republic must be informed about this through the mass media or by some other way. The issue of a state of emergency may be considered according to the decision of the Council of the Republic without any preliminary examination in commissions of the chamber. Concerning the approval of the decree of the President on the declaration of emergency order and the measures taken by the Council of the Republic, only the approved provisions shall become effective. The Council of the Republic should inform the President on the decision taken and make an announcement through the mass media.

1027. According to the Law 'On a State of Emergency', if a resolution on the approval of decree of the President on the declaration of a state of emergency finds no majority votes from the full composition of the Council of the Republic, a decision on the declaration of a state of emergency shall not be subject to approval and shall be drawn up by the ruling of the Council of the Republic. In this case decrees of the President shall have no legal force. In our opinion, the law in question should settle a situation where the decree of the President on the declaration of a state of emergency shall have legal force if the Council of the Republic failed to hold its session in its required composition and this was the reason of lack of the required number of votes. Running a few steps forward, it should be noted that a similar approach must be also stipulated as regards the declaration of martial law. Possibly, for the indicated instances, the Constitution must fix the effect of decrees of the President, if they could not be approved by the Council of the Republic due to lack of a quorum or to reduce it (quorum) significantly (At present, Parliamentary sessions are legally valid in the presence of not less than two-thirds of members of the chamber and the decision is considered to be adopted, if it has a majority of votes of the full composition of the chamber).

1028. The time period of a state of emergency in the whole territory of the Republic should not be more than thirty days, and sixty days in certain localities. After the expiration of the specified periods, a state of emergency is considered to be terminated. If, during the given period, the purposes of a state of emergency were not achieved, the period may be subject to prolongation by decree of the President of the Republic of Belarus in accordance with the law on a state of emergency (Article 9 of the Law 'On a State of Emergency').

1029. A state of emergency may be annulled by the President of the Republic of Belarus before the period specified by the law, if the circumstances that caused it were removed. The population of the Republic of Belarus should be informed about it by the same way as they were informed about declaration of a state of emergency.

1030. It is important that the law specifies guarantees of the rights of citizens and officials under conditions of a state of emergency, including a specification of the limits of emergency measures and temporary limitations thereof, guarantees of property and social rights, the procedure of detention of citizens who violated the curfew, the responsibility of persons who would secure conditions of a state of emergency, and envisages normal functioning of the court system and prohibition of creation of extraordinary courts.

1031. Under Article 84.23 of the Constitution the President is entitled, in instances specified in the law, to defer a strike or suspend it for a period not exceeding three months. Thus, the law should define the instances when a strike specified by Article 41 of the Constitution will be deferred or postponed, but not more than for three months.

1032. A strike may be held within a three month period of time after the rejection of proposals of the mediation commission and, if the parties made their applications to a mediator or to arbitration, then after rejection of proposals of a mediator or disagreement with a decision of arbitration, except for the instances when it is obligatory for the parties. Strikes are prohibited in the Armed Forces, bodies of internal affairs, civil defence, state security, the office of Public Attorney, state power, at energy-producing companies, central heat and gas supply, in the establishments of medical first aid, as well as at the enterprises where termination (suspension) of their work shall make the threat of life and health of people.

1033. In the event of a natural disaster, serious accidents and catastrophes, epidemics and mass disorders, the President of the Republic of Belarus may postpone the strike for two months or to suspend it, if the strike has already been started.

1034. The Head of State in presidential republics is the Commander-in-Chief of the Armed Forces. He shall appoint and release the Supreme Command of the Armed Forces. Therefore, it is relevant to specify in the Constitution of the *above* mentioned competences (Article 84.28).

1035. The Armed Forces of the Republic of Belarus shall serve for the protection of the Republic of Belarus, to secure its borders, sovereign and territorial unity. Under the Law of 24 July 2002 'On the Armed Forces' with further alterations and addenda it is the Ministry of Defence of the Republic of Belarus that is responsible for fighting and mobilizing, training the Armed Forces for war time, technical equipment, structural development, arms and munitions, strategic and tactical training, military discipline, protection of confidential information and counteracting foreign intelligence and the observation of legislation.

1036. The President, as the Commander-in-Chief of the Armed Forces of the Republic of Belarus, is responsible before the people for the reliable defence of the country, the honouring of international treaties as regards security, and shaping and carrying out the military policy of the Republic of Belarus. He appoints the Supreme Commander of the Armed Forces of the Republic of Belarus.

1037. The Law 'On Military Doctrine of the Republic of Belarus', as a programme law, specifies the principles of carrying out military security operations of the State by applying political and military measures. This is a programme law and was approved by the majority of the Parliament. There are also significant laws directed to the security of the country. These are the Law of 17 July 2002 'On Defence' with further alterations and addenda and the Law of 22 July 2003 'On Military Obligation and Military Service' with further alterations and addenda.

1038. In the event of military threat or attack, the President shall impose martial law in the territory of the Republic of Belarus and announce general or partial mobilization with the submission of the decision taken for its approval by the Council of the Republic within three days.

1039. In accordance with the Law of 13 January 2003 'On Martial Law', martial law in the territory of the Republic or in some areas thereof shall be imposed in the event of military threats or attacks. Military threats shall be any actions such as the following: a declaration of war with respect to the Republic of Belarus on behalf of another state; a concentration of the armed forces of another state along the state border of the Republic of Belarus that indicates a real intention to use armed force against the sovereignty, independence or territorial integrity of the Republic of Belarus; the planning for possible armed conflicts with the Republic of Belarus; mobilization in another state aimed to attack the Republic of Belarus; intensification of the activity of international terrorism against the Republic of Belarus, its sovereignty, independence and territorial integrity; other actions of another state, extremist, religious, or separatist movements, organizations located in the territory of another state (other states), including statements and display of power that violate the Statute of the United Nations Organization and which signify preparation to attack the Republic of Belarus.

1040. According to the universally acknowledged principles and norms of international law, any of the following actions regardless of announcement of war by another state shall be considered as attack: invasion of the territory of the Republic of Belarus of armed forces of another state or any military occupation, even if it is of temporary character, any annexing of the territory of the Republic of Belarus or a part thereof with use of armed forces; rocket attacks and bombing raids of armed forces of another state against the territory of the Republic of Belarus or the use of any other weapon by another state against the Republic of Belarus; use of armed forces of another state against the Armed Forces of the Republic of Belarus, other troops and military units formed in accordance with the legislation of the Republic of Belarus (hereafter is also referred to as the Armed Forces, troops and other military units); the actions of another state permitting its territories that it placed at disposal of another state to use for the attack against the Republic of Belarus; sending armed bands, irregular forces, mercenaries or regular troops that carry out military attacks against the Republic of Belarus that are equal to those specified in this article by another state or on behalf of another state; use by another state of armed forces against the sovereignty, independence or territorial integrity of the Republic of Belarus by some other way that is incompatible with the Statute of the United Nations Organization.

1041. The decree of the President of the Republic of Belarus on the imposition of martial law, as a rule, shall specify: circumstances that were the grounds for the imposition of martial law; forces and means that secure the conditions of martial law; the list of measures that provide for the conditions of martial law; state bodies and military organs that are responsible for the measures on securing the conditions of martial law, as well as the competences of the specified bodies as regards the application of those measures; the date and time of the beginning of effect of martial law and the date of enforcement of the decree. The decree of the President of the Republic of Belarus on the imposition of martial law shall be subject to official publication and distributed through all the other mass media and means of communication. After the promulgation of the decree of the President of the Republic of Belarus, the Council of the Republic should be obliged to arrive at the place of the holding of the meeting of the Council of the Republic as soon as possible without any special call. The Council of the Republic shall consider the decree of the President of the Republic of Belarus on the imposition of martial law and no later than three days after its submission shall take the relevant decision. The decree of the President of the Republic of Belarus on the imposition of martial law that was not approved by a majority of votes of the full composition of the Council of the Republic shall lose its legal force immediately after the adoption of the relevant decision by the Council of the Republic and the population of the Republic of Belarus shall be informed about this in the same way as it was informed about the imposition of martial law.

1042. During the period of martial law the rights and liberties of citizens shall be subject to essential restrictions in accordance with the law. It is significant that during the period of martial law justice is administered by the court only according to the legislation that is effective at the moment of the imposition of martial law. Due to the fact that under conditions of martial law it is hardly likely to suppose any improvement of legal status of citizens, the specified norm may be considered not as a limitation of the right of the law maker to the development of the legislation, but as the most important guarantee of the rights and liberties of citizens. The formation of special courts shall be prohibited.

1043. Martial law imposed in the territory of the Republic of Belarus in accordance with the law may be abolished by decree of the President of the Republic of Belarus after removal of the circumstances that were grounds for it. The population of the Republic of Belarus shall be informed about this in the same way as it was informed about imposition of martial law. After the abolition of martial law all the normative legal acts of the Republic of Belarus adopted to secure martial law shall be subject to no application, but shall be subject to abolition by the state bodies who adopted them, unless otherwise is specified by the legislative acts of the Republic of Belarus. After abolition of martial law the state bodies and organs of military administration shall terminate their powers in the field of securing the conditions of martial law in accordance with the procedure set by the President of the Republic of Belarus.

1044. Legislative acts shall specify the powers of other state bodies in detail. The Constitution resolves the most significant issues. Thus, if under the common rule the term of office of the Parliament is four years, then in the event of war it may be subject to prolongation.

1045. The Council of the Republic and the House of Representatives may not be dissolved during martial law, and the holding of elections and referendum shall be inadmissible.

1046. In case of expiration of the term of office of elective state bodies and officials during the period of martial law, their term of office may be prolonged until the end of the effect of the martial law, unless their powers are suspended in accordance with the procedure specified by the law.

1047. From our point of view, the problem of state security is multilateral and may not come only to the indicated *above* aspects. It also comprises the issues of economic, ecological safety, social peace and religious tolerance, demographic security.

1048. It is important for the State to build relations with other objects of international relations on the basis of peace and cooperation. It should be noted here that in accordance with the requirements of the Constitution, the Republic of Belarus in its foreign policy should follow the principles of equality of the States, non-use of force or threat of force, non-trespassing, friendly settlement of disputes, non-interference into the national affairs of the country and other universally acknowledged principles and rules of international law (Article 18 of the law).

1049. The Republic of Belarus aims to make its territory nuclear free and the State to be neutral. To achieve the nuclear-free status, in 1996 Belarus had withdrawn the nuclear weapons that were present in the Soviet era from its territory. Under conditions of peaceful and neighbouring cooperation, now the forefront issues are the development of an economic system, the improvement of the political and legal system, development of a national culture and language, prevention of crime, strengthening relations with European structures, and first of all, with the Council of Europe and the European Union. To be in the European family, to develop international relations with Russia and other CIS countries shall be the major guarantee of sovereignty of Belarus and its safety.

Chapter 4. The Power of the Military

1050. The military, as the Belarusian history signifies, shall be outside politics and shall execute their own professional duties only in case of necessity to protect state sovereignty and the territorial integrity of the country. First and foremost, the military deals with defence.

1051. Article 1 of the Law 'On Defence' gives definition of this notion. The defence of the Republic of Belarus shall mean the system of legal, political, economic, military, social and other measures that secure the military safety of the State. Legal grounds of the defence are formed from the Constitution (Article 57 and others), the Law 'On Defence' with further alterations and addenda, the Law 'On Mobilization, Preparation and Mobilizations', the Law 'On Military Obligation and Liability for Military Service', the provision on military service of officers of the Armed Forces of Republic Belarus, etc.

1052. In accordance with Article 4 of the Law 'On Defence', organization of defence shall include: analysis, estimation and forecasting of the military and political situation; elaboration of major trends of military politics and Military doctrine of the Republic of Belarus; legal regulation in the field of defence and military construction; creation and ensuring the efficient operation of military organization of the State; creation, preparation and maintenance of required mobilization readiness at state bodies as well, and in other organizations that are involved in the military organization of the State, for example, the transport and communications industries; construction and development of the Armed Forces, other troops and units, as well as planning for their use; improvement and preparation of the administrative system of the military organization of the State, as well as the economy of the Republic of Belarus for operations under conditions of peacetime; safety of State borders of the Republic of Belarus and securing armed protection of the Republic of Belarus; elaboration of main trends of development of arms, military technology, forming and realization of arms programmes; State defence orders on product development, production, supplies, improvement and repair of arms, military machinery; the development and improvement of the system of data security activities of the military organization of the State; the planning and realization of actions as regards territorial and civil defence; the coordination of activities of state bodies and other organizations on issues of preparing the population and territory for battle; planning of transfer of state bodies and other organizations and economy of the Republic of Belarus for work under conditions of wartime; making a stock of material facilities in state and mobilization reserves; the carrying out of scientific research and experimental construction works for purposes of ensuring defence; financing of defence expenditure; control over spending the facilities allocated for defence, and other activities of the Armed Forces, other troops and units; protection of information that is of State and official secret status in the sphere of defence; international cooperation for purposes of collective military safety, participation in the development and realization of international agreements in the field of disarmament and arms control; accumulation, accounting for and preparation of mobilization resources from citizens called up and those who are liable for military service; pre-conscription and physical training in institutions of education, providing for secondary and special vocational education in accordance with educational standards; other actions stipulated by the legislation of the Republic of Belarus. Legislation shall determine the powers of the state authorities of the Republic of Belarus in the field of defence.

1053. Under Article 84 of the Constitution of the Republic of Belarus, the President shall be the Commander-in-Chief of the Armed Forces of the Republic of Belarus, appoint and dismiss the Supreme Commander of the Armed Forces; impose, in the event of military threat or attack, martial law on the territory of the Republic of Belarus and announce general or partial mobilization with the submission within three days of the taken decision for its approval of the Council of the Republic.

1054. Moreover, according to the Law 'On Defence' the President shall form and is the Head of the Security Council of the Republic of Belarus, and shall define the tasks to carry out for state bodies as regards the organization of armed protection of the Republic of Belarus; approve the concept of military construction and structure of the Armed Forces; approve the structure and strength of the Armed Forces; approve the Provision on the Ministry of Defence of the Republic of Belarus, General Staff of the Armed Forces, Department of Railway Forces of the Ministry of Defence of the Republic of Belarus, Ministry of Interior of the Republic of Belarus, Main Department of Chief of Internal forces of the Ministry of Interior of the Republic of Belarus, Ministry of Emergencies of the Republic of Belarus, KGB of the Republic of Belarus, State Committee of Border guards of the Republic of Belarus, as well as Railway Forces of the Republic of Belarus; issue decrees on the transfer of the servicemen who have already served the fixed period of military service to the reserve and on call for the people of the Republic of Belarus for fixed term military service; confer the military rank of 'colonel', as well as military ranks of superior officers; hold negotiations and sign international agreements in the field of defence; exercise other powers stipulated by the Constitution and legislation of the Republic of Belarus in the field of defence.

1055. The higher collective coordinating and political body for the purposes of exercise of the authority of the President of the Republic of Belarus as the Head of State and Commander-in-Chief of the Armed Forces in the sphere of ensuring national security of the Republic of Belarus is the Security Council of the Republic of Belarus.

1056. The Security Council of the Republic of Belarus shall make proposals to the President of the Republic of Belarus on the issues of state policy in the field of military safety of the State; organize an efficient operation of the military system of the State under any military and political conditions; coordinate transfer of the economy of the Republic of Belarus for work under conditions of wartime; hear the heads of the national state bodies on the issues of defence and ensure the military safety of the State; define the main trends of international military and political activities; work for the development of inter-allied and partner relations with other states; exercise other authorities stipulated by the legislation of the Republic of Belarus in the field of defence.

1057. According to Article 7 of the law the House of Representatives of the National Assembly of the Republic of Belarus shall consider draft laws in the field of defence, including declarations of war and of peace, on martial law and on a state of emergency.

1058. The Council of the Republic of the National Assembly of the Republic of Belarus shall approve or reject the draft laws in the field of defence adopted by the House of Representatives of the National Assembly of the Republic of Belarus; conceal decisions of local Councils of Deputies on the issues of defence that are not in line with the legislation of the Republic of Belarus; consider decrees of the President of the Republic of Belarus on the declaration of martial law and on a state of emergency, on full or partial mobilization and, within three days period of time after their submission, shall adopt the relevant decision.

1059. The law shall also specify the powers of the Council of Ministers of the Republic of Belarus in the field of defence. The Government shall settle issues within its competences and has responsibility for covering the needs of the Armed Forces, other troops and military units as regards necessary financial and material resources for the protection of the Republic of Belarus, execution of international agreements on the issues of collective safety, disarmaments and arms control.

1060. The Council of Ministers of the Republic of Belarus shall organize the development and formation of the state defence order, equipment of the Armed Forces, other troops and military units by arms, military technologies and other material facilities and resources; upon the laws shall define the scope of material resources and budgetary funding on defence needs, research and design in the field of defence; specify the procedure of account of draftees and persons in reserve, in military commissariats and organizations; administer military training of citizens of the Republic of Belarus for military service, their call to military service, service in reserve and secure creation of reserves with military educated personnel; submit for the approval by the President of the Republic of Belarus of mobilization plans of the Republic of Belarus and plans of creation, accumulation, conservation and timely renovation of supplies of material facilities in state and in mobilization reserves, organize elaboration of mobilization plans of economy of the Republic of Belarus, its transfer to the work under conditions of wartime; create necessary supplies of material facilities of state reserve in stores and bases, secure its maintenance, administer mobilization preparation of economy of the Republic of Belarus and transfer its work under conditions of wartime; realize within its powers control over army mobilization; confirm the state programmes of research and design projects in the interests of defence and safety of the Republic of Belarus; take decisions on the creation in the territory of the Republic of Belarus of defence objects, adopt the procedure of their usage; conclude and denounce within its powers international agreements in the field of defence; organize execution of international agreements as regards the issues of securing collective safety, disarmament and arms control; take decisions and organize their execution on the issues of living conditions, material and financial supply of servicemen, discharged persons and members of their families; administer civil defence; organize supervision over execution by organizations of the state defence order, exporter of arms, military technologies, strategic materials, technologies and products of double purpose; carry out other powers enshrined by the Constitution and legislation of the Republic of Belarus in the field of defence.

1061. The Ministry of Defence of the Republic of Belarus is a national state body that shall administer the Armed Forces and their training for solving the problems of security of military safety and armed protection of the Republic of Belarus. The Ministry of Defence of the Republic of Belarus shall elaborate the proposals on the issues of defence, and on formation of the military policy and military doctrine of the Republic of Belarus; adopt legal acts within its powers on the issues of defence; organize interaction and coordination of activities of the state bodies and other organizations on the issues of defence; elaborate long-term state programmes and annual plans of projects in the interests of securing a comprehensive defence system, proposals on forming of the state defence order; organize administration fighting activities of the Armed Forces, operative training of administrative bodies of the Armed Forces; prepare proposals within its powers about expenditure on the defence in the draft budget of the Republic of Belarus for the financial; participate in the elaboration of the concept of development of the Armed Forces and carry out its provisions; participate in the organization of mobilization of the economy of the Republic of Belarus, realize control over the preparation and performance of mobilization tasks; administer development of military science, organize study on the modernization of existing and creation of perspective samples of arms and military technologies; organize supply of the Armed Forces with arms and military technologies, by all means of material and technical facilities and allowances; develop and submit for consideration to the Council of Ministers of the Republic of Belarus of the nomenclature, amount, rates and order of supply, storage, transportation, maintenance and use of supplies of material facilities in state reserves; participate in the realization of military and technical cooperation of the Republic of Belarus with other states and international organizations, realize cooperation with military departments of other states; secure social protection of servicemen, civil personnel of the Armed Forces, discharged persons and members of their families; organize and realize training of military personnel for the Armed Forces and under the contract basis for other troops and units; exercise other powers stipulated by the legislation of the Republic of Belarus in the field of defence.

1062. The General Staff of the Armed Forces (hereinafter is also referred to as the General Staff) is the central body of the military administration that shall realize operative functions as regards the administration of the Armed Forces, secure its high fighting efficiency, organize interaction and coordinate activities of structural elements of the military system of the State to tackle problems in the field of defence both during peace and during wartime. The General Staff in concert with the bodies of military administration and other troops and units shall carry out analysis of military and political situations, theoretical development of the issues of improvement of defence capacity of the State; support fighting efficiency and order of the Armed Forces at the level that guarantees military safety and armed protection of the Republic of Belarus; coordinate activities of the bodies of military administration, other troops and units in the course of strategic and operative planning of using the Armed Forces, other troops and units both during peace and wartime; work out plans of using the Armed Forces, other troops and units during wartime, mobilization plans, as well as the plans of operative equipment of the territory of Republic Belarus for the purposes of defence; secure the strategic administration of military organization of the State during wartime on behalf of the President of the Republic of Belarus; elaborate and carry out the plan of construction of the Armed Forces, provisions on the structure, strength, fighting composition and distribution of the Armed Forces; organize territorial defence; plan and organize measures on data awareness in the Armed Forces, coordinate activities of bodies of military administration, other troops and units in the sphere of information counteraction; organize interaction of the Armed Forces with other troops and units in the sphere of defence; carry out organization of operative equipment of the territory of the Republic of Belarus and development of communications, optimize the system of distribution of the Armed Forces, organize the development of military infrastructure of the Republic of Belarus; plan and organize measures on the support of fighting and mobilizing orders of the Armed Forces, other troops and units for the purposes of defence, control its good condition; realize current and perspective planning of provisions destined to mobilizing deployment of the Armed Forces; define within the size of personal composition of the types of the Armed Forces, sorts of troops, special troops, military educational institutions and organizations of the Ministry of Defence of the Republic of Belarus in accordance with the concept of the structure of the Armed Forces; plan and organize the referral of citizens of the Republic of Belarus called to military service and service in reserve, to military units, as well as placing servicemen and reservists in reserve; plan and organize preparation and refresher courses of those liable for military service on the reserved list, plan and organize training and retraining of men liable for call-up (including reservists), conscription of citizens of the Republic of Belarus to military service on mobilization and placing of servicemen on demobilization in accordance with the legislation of the Republic of Belarus; take measures on keeping state and official secrets in the Armed Forces and counteract foreign technical reconnaissance; exercise other powers stipulated by the legislation of the Republic of Belarus in the field of defence.

1063. Bodies of local government, within their powers, shall take part in state and public arrangements in the field of defence. Bodies of local government shall: secure the needs of the Armed Forces, other troops and units as regards material facilities, energy and other resources and services upon their orders, allocate plots of land for the needs of defence; provide office premises and housing floor space, communal and other facilities in accordance with the legislation of the Republic of Belarus for military units, military educational institutions and organizations of the Armed Forces, of other troops and units; in accordance with the legislation of the Republic of Belarus organize and hold pre-conscription training and military training of draftees, patriotic education of the population, call of the citizens of the

Republic of Belarus to military service, render assistance related to military, academic and special periodical training of citizens who are liable for military service, including academic periodical training of citizens who study at military departments of civil, higher and secondary special educational institutions; guarantee social protection of servicemen, persons discharged from military service, persons who are liable for military service, members of their families; carry out the powers and functions vested in them in the field of mobilization training and mobilization; secure the execution of the state defence order in the relevant territory; organize planning and secure execution of measures related to territorial defence; organize the execution of measures of civil defence stipulated by the plans of civil defence; coordinate its own activities during wartime with the bodies of military administration in accordance with the plan of defence. Bodies of local self-government shall take part in the actions on ensuring defence within their powers in accordance with the legislation of the Republic of Belarus.

Chapter 5. The Constitutional Relationship between Church and State

1064. Under Article 16 of the Constitution religions and faiths shall be equal before the law. Relations between the State and religious organizations shall be regulated by the law according to their influence on the formation of the spiritual, cultural and state traditions of the Belarusian people. The activities of confessional organizations, their bodies and representatives, that are directed against the sovereignty of the Republic of Belarus, its constitutional system and civic harmony, or involve a violation of civil rights and liberties of its citizens, or which impede the execution of state, public and family duties by its citizens or are detrimental to their health and morality shall be prohibited.

1065. The Republic Belarus is a secular state. Under Article 4 of the Constitution, the ideology of religious associations may not be made obligatory for citizens. The legislation shall fix, in turn, the responsibility for any direct or indirect restriction of the rights of citizens depending on their attitudes to religion, as well as for kindling feud and hatred or insults to people in connection with their religious beliefs.

1066. As of 1 January 2015 in the Republic of Belarus there were 3,482 religious communes, including 1,643 Orthodox communes and 491 Catholic communes. Also represented, are Communes of Old Belief (33), Christians of Evangelical Belief (522), Evangelic Christians-Baptists (288), Greek-Catholic (14), New Apostolic (21), Judaic (52), Islamic (25), Jehovah Witnesses (26), Baha'i (6), Mormon (3), Society of Krishna Conscience (6). In the territory of the Republic of Belarus there are more than 1,300 Orthodox Churches, about 460 Catholic Churches and about 500 other churches or religious meeting places.

1067. In the republic there are religious organizations such as Orthodox and Catholic Theological Seminaries, Orthodox Academy and Theological School, Orthodox Monasteries (31) and Catholic Abbeys (9), Protestant Missionary organizations (25), religious centres (45) and administrations (republican and regional), amongst them Orthodox (12) and Catholic dioceses (5). There are 3,036 priests, including 1,564 Orthodox priests and 414 Roman-Catholic priests (192 of whom are foreign citizens).

1068. The State shall not entrust religious organizations with the execution of certain state functions, and shall not interfere with the activities of religious organizations, if their activities are in line with the legislation. The State shall not finance activities of religious organizations.

1069. Religious organizations do not perform state functions. They have the right to participate in public life, as well as to use the mass media equally with other public associations. Religious organizations do not participate in the activities of political parties and other public associations that pursue political purposes and do not give them financial and other support.

1070. In places of public worship it is prohibited to use state symbols, holding of meetings, other actions of political nature, as well as appearances or expressions that insult representatives of the state bodies, officials and individual citizens.

1071. The State shall promote establishment of relations of tolerance and respect among the citizens, who believe in a religion and those who do not, between religious organizations of various confessions, as well as among their followers.

1072. Religious organizations are obliged to adhere to the requirements of the Constitution of the Republic of Belarus and effective legislation.

1073. Religious organizations in the Republic of Belarus are voluntary associations of citizens of the Republic of Belarus (religious communes) or religious communes (religious associations) united on the basis of community of their interests for satisfaction of religious needs, as well as monasteries and monastic communes, religious fraternities and sisterhoods, religious missions, and theological educational institutions.

1074. Religious organizations shall have the following signs: confession; elaborated cult practice; holding of worships; religious enlightenment and education of their own followers.

1075. It is important to bear in mind that the leader of a religious organization may only be a citizen of the Republic of Belarus.

1076. According to the new wording of the specified law, religious communes shall be formed on the initiative of not less than twenty citizens of the Republic of Belarus who reached the age of 18 and reside in one or in several localities with adjacent territorial limits and that function only in their territory.

1077. Religious organizations shall be subject to obligatory state registration. The status of a legal person shall be obtained by them since the moment of their state registration. State registration of religious organizations shall be carried out: religious communes – by the regional and Minsk City Executive Committees; religious associations, as well as monasteries and monastic communes, religious fraternities and sisterhoods, religious missions, theological educational institutions, created as a result of decision of administrative bodies of religious associations – by a national body of state administration on religious issues.

1078. A religious organization shall carry out its activities on the grounds of the charter. Charters of religious organizations shall define their legal capacity in accordance with the civil legislation. These charters shall contain information about the type, location and region of activities of religious organizations, their confession affiliation, about the organizational structure of the religious association, about property status, and other issues in the event of cessation of their activities, as well as other provisions related to peculiarities of activities of the given organizations.

1079. For registration of religious communes, the founders shall submit the application about its registration signed by all the participants (members) of the specified commune to the city or district Executive Committee or local administration offices in accordance with the place of anticipated activities of the commune. The application shall include: list of citizens; charter of the religious commune in three copies; the protocol of meetings of participants; a document confirming the right of placement of the religious commune in the location specified in charter. These documents shall be subject to consideration within one month and shall be forwarded together with the relevant conclusions to the regional or Minsk City Executive Committee that shall take decision about registration or about refusal of registration of the religious commune, and the applicants shall be informed thereof. For the registration of a religious association its founders shall submit the application and necessary documents to the national state body on religious issues that shall take decision within one month.

1080. A refusal, as well as the unwillingness of an official to register the association in the state register of religious organizations may be subject to appeal to the court.

1081. The law shall stipulate the reasons for refusal of the state registration of religious organizations, as well as the grounds for its possible liquidation.

1082. The court shall consider cases about the cessation of activities of religious organizations under the procedure stipulated by the Civil Code of Procedure of the Republic of Belarus upon the motion of the body authorized to register their charters or the Public Attorney.

1083. Property of religious organizations may include buildings, icons, objects of production, of social and charitable purpose, monetary funds and other property that is necessary for their activities.

1084. Citizens and religious organizations shall have the right to acquire and use religious literature in the language at their choice, as well as other subjects and materials of religious purpose.

1085. Religious organizations shall have the right under the procedure stipulated by the effective legislation to produce, export, import and distribute subjects of religious purpose, religious literature and other religious information materials. Issue of the periodicals of religious nature and other religious literature of no public worship purpose shall be realized in accordance with the legislation about the press and the mass media.

1086. The legislation stipulates holidays and free days that fall on some religious holidays of Orthodox and Catholic confessions: Christmas, Easter, Radunica (Parents Day), Memory Day (Decree of the President of the Republic of Belarus of 26 March 1998 No. 157 'On State Holidays and Free Days in the Republic of Belarus' with the *following* alterations).

1087. Everyone shall have the right to independently determine one's attitude towards religion, to profess any religion individually or jointly with others, or to profess none at all, to express and spread beliefs connected with one's attitude towards religion, and to participate in the performance of the acts of worship and religious rituals and rites that are not prohibited by the law.

1088. Each person shall have the right to adopt a religion or beliefs at one's choice; have a religion or beliefs; profess a religion or beliefs both individually and jointly, publicly or privately; execute religious rites; and give their own children religious and moral education in accordance with beliefs.

1089. According to the law citizens of the Republic Belarus are equal before the law in all the areas of civil, political, economic, social and cultural life regardless of the attitude towards religion. It enshrines that specification in official documents of the attitude of a person towards religion is prohibited except for the instances where a person wishes it himself/herself.

Selected Bibliography

Although the literature on state conditions and state constitutionalism is vast and increasing, listed below are some basic sources:

Vasilevich, G.A. *Constitutional Law of the Republic of Belarus*. Minsk: Knizhny Dom (Book House), 2010.

Vasilevich, G.A. *Constitution of the Republic of Belarus. Scientific and Law Comments*. Minsk: BSU Belarusian State University, 2005.

Vishnevskaya, I.V. *Historia Politychnai i Pravavoi Dumki*. Minsk: Theseus, 2004.

Demichev, D.M. *Constitutional Law*. Minsk: Vysheishaya shkhola, 2012.

Kuntsevich, K.N. *Comparative Constitutionalism*. Minsk: Publishing House of MIM (Minsk Institute of Management), 2003.

Index

The numbers here refer to paragraph numbers.

Index